THE
MGM
STORY

THE MGM STORY

THE COMPLETE HISTORY OF SIXTY-FIVE ROARING YEARS

JOHN DOUGLAS EAMES

PYRAMID BOOKS

This revised edition published in 1990
by Pyramid Books, an imprint of the
Octopus Publishing Group,
Michelin House, 81 Fulham Road,
London SW3 6RB

Text © 1975, 1979, 1982, Sundial Publications Limited
Additional text © 1990 Octopus Group Limited
All photographs © Metro-Goldwyn-Mayer Inc.
ISBN 1871 307 775
Produced by Mandarin Offset Printed in Hong Kong

This book is for Jane Williams

27489

Furthermore, Leo wasn't collecting his usual lion's share of Academy Awards. Mayer had to find 'another Thalberg' to replace the cabal of executive producers which had been operating under his supervision. The choice was Dore Schary, a young man with ideas who had once been a writer at the studio, and who had risen to become production chief of RKO-Radio. Nicholas Schenck, the president of Loew's since the death in 1926 of Marcus Loew (genuinely mourned by the whole trade), approved the choice.

After a honeymoon period, Mayer and Schary came into conflict with increasing frequency and Schenck had to assert himself as peacemaker. This duplicated a situation which had cropped up from time to time between Mayer and Thalberg, even though the former held the latter in higher esteem than he did Schary. Now Mayer was also often at loggerheads with Schenck. Their hidden enmity had its roots in 1928 when Schenck and Loew's heirs had secretly sold the entire company to William Fox. (The deal was aborted by Fox's tangled finances and a US anti-trust investigation.) Mayer had then been mollified by a liberal anointment of money, but in 1951 he finally defied Schenck to choose between him and Schary. The president chose Schary: incredibly, Mayer was out. Five years later, in 1956, so was Schary.

Just as MGM had been the Hollywood studio *par excellence*, so it typified the gradual decline of the film city and its big-studio system of mass production and long-term contracts. Competition from television reduced income while ever-inflating costs increased outgoings. Studio chiefs came and went: an independent producer, Sol C. Siegel, took over in 1958, Robert Weitman followed in 1962, and Herbert Solow reigned briefly in 1969. Significantly, both the latter came from television, the movies' successor in public hypnosis. Stars, directors and producers launched out on their own; profit participation instead of (or in addition to) salary became the vogue. Although they retained a proportion of their customary production activity, the big companies increasingly turned to financing and distributing independent film-makers' products.

Meanwhile in New York the control of MGM underwent equally drastic changes. The government's anti-trust laws, which had helped to save the company in 1928, cut it in half 30 years later. Loew's became an entirely separate firm owning the theatre chain and radio station WMGM. Metro-Goldwyn-Mayer retained the studio, the distributing organization and such subsidiaries as MGM International, the overseas theatre and distribution wing developed by Arthur Loew, one of Marcus' twin sons; MGM Records; the consistently profitable Robbins–Miller–Feist music publishers; and MGM TV. This last, an example of 'if you can't beat 'em, join 'em', prospered by leasing the vast MGM backlog of movies to television (they never sold outright as some of the majors did); they also made films specifically for the medium.

Crises and convolutions in ownership and management have periodically rocked the MGM boardroom. Schenck, who had resisted changes longer than any other company's chief executive, relinquished the presidency in 1955. Arthur Loew was persuaded to take over, but had had enough within a year and resigned in favour of Joseph Vogel, a Loew's Theatres veteran of 40 years. His tenure was marked by a dramatic attempt by outside interests to gain control; among its instigators was none other than Mayer. This try for revenge was a failure, and Mayer died in 1957, an unhappy millionaire. Vice-president Robert O'Brien ascended to the presidency in 1963, followed in 1969 by James Polk Jr, another who lasted less than a year; then came James T. Aubrey Jr, ex-television executive.

Share deals and proxy battles gave behind-the-scenes control to Polk's sponsor, distillery magnate Edgar Bronfman; then to Aubrey's backer, hotel and airline financier Kirk Kerkorian, whose shareholding dominance from late 1969 continues at the present writing. Aubrey shifted MGM's headquarters from New York to the Culver City studios, where sales of company assets were announced with depressing frequency. Theatres in Australia and India, the British studio, the London-based overseas music publishers (Robbins, etc.), the MGM Record company, and parts of the Culver City acreage were liquidated. Annual reports to stockholders were saying less about films and more about the new MGM Grand Hotel in Las Vegas, into which $120m. was poured.

Finally, in October 1973, Aubrey announced the complete withdrawal of MGM from distribution. The company's product, new and old, was handed over for a ten-year period to United Artists in the USA and Canada, and to Cinema International Corporation (which already handled Paramount and Universal abroad) in the rest of the world. Simultaneously, UA bought the American arm of MGM's music publishers and CIC bought MGM International's theatres, including the Empire and Ritz in London. These transactions brought in a total of $32½m. plus a share of UA and CIC rentals from future MGM cinema and television bookings.

Aubrey resigned. Frank E. Rosenfelt, who had joined MGM's legal department in 1955, was appointed president, while Kerkorian made his control less anonymous by taking the title of chief executive for a short while. With hotels thriving and film overheads slashed, they reported booming profits.

With the forming of a new company, MGM/UA Entertainments, in 1981, this healthy state of affairs continued. During the rest of the '80s, the famous company had its ups and downs, and changed hands a number of times, but still kept its separate identity and logo.

The days when the dream factories were running full blast, peopled by almost mythical celebrities who thrived on a strange mixture of hardworking efficiency and lunatic extravagance, are long gone. The MGM lion's roar continues nevertheless—muted perhaps, but still echoing those heady decades when the studio's motto was: 'Make it good . . . make it big . . . give it class!'

IN THE BEGINNING
1924

MGM entered a growing industry. Motion pictures were the No. 1 mass entertainment and more theatres exclusively devoted to them opened every week. In the USA the total approached 20,000; in Britain it passed 4,000. Going to the movies was an all-age habit.

But the mounting rivalry of radio had to be met by making pictures bigger: the 1923 success of Cecil B. DeMille's spectacular *Ten Commandments*, and James Cruze's *Covered Wagon*, the first epic Western, inspired more big-scale productions in 1924: Rudolph Valentino in *Monsieur Beaucaire*, Mary Pickford in *Dorothy Vernon of Haddon Hall*, Douglas Fairbanks in *The Thief of Bagdad*, John Barrymore in *Beau Brummel*; D. W. Griffith's *America*, John Ford's *The Iron Horse*.

In Europe the dominant film nation was, strangely enough, Germany. A shambles five years earlier, the defeated country was creating stars and fine directors (Pola Negri, Emil Jannings; Ernst Lubitsch, Fritz Lang) faster than Hollywood could lure them away.

Besides such assets as studio equipment, stars, directors, writers and technical personnel, MGM inherited from its component companies some valuable properties for re-issue. Foremost among them were the splendid productions Rex Ingram made for Metro. The new combine successfully revived Valentino in **The Four Horsemen of the Apocalypse** *(right), which had shot him to the zenith of stardom in 1921; and* **Scaramouche** *(left), which to a less sensational degree had done the same for Ramon Novarro in 1923. This scene of Lewis Stone and Alice Terry illustrates Ingram's elegant pictorial style.*

Norma Shearer, already a popular leading lady, had only professional interest for Thalberg, her future husband, during their first busy MGM years. In **Broken Barriers** *all hell burst loose when Miss Shearer revealed to father George Fawcett, sister Ruth Stonehouse and mother Margaret McWade that she was in love with a married man. Reginald Barker, Scottish-born maker of American films since 1913, directed this emotional drama with Miss Shearer, Adolphe Menjou, James Kirkwood and Mae Busch in the major roles. Script: Sada Cowan, Howard Higgin.*

Excuse Me *was a farce about a naval officer (Conrad Nagel) and his would-be bride (Miss Shearer) who spent most of their time running up and down a train looking for a clergyman to marry them. Best-selling novelist Rupert Hughes wrote it on an off-day and it was directed by Alf Goulding, an Australian who subsequently made many movies in Britain. Also cast: Renee Adoree, John Boles, Walter Hiers, Bert Roach.*

He Who Gets Slapped *was the first film entirely* ▷ *prepared and produced by MGM. The six months preceding its delivery to the distributing organization in October 1924 were also occupied in completing, editing and releasing pictures originated by the Metro, Goldwyn and Mayer companies. But Mayer and Thalberg always kept in mind the importance of making this film an impressive demonstration of the new studio's powers. They assigned three stars— John Gilbert, Norma Shearer and Lon Chaney —and the celebrated Swedish director, Victor Seastrom (who also wrote the screenplay with Carey Wilson) to the story of a scientist who started a new life as a circus clown. Cast included Tully Marshall, Marc MacDermott, Ford Sterling, Paulette Duval. It was based on a Russian play staged a few years before on Broadway by the Theatre Guild: a risky choice for the studio's debut because, while it dealt with such melodramatic elements as a wicked baron pursuing the equestrienne heroine, and murder by means of a hungry lion, its effect had to be that of a moody, poetical tragedy. Happily it proved to be both an artistic and a commercial success. MGM was on its way.*

Already a major star, but with his biggest hit still in his future, Ramon Novarro had a success in **The Red Lily**, written and directed by Fred Niblo – who indeed had the same triumph yet to come in 1925: Ben Hur. Ramon and Enid Bennett played penniless lovers who eloped to Paris, she to become a prostitute known as 'the red lily', he to learn the ways of the underworld from Wallace Beery. Then usually cast as a villain, Beery in 1924 had been acting in movies for 11 years and had another quarter-century to go, the final 19 years as an MGM star. Also cast: Frank Currier, Rosemary Theby, Mitchell Lewis, Emily Fitzroy.

One of the most popular 1924 releases was Mr and Mrs Marshall Neilan's film version of Thomas Hardy's formidable novel **Tess of the d'Urbervilles** (scripted by Dorothy Farnum). Neilan was one of Hollywood's top directors, while Mrs was Blanche Sweet (her real name, believe it or not), then aged 28 and already a veteran of 15 years' filming, having started at the Biograph studio along with Mary Pickford and the Gish sisters. In this scene Tess reveals to her husband (Conrad Nagel) the shameful truth about her seduction by d'Urberville (Stuart Holmes) when she was a servant in his house. After the film was completed Mayer changed the tragic ending to a happy one, much to the annoyance of Neilan – and Hardy.

Magnificently produced and beautifully photographed in Italy, George Eliot's **Romola** was the second film in which Henry King directed Lillian Gish and Ronald Colman for Inspiration Pictures, an independent production company which chiefly consisted of King, one Charles Duell and stars Lillian Gish and Richard Barthelmess. The first was The White Sister, a successful Metro release. After Romola, Inspiration was disrupted by a sensational lawsuit brought by Lillian against Duell charging that she had been defrauded of a great deal of money due under her contract. She won. Director King and Dorothy Gish were then signed by MGM to do two pictures (neither was ever made) and in 1925 Lillian joined the MGM roster. Romola also starred Dorothy Gish and William H. Powell (that's the way he was billed then). Seen here in the wedding scene are Lillian in the title role and Powell as the villain, actually the best part in the picture.

One of the films already produced by the companies forming MGM and released just after the amalgamation was Metro's **Mademoiselle Midnight**. It was a trifle written by John Russell and Carl Harbaugh and starring Mae Murray (here with Johnny Arthur and Monte Blue) as the French heiress of a Mexican ranch. Robert Z. Leonard, the star's husband at that time, directed it. They had made a succession of popular but unmemorable pictures together under their Tiffany Productions banner, named after the famous jewellery shop rather than the gauze through which Miss Murray's close-ups were photographed.

The Valentino influence was still at full strength when Rex Ingram wrote and directed **The Arab**, with Ramon Novarro as a Bedouin tribe leader's son flaring his nostrils at the sight of Christian missionary Alice Terry. It was filmed in North Africa just before the MGM merger and Ingram edited it under the new regime. However, this fiery Irishman bridled at the very idea of supervision by studio bosses Mayer and Thalberg. He was backed by MGM's New York overlords Marcus Loew and Nicholas Schenck in his emigration to the French Riviera, where all his subsequent pictures were made.

To ensure an auspicious start with MGM, William Randolph Hearst's Cosmopolitan production company shot the works on **Janice Meredith**/The Beautiful Rebel, a great big splashy 'costume drama' directed by E. Mason Hopper and scripted by Lillie Hayward. The star was of course Marion Davies, at the centre of an American Revolution story involving the midnight ride of Paul Revere (Ken Maynard), the Boston Tea Party, a comic British sergeant (W. C. Fields) and several famous battles, not to mention Louis XVI and Marie Antoinette. It was a bit of a flop. Marion was really not at her best in the romantic dramas with which Hearst tried to make her a superstar.

Jackie Coogan, one of Hollywood's greatest child stars, was an important box-office asset for MGM during its early years. He had been famous ever since Chaplin chose him to team with him in The Kid (1919) and was still busy as a character actor in minor roles 50 years after his debut. Edward Cline directed Jackie in **Little Robinson Crusoe** as an orphan shipwrecked on an island whose natives made him a captive war god. Tom Santschi, Noble Johnson and Gloria Grey were also in Willard Mack's screenplay.

Jackie Coogan's first film made entirely under the MGM banner was **The Rag Man**. Edward Cline directed him in Willard Mack's screenplay as a kid who ran away from an orphanage fire and took refuge with a junk man (Max Davidson). Jackie was now a superstar needing an entourage of managers, press agents, secretaries, etc. He wore his Rag Man costume for this shot with his publicity chief, Lawrence Weingarten, who was soon to begin a 32-year stretch as one of MGM's most active producers – and become the husband of Sylvia Thalberg, Irving's screenplay-writing sister.

Wine of Youth was directed by King Vidor, who didn't consider it important enough to mention in his autobiography. However, it did advance the careers of three young stars-to-be: Ben Lyon, who had played the same role in the Rachel Crothers play on which the film was based, Eleanor Boardman and William Haines. Eleanor played a girl wooed by two suitors but made afraid of marriage by the quarrelling of her parents. Others in Carey Wilson's screenplay were Pauline Garon, Creighton Hale and William Collier Jr.

Virtually forgotten today, Viola Dana ranked as one of the top stars of the newly-amalgamated MGM. A lively comedienne, she enjoyed a long career which lasted until the fade-out of silent films. In **Along Came Ruth** *she played a small town's live-wire who took over a furniture shop and its owner's nephew. Walter Hiers, Tully Marshall and Raymond McKee were also in the Winifred Dunn screenplay. Edward Cline directed . . . Miss Dana had to do some heavy emoting in* **Revelation.** *One of the dottier plots of 1924 cast her as a profligate Montmartre dancer who left her illegitimate child in a convent. An American artist was so smitten by her that he used her as the model for his painting of the Madonna, which miraculously made her reform, reclaim her child and marry the artist. George D. Baker directed from his own script based on a popular novel, 'The Rosebush of a Thousand Years'. Monte Blue and Lew Cody supported Miss Dana, seen here essaying an apache dance in the cabaret sequence.*

One Night in Rome *was no masterpiece, but it served to bring a great name of the American theatre to nourish MGM's budding prestige. Laurette Taylor made only three films during a triumph-studded career, all of them derived from plays by her husband, J. Hartley Manners, in which she had starred on Broadway. The first two were directed by King Vidor for Metro (Peg O' My Heart and Happiness); this third was shot in 1924 by Clarence Badger for MGM. She played a fortune-teller whose client (Warner Oland, the Swedish actor who was later to become the screen's most famous Oriental in the 'Charlie Chan' series) recognized her as the woman who had disappeared in a cloud of scandal after her husband's suicide. Tom Moore, Alan Hale and the lady billed as Miss Dupont were also in the cast.*

Pauline Frederick, at the height of a long and illustrious career, made **Married Flirts** *for the new company. It was one of those 'sophisticated' dramas, considered quite daring in those days, of husbands being lured from wives. She played a novelist who lost her husband to a vamp, who thereupon rejected him to marry another man, who subsequently was enticed away by the novelist, who . . . Left to right: Mae Busch, Conrad Nagel, Pauline Frederick. Robert Vignola directed Julia Ivers' script from a current best-seller by Louis Joseph Vance.*

Robert Z. Leonard directed **Cheaper to Marry,** *from a play by Samuel Shipman, in the first of his 31 MGM years, the industry's longest association of any studio and director. That matrimony was not only a Good Thing but also a good financial deal was the moral of the film, with lawyer Conrad Nagel here making his merger bid for artist Marguerite de la Motte. Meanwhile his partner (Lewis Stone) was squandering their firm's assets on a gold-digger (Paulette Duval) and heading for suicide. Also cast: Louise Fazenda, Claude Gillingwater. Alice D. G. Miller scripted.*

One of the biggest moneymakers in American theatres at the time of the MGM amalgamation was Goldwyn's Three Weeks, written by Elinor Glyn and starring Aileen Pringle. Its follow-up, **His Hour,** *was released in September 1924, with the box office lure of Glyn and Pringle augmented by that of John Gilbert, now just emerging as a major star, plus direction by King Vidor. Best-selling Madame Glyn (an English-woman, but always referred to as 'madame') and the Hollywood of the Twenties were made for each other. Both purveyed Glamour with a capital 'Gee', and never more so than in His Hour. Emily Fitzroy, Lawrence Grant and Jacqueline Gadsden supported Gilbert and Miss Pringle, who are seen here in a scene captioned: 'Gritzko manoeuvres Tamara to his lodge. She resists his advances until she collapses from exhaustion.' . . . Well, she tried.*

A clutch of 1924 melos: In **The Bandolero,** *Gustav von Seyffertitz (bearer of one of the screen's truly memorable names) had a difficult scene when he had to register conflicting emotions while watching Manuel Granado, as the son he thought had died years before, being married by Gordon Begg to Renee Adoree, daughter of the bandit who had kidnapped the son and reared him as a matador. Complicated, but commercial. Tom Terriss directed, mostly in Spain, from his script . . . Alice Terry was*

the gentlewoman rescued from the fate worse than death by goldminer Conway Tearle in **The Great Divide,** *with Wallace Beery as the nastiest man in the West. Reginald Barker directed this robust melodrama, adapted by Benjamin Glazer and Waldemar Young from a stage blood-and-thunderer that had been touring the USA for a dozen years. In 1929 he repeated the chore for First National with Dorothy Mackaill starring. It was a moneymaker every time . . .* **The Dixie Handicap** *was*

unabashedly old-fashioned drama with everybody right in there acting for dear life. Left to right: Lloyd Hughes (hero), Otis Harlan (old retainer), Joseph Morrison (errant groom), Frank Keenan (racehorse owner), Claire Windsor (his daughter). In those days, the movies saw nothing incongruous in casting white (Harlan) and black (Morrison) actors together as Negroes. Reginald Barker directed; Waldemar Young scripted.

Sherlock, Jr, *made by Buster Keaton for Metro, was another of the early attractions to come through the new distribution set-up. It was one of the comedian's most imaginative feature-length films, with unusual photographic effects as well as the hair-raising stunts and chases that Keaton delighted in doing (without the aid of a double). He played a sleepy projectionist dreaming his way into his theatre's screen as a daredevil hero foiling the villain who kidnapped his girl. This shot shows the hero's valet, disguised as a motorcycle cop, just before he fell off the machine leaving Buster on the handlebars to hurtle through a glorious sequence of near-disasters. Jean Havez, Clyde Bruckman and Joseph Mitchell wrote the Joseph Schenck production.*

The most successful financially of all the feature-length pictures produced at Buster Keaton's studio for Metro or MGM release, **The Navigator** was, and is, considered by many Keaton buffs to be the funniest film he ever made. He played a dimwitted millionaire adrift in an ocean liner with no one else aboard but Kathryn McGuire. Approaching land, they were attacked by cannibals and escaped into the sea; the movie ended with a marvellous underwater sequence. Buster co-directed with Donald Crisp, better known as an actor, and the usual Keaton team of Jean Havez, Clyde Bruckman and Joseph Mitchell scripted.

'Sheer beauty is the only way to describe these gorgeous creatures!' said the caption for this still from **The Beauty Prize**. Lloyd Ingraham (actor of many supporting roles in later years) directed Viola Dana, Pat O'Malley, Eddie Phillips and Edward Connelly in the story of a manicurist who won a beauty contest while posing as a debutante and revealed her deception via that new craze, the radio. Written by Nina Wilcox Putnam and Winifred Dunn.

In **Lady of the Night** Norma Shearer had a shot at a dual role, playing a girl of the underworld and a daughter of luxury. The former was discharged from a reformatory on the same day as the latter graduated from finishing school. By another thumping coincidence, they both encountered a young inventor (Malcolm McGregor, here) who, bewildered by their resemblance, fell in love with both. George K. Arthur was the recipient of the bad Norma's kiss. Monta Bell directed Adela Rogers St Johns' dotty story.

Eleanor Boardman, a cool, charming actress of considerable skill, was extremely useful to MGM. Three 1924 movies were: **So this is Marriage** with Conrad Nagel. 'You're not fit to be his mother,' he snarled at her, playing domineering husband to her frivolous wife in this Hobart Henley production, which surprisingly climaxed with a biblical sequence depicting the story of David and Bathsheba. Seems that Eleanor, wearied of connubial rows, toyed with the idea of divorcing Conrad and marrying Lew Cody. The latter, noble fellow, thereupon read her the bible story, filmed in colour. Impressed, she went back to her husband, in black-and-white. Script: Carey Wilson, John Lynch, Alice D. G. Miller. Also cast: Warner Oland, John Boles, Clyde Cook, Edward Connelly, Miss Dupont, Francis McDonald, Tom O'Brien . . . Miss Boardman

took a rather unconvincing fling at male impersonation in **The Silent Accuser**. She was searching for the murderer of her stepfather. Filling her lap in this Mexican tavern scene is Edna Tichenor; dog star Peter the Great woofed through the title role as the only witness of the murder. Director was Chester Franklin, who also wrote the script with Frank O'Connor. Raymond McKee was the hero . . . Below,

Sinners in Silk: 'Here is the truth about today's flappers and lounge lizards!' claimed the advertising for this gee-whiz drama by Benjamin Glazer and Wilson. Adolphe Menjou, here playfully spiking the drinks of Hedda Hopper and Bradley Ward at a wild party, was a roué who then continued to celebrate his successful rejuvenation surgery by taking a girl home with him. His sinful intentions were thwarted when she revealed herself to be the sweetheart of his son. Miss Boardman (girl), Nagel (son), Jean Hersholt and Miss Dupont were others in the cast, directed by Henley.

Victor Schertzinger, who was to become more famous in the talkie era, directed **Bread**, a domestic drama scripted by Lenore Coffee and Albert Lewin from the best-selling novel by Charles G. Norris. He shared with Charles Chaplin the distinction of being the music composer as well as the director of his pictures. In fact, he wrote the first score for theatre musicians to play during a film: Thomas Ince's Civilization in 1916. Mae Busch and Pat O'Malley, already veterans of the silent screen, had the leads. Also cast were Robert Frazer, Wanda Hawley and Hobart Bosworth.

Robert Z. Leonard directed Mae Murray for the last time in Ibanez's story **Circe the Enchantress**; they were divorced soon afterwards. The legendary Circe could turn men into swine, and so could her 1924 counterpart as portrayed with gusto by Miss Murray. The heroine, having been corrupted by a cad when she was an innocent convent girl, proceeded to tempt and torment all the males in sight. Suddenly repenting in the middle of an orgy, she fled back to the convent, only to be paralyzed by a car crash on the way. The film ended with that 'Walk towards me . . . you can do it' treatment that has cured many a movie cripple, this time applied by hero James Kirkwood. William Haines had a featured role.

Although neither was the superstar each was soon to become, Norma Shearer and John Gilbert drew large crowds to **The Snob**, which opened in the same month (November 1924) as the more ambitious He Who Gets Slapped. This quick successor to their first romantic teaming was directed by Monta Bell from his own script, and is an example of that era's movie preoccupation with marriage and divorce. They played schoolteachers, married for love, parted by his obsessive desire for wealth and social position. Phyllis Haver, playing the blonde heiress who lured him away, shared featured billing with Conrad Nagel and Hedda Hopper (who eventually became a much-feared gossip columnist).

When MGM opened shop it found some problem items on the shelves stocked by former proprietors. A major one was Erich von Stroheim's **Greed**, which he had finished shooting for the Goldwyn company in 1923. A year passed before its release, during which time it was cut from its original, impossible 42 reels (about four times as long as a long film should be) to 24. At this stage von Stroheim baulked, saying that this was his masterpiece and it would be ruined by further editing. He was half right: it was his masterpiece, but it wasn't ruined even after he allowed Rex Ingram to cut six reels and June Mathis, without his permission, whittled off eight more. It was an unremittingly realistic filming of a sordid novel, Frank Norris' 'McTeague', first done by World Films in 1915, and dealt with sleazy characters living in squalor, obsessed by money-love to the point of insanity. In a company and an industry dedicated to mass entertainment, Greed was a freak, and, as Mayer predicted, audiences found it repellent: it never recovered its cost. Nevertheless, it stands among the memorable artistic achievements in Hollywood's history. ZaSu Pitts (left with Dale Fuller) gave a dramatic performance of harrowing intensity as McTeague's wife, murdered for the money she hoarded. Von Stroheim's script also spotlighted Gibson Gowland (McTeague) and Jean Hersholt.

The Prairie Wife, made for MGM by a one-picture independent outfit (oddly, in view of the locale, named Eastern Productions), co-starred English actor Gibson Gowland as a result of his powerful performance as the wife-murdering dentist in Greed. Gowland played for almost every Hollywood company during a long career, but never had another opportunity as great as von Stroheim had given him. In the new film he was the brutal caretaker of a Western homestead, terrifying the society girl brought to it as a bride. Hugo Ballin scripted, and directed a cast that also included Dorothy Devore, Herbert Rawlinson and Boris Karloff.

Wife of the Centaur was King Vidor's second sex drama in succession (after His Hour) to star John Gilbert and Aileen Pringle. Cyril Hume's book, on which it was based, was pretty outspoken stuff for 1923 and the sensation it caused did no harm at all to the box office take of the following year's film version. Gilbert and Eleanor Boardman (together here) played a neurotic novelist and his unsophisticated wife who almost lost him to Pringle, drink and debauchery. William Haines had a supporting role in the film.

SILENTLY EPIC
1925

MGM-Loew's Inc. made a profit of $4,708,631 in the studio's first full year, easily surpassing all but Paramount, which reported a million more.

Paramount had a strong star list, with Gloria Swanson, Richard Dix, Rudolph Valentino, Bebe Daniels, Thomas Meighan, Nita Naldi, Rod La Rocque, Jack Holt and the new sensation, Pola Negri.

Other studios prospered with Colleen Moore in *So Big*, Corinne Griffith in *Declassée* (with an extra named Clark Gable), Harold Lloyd in *The Freshman*, Lon Chaney in *The Phantom of the Opera*, Charlie Chaplin in *The Gold Rush* and brother Sydney in *Charley's Aunt*. Sam Goldwyn expanded his bank balance with mother-love sacrifice in *Stella Dallas* and the throbbing Vilma Banky–Ronald Colman romance of *The Dark Angel*.

They were all pretty harmless, but influential critic G. A. Atkinson told his London wireless listeners: 'Hollywood is pouring out a torrent of sophisticated barbarism . . . diabolically cynical!'

The biggest gamble of MGM's first year was inherited from the Goldwyn company. In 1923 that organization (Samuel Goldwyn had no connection with it by then) had propped up its tottering prestige by obtaining movie rights to **Ben-Hur**. Lew Wallace's fabulous best-seller was also a huge moneymaker on the stage, and Goldwyn had had to sign away an unheard-of 50 per cent of the film's future income to get it. A massive production budget had been required: a company headed by director Charles Brabin, writer-supervisor June Mathis and star George Walsh trekked to Rome, where enormous sets were constructed. Cameras had been rolling spasmodically for three months when Goldwyn became part of MGM. News of sluggish progress so disquieted the new firm that president Marcus Loew himself sailed to the rescue with replacements: director Fred Niblo, writers Bess Meredyth and Carey Wilson, and star Ramon Novarro (here as Ben-Hur, with Francis X. Bushman as the villainous Messala). But before long there were signs that the new key people were having as disastrous a time as the old, and early in 1925 Mayer and Thalberg prevailed upon Loew to order the whole enterprise back to California where they could keep an eye on it. They did so with such efficiency – and lavish expenditure – that Ben-Hur emerged as the greatest world-wide success the movie industry had ever produced (except, possibly, The Birth of a Nation). However, its $6m. cost was never entirely recouped, thanks to that original 50 per cent royalty deal. Also cast: May McAvoy, Carmel Myers, Mitchell Lewis, Betty Bronson, Nigel de Brulier.

The other film that really put MGM on top ▽ was **The Big Parade**. Its twin New York premieres on November 19, 1925 at the Astor (where it ran 96 weeks and grossed $1.5m.) and the Capitol were the start of a furore which swept most of the world's filmgoers and critics into ecstasies of praise. In all, $15m. worth of customers loved it, and so did MGM: it had cost only $250,000 to make. When King Vidor had finished filming, Mayer realized the movie's immense potential and persuaded him to accept a flat payment instead of his contractual 20 per cent of profits, which would have given him ten times as much. Mayer talked directors

Victor Seastrom and Erich von Stroheim into similar revisions when it appeared beneficial to the company. A 1971 television screening of The Big Parade (rare indeed for a silent feature) showed it to be still a moving depiction of one man's World War I, if not the towering master-work it once seemed. The love scenes of John Gilbert and Renee Adoree (right), alternately tender and vivacious, still shine; the panoramic shots of an army on the move and the closer incidents of battle remain impressive. However, the comic bits by Gilbert's buddies, Tom O'Brien and Karl Dane (second and third from left) now look pretty crude. Hobart Bosworth and Claire McDowell had parts in the Laurence Stallings–Harry Behn screenplay.

A year after He Who Gets Slapped, *Victor Seastrom* completed **The Tower of Lies**, *another impressive drama in which Lon Chaney again suffered, was driven to madness, and died. And again these two fine artists struck just the right note of brooding tragedy in spite of plot elements that were sheer nickelodeon. Norma Shearer repeated her earlier success opposite Chaney; he was a Swedish farmer and she the beloved daughter who saved him from bankruptcy by eloping to the big city with their rapacious landlord. Ian Keith played the villain and William Haines, David Torrence and Claire McDowell were also involved. Mayer took producer credit for the Seastrom–Carey Wilson screenplay.*

One of the biggest hits in Lon Chaney's career was **The Unholy Three**, *a weird story written by Clarence Robbins and Waldemar Young and directed by Tod Browning. It was about circus sideshow performers: a ventriloquist (Chaney), a strong man (Victor McLaglen) and a midget (Harry Earles). Assisted by a light-fingered lady (Mae Busch) they augmented their income by picking pockets, which progressed into burglary and finally murder. Miss Busch (here with Chaney) was an Australian actress specializing in vamps and villainesses. Matt Moore and Edward Connelly were also cast.*

Lon Chaney was the Limehouse thief known as **The Blackbird**, *who used a second identity when necessary: a rescue mission keeper with contorted legs. After one robbery he killed a policeman and took cover under his usual crippled disguise, then found his joints had become permanently locked. This typical example of the writing and directing style of Tod Browning, often Chaney's collaborator, had Renee Adoree and Owen Moore (here) for romantic interest, with Doris Lloyd, Sidney Bracey and Lionel Belmore supporting.*

The Monster *is a title that might have served for four out of five Lon Chaney movies. No villainy was too vile for Lon, no disguise too grotesque. Unusually, he wore very little make-up as this particular monster (looking, in fact, remarkably like his future successor in monstership, Boris Karloff). He played an insane surgeon who abducted passing motorists for experiments in bringing the dead back to life. Here he is seen hypnotizing Walter James, who got all the make-up that was going in this one. Gertrude Olmstead, Hallam Cooley and Johnny Arthur were featured, and Roland West directed the Willard Mack–Albert Kenyon script, from a play by Crane Wilbur.*

23

In **Dance Madness** Claire Windsor played a dancer married to an alcoholic hell-raiser (the ubiquitous Conrad Nagel, cast against type). During one of their riotous parties she tested his fidelity by impersonating a notorious masked dancer (Hedda Hopper) and trying to seduce him. Those wild young pleasure-seekers of the roaring Twenties were displayed in a film which could have been inspired by the contemporary life and/or works of Scott Fitzgerald. Director Robert Z. Leonard; author, S. Jay Kaufman.

During MGM's first two years Eleanor Boardman was starred, or featured, in 11 releases. **The Way of a Girl** led her down the highway, through city streets in a mile-a-minute auto. As a speed-crazed flapper Miss Boardman survived arrests and smash-ups, only to become a hostage held by escaping convicts. Robert Vignola directed the thriller, with Matt Moore and Matthew Betz (here with Eleanor) featured. Also cast: William Russell, Charles French, Kate Price. Writers: Katherine Newlin Burt, Albert Le Vino . . . In **An Exchange of Wives** Boardman was involved in the fun and games which became commonplace in certain circles four decades later, but were a novelty in 1925. The daring (really innocent) goings-on were conducted by Hobart Henley, with the plot coming from Cosmo Hamilton's Broadway play, scripted by Frederic and Fanny Hatton. Her fellow mate-swappers, Lew Cody, Renee Adoree and Creighton Hale, were also kept very busy by MGM. The studio's stock company of contractees was much smaller than it later became.

How to keep a husband—and how to get one: the screen fairly radiated mature charm when **Daddy's Gone A'Hunting**/A Man's World brought Alice Joyce and Percy Marmont together. She had been a leading lady since the heyday of the Vitagraph company, and the English actor had recently scored a hit in If Winter Comes. The new picture—the only one either star made for MGM—was from a play by Zoe Akins, a drama of bohemian husband

versus homeloving wife. Frank Borzage directed with the accent on sentiment and with Virginia Marshall, Ford Sterling and Holmes Herbert in the cast. . . . The decor destined to be dubbed 'Early MGM' by future connoisseurs was seen in all its glory in **A Slave of Fashion**. William Haines, Lew Cody and Norma Shearer are nearly overwhelmed by the set in this scene from Hobart Henley's production, a comedy (by Samuel Shipman, Bess Meredyth, Jane Murfin) about a small-town girl who stole a train-wreck victim's lease on a New York flat in order to taste the life of luxury. When her family turned up she pretended to be the wife of the absent owner; then the owner turned up. Reader, she married him.

Victor Seastrom directed **Confessions of a Queen**, from Alphonse Daudet's 'Les Rois en Exil'. His moody Scandinavian artistry combined oddly with the French writer's ironic humour, and the film was something like an operetta without music. Left to right: Lewis Stone, Alice Terry and John Bowers, as the king-queen-prince triangle. Eugenie Besserer and Andre de Beranger were also in the Agnes Christine Johnston screenplay. After a few years with MGM, Seastrom returned to Sweden and his real name (Sjostrom); three decades later, at 77, he won world acclaim as an actor in Bergman's Wild Strawberries.

Claire Windsor was a charming beauty who held her place in the second flight of stars for many years. **The Denial** gave her a strong role. As the stern mother in this early scene she is confronted by her daughter (Lucille Rickson) asking for consent to marry a young officer (Robert Agnew). Flashback related the tragic consequences of her own mother (Emily Fitzroy) opposing her and her lover (William Haines) in the same situation. Hobart Henley directed; Agnes Christine Johnston adapted Lewis Beach's play.

Rex Beach's novel **The Auction Block** had made a hit for Goldwyn Pictures in 1917, so eight years later MGM gave it another whirl, re-scripted by Frederic and Fanny Hatton with Charles Ray and Eleanor Boardman forming a new co-starring team and Hobart Henley directing. The story—about a rich New Yorker (unusual role for Ray) and a Southern beauty contest winner who considered him an idle wastrel until he took a job in a shoe shop—was pretty thin for a novel, let alone two films. Sally O'Neil (here), as Eleanor's man-chasing friend, helped to pep it up, with David Torrence and Ned Sparks also cast.

The well-knit plot of Somerset Maugham's 1921 stage success **The Circle** provided Miss Boardman (centre) and (from left) Hale, Eulalie Jensen, Malcolm McGregor and Alec B. Francis with excellent parts. The film was directed by Frank Borzage, later to be Hollywood's foremost specialist in romantic pathos. It nicely fitted the 1925 vogue for marital infidelity in films, although it suffered by losing Maugham's urbane dialogue. Note the studio's favourite chair, last seen bearing Norma Shearer in Slave of Fashion.

In contrast to the quiet advent of Garbo, the arrival of Lillian Gish at the studio for **La Boheme** was that of a queen (their films were in production simultaneously in autumn 1925). The spotlight was on the Gish set, where King Vidor was directing the illustrious star whose signing to a long-term contract was a major MGM coup. Aided by Vidor and a passionate performance by co-star John Gilbert, Lillian gave one of her most affecting portrayals of tremulous pathos. Her technique in achieving its realism startled all concerned: for example for three days before filming Mimi's death scene she parched her lips by allowing no liquid to touch them, and trained herself to breathe without visible movement. Other characters in the Harry Behn–Ray Doyle script from Murger's 'Vie de Bohème' were played by Renee Adoree, Roy D'Arcy and Edward Everett Horton.

The Lionel Barrymore of the Twenties was an absolute rotter, never the lovable old grouch he became in later decades. In **The Thirteenth**
◁ **Hour**, directed by Chester Franklin, he was a criminologist unmasked as a crook and a murderer by detective Charles Delaney and police dog Napoleon in the nick of time: here he was about to wreak further evils upon lovely Jacqueline Gadsden. The film was a baddie too. Franklin wrote it with Douglas Furber, and cast Polly Moran and Fred Kelsey in support. Barrymore had a fine old time as the heavy in
▷ the all-stops-out melodrama of **Body and Soul**, a remake of Goldwyn's 1920 The Branding Iron. First he behaved disgracefully as a doctor, then he fled to Switzerland to lust after an inn servant (Aileen Pringle), trick her skiing lover (Norman Kerry) into an accident, and finally, in an alcoholic rage of jealousy, brand the lady. Reginald Barker directed; Elliott Clawson revised Katherine Newlin Burt's original.

Ramon Novarro and Alice Terry were reunited in **Lovers?**, but the result couldn't compare with their Scaramouche, Prisoner of Zenda or The Arab. Maybe it was the absence of Rex Ingram (John Stahl directed this one), or perhaps it was the so-what story of a scandal aroused by a young man falling in love with his guardian's wife. Also cast: Edward Connelly, John Miljan and George K. Arthur. Script: Sylvia Thalberg and Douglas Furber.

Heaven on Earth was an oddity. Supposedly a brand-new production in 1927, it had the same co-stars (Renee Adoree, Conrad Nagel) and the same film editor (John English) as the 1926 Exquisite Sinner, which had been completed by the same director (Phil Rosen, who took over from Josef von Sternberg). Both were about a young Frenchman, bored with his family and their silk-mill business, running off with a band of gypsies. The different supporting cast in Heaven on Earth (Gwen Lee, Julia Swayne Gordon) indicated that Messrs Rosen and English had not quite made two movies for the price of one. Script: Harvey Gates.

'Don't step on it, it might be Lon Chaney' was a 1927 quip. Lon threw Polly Moran and millions of ticket-buyers into delicious spasms of terror in **London After Midnight**. Conrad △ Nagel, Marceline Day and Henry B. Walthall were also involved in the Tod Browning thriller about murder disguised as suicide and solved by hypnotism. Browning wrote the script with Waldemar Young.

Tod Browning whipped up another offbeat recipe for Lon Chaney in **The Unknown**, using a Waldemar Young script. The star played a fake armless wonder in a sideshow, mad about a girl (Joan Crawford) who couldn't bear the touch of a man's hand. So he had his arms amputated for real. Then the girl fell for an acrobat in their circus (Norman Kerry) and her peculiar aversion vanished overnight, so to speak. That's show business.

The celebrated stage thriller **Mr Wu**, filmed in Britain in 1921, was remade with Lon Chaney in Matheson Lang's old part. It was well directed by William Nigh and acted with bravura by the star and Louise Dresser (shown

here) as the English gentlewoman who stabbed him in the last reel. Her son (Ralph Forbes) wanted to marry his daughter (Renee Adoree with tilted eyelids) and Wu reacted by killing the girl and threatening the boy's family (also including Holmes Herbert and Gertrude Olmstead). Anna May Wong brought a genuine Oriental touch to the cast in Lorna Moon's version of the Maurice Vernon–Harold Owen play.

Mockery was too heavy for popular success although it was written and directed by Benjamin Christensen with dramatic power and visual beauty. Lon Chaney was impressive as a peasant who twice rescued a countess (Barbara Bedford) from Russian revolutionaries, despite having become a Bolshevik himself. Also cast: Ricardo Cortez and Emily Fitzroy.

The Big City was one of the less memorable efforts by Lon Chaney, author-director Tod Browning and scripter Waldemar Young. The star played a cabaret owner with a jewel-robbery gang as a sideline; the swag was stashed in a costume shop run by Betty Compson (here). Young love was supplied by James Murray and Marceline Day. Miss Compson, who had been in pictures since 1915, had scored opposite Chaney in The Miracle Man (1919); she continued well into the talkie era.

1927

King Vidor's **The Crowd** *was one of the most*
highly praised pictures in the whole history of
MGM. A far cry from his Big Parade *in scope,*
it was similar in that it centred on an average
man pitted against situations he could not
control. This postwar everyman fought on the
battleground of economic serfdom. James
Murray, an extra who happened to walk by
when Vidor was looking for an unknown lead-
ing man, was amazingly good as the clerk with a
little job in a huge office, and a little apartment
in a vast city. Eleanor Boardman gave the
performance of her life as his wife. Vidor wrote
the story early in 1926 and worked on the film
intermittently until the end of 1927. It was
scripted by him with Harry Behn and John
V. A. Weaver. Much of it was shot in New York,
where hidden cameras recorded street scenes of
a realism not seen on the screen before. The
painstaking production was so unhurried that
Miss Boardman (Mrs Vidor) took time out to
have a baby, between scenes as it were, and
Murray acted in a few lesser movies. Seven
different endings were shot and it went into
release with two; one left Murray as a cipher
in the crowd, the other 'happy' ending gave him
an unexpected windfall: exhibitors could take
their choice. Although generally regarded as an
artistic triumph with no paybox appeal, the
film actually returned twice its cost. Minor
successes were scored by Bert Roach as the
boy's office pal, Del Henderson and Lucy
Beaumont.

During the leisurely production of The Crowd
its leading man, James Murray, had time for
other assignments. The best of them was **In**
Old Kentucky, *a rewrite by A. P. Younger*
and Lew Lipton of a 1919 movie Mayer
produced for First National. Murray played a
drunken young war veteran who returned to
find his horse-breeding family facing ruin.
After their last horse won the Kentucky Derby,
he reformed. Dorothy Cumming (with him
here) scored a hit as his mother; others in the
John M. Stahl picture were Helene Costello,
Wesley Barry and Stepin Fetchit.

Seven months elapsed between the completion of
Flesh and the Devil *and the start of* **Love**.
Theatre owners and their patrons were loudly
demanding another Garbo picture, MGM was
longing for another Garbo picture, and Garbo
was refusing to make another Garbo picture.
Mayer tried persuasion, promises, threats, but
for once he had met his match. 'That dumb
Swede', as someone had called his young dis-
covery, unexpectedly displayed a shrewd busi-
ness sense and inflexible willpower. She had
decided that $600 a week wasn't enough for a
star millions were talking about and paying to
see; $5,000 a week would be more appropriate.
She got it, and **Love** *went into production with*
John Gilbert (whom she was still on the verge of
marrying, according to the headlines) co-
starring and Edmund Goulding directing. As in
this scene, in which the disgraced Anna
Karenina steals into her former home to see
the son she has abandoned, the film was less
affecting than the second version of Tolstoy's
tragedy which Garbo made eight years later.
But it was a box-office smash. How could the
masses resist billing like 'Gilbert and Garbo in
Love'? Brandon Hurst as Karenin and Philippe
de Lacy as the child won praise; George
Fawcett and Emily Fitzroy supported in the
Lorna Moon–Frances Marion screenplay.

ing. Theatres, emblazoned with 'All Talking! All Singing! All Dancing!', were filled and encircled by excited crowds. It was not just a stunt, it was also excellent entertainment for its time and won the 'best picture' Academy Award of 1929. Edmund Goulding's simple but effective story of a sister act (Anita Page and Bessie Love, here) broken up by an amorous songwriter (Charles King) was the framework for hit numbers by Nacio Herb Brown and Arthur Freed, including the title song and 'You Were Meant for Me'. The big Technicolor production number, 'Wedding of the Painted Doll', was deemed too static by Irving Thalberg after a preview, and he ordered it to be re-shot. Sound engineer Douglas Shearer thereupon had an idea which has been used ever since. He suggested that as there was nothing wrong with the music already recorded, it should be played through loudspeakers on the set while the performers got the number right for the cameras, and the film could then be married to the pre-recording. Harry Rapf produced and Harry Beaumont was the director; his cast

included Jed Prouty, Kenneth Thompson, Mary Doran and a big chorus. The lyricist, Freed, was later to become the producer most responsible for MGM's pre-eminence in musicals.

Joan Crawford became a major star with the release of **Our Dancing Daughters**, the ideal △ screen expression of the Jazz Age, which was just then reaching its climax. Girls were cutting their hair shorter, mixing their drinks stronger, changing their bedmates faster – and millions of moviegoers rushed to see how they did it, MGM style. Miss Crawford played a wild deb who lured John Mack Brown from his hard-drinking wife, Anita Page (left). Harry Beaumont directed and Nils Asther, Dorothy Sebastian; Eddie Nugent and Dorothy Cumming were also cast. Josephine Lovett's screenplay was produced by Hunt Stromberg, but in those days he and other production supervisors (Harry Rapf, Albert Lewin, Bernard Hyman, Paul Bern) got no more screen credit from Thalberg than he gave himself: none.

Give MGM credit for developing and maintaining the superstar of stars. But there's no denying that some of Garbo's vehicles would have been novelettish nothings without her. **Wild Orchids**, scripted by Willis Goldbeck from John Colton's story 'Heat' (a title which presented billing embarrassments), was a triangle piece about a plantation owner visiting Java with his wife, who indulged in a steamy affair with a native prince. Lewis Stone and Nils Asther as husband and lover were the only others cast-listed. With Sidney Franklin directing, Garbo mesmerized her audiences once more, and again the box-office responded.

Three movies starring Ramon Novarro: **Across to Singapore** was a new version of Ben Ames Williams' sturdy yarn, 'All the Brothers Were Valiant', first filmed by Metro in 1923. The rival sailing-ship brothers, one saintly, one devilish, were respectively and vigorously played by Ramon Novarro and Ernest Torrence. Storms at sea – emotional and climatic – were directed with gusto by William Nigh. Left to right: Joan Crawford, Frank Currier, Novarro, Edward Connelly. Script: Richard Schayer . . . **Forbidden Hours** scored below the

Novarro average at the paybox, although he and Renee Adoree (here) did their best. The script by A. P. Younger had a distinct whiff of mothballs; one of those Ruritanian fancies about a king in love with a commoner who sacrificed herself to save his throne. Dorothy Cumming and Roy D'Arcy supported. Harry Beaumont directed . . . Novarro went back into the Navy in **The Flying Fleet**, and if it didn't prove as big a hit as his Midshipman, blame it on the absence of dialogue when talkies were the new rage. It was written by Frank Wead and Schayer, excellently directed by George Hill, and produced with the co-operation of the US Naval Academy's flying school. Novarro is here getting his reward from Anita Page for surviving a perilous California–Hawaii flight with Ralph Graves, Eddie Nugent and Carroll Nye.

Undeterred by the disappointment of The Callahans and The Murphys, Thalberg gave Marie Dressler (centre) another and more successful chance in **Bringing Up Father**. She and Polly Moran (left) were teamed again, as they were to be many more times. Frances Marion's broad comedy was based, like Tillie the Toiler, on a famous Hearst comic strip: J. Farrell MacDonald played the henpecked Jiggs, Polly was Maggie, the social climber. Jack Conway directed them and Gertrude Olmstead, Grant Withers and Rose Dione (right).

A Woman of Affairs was really The Green Hat, Garbo version. Michael Arlen's novel, which sold in fantastic numbers, was considered so daring that the character names as well as the title had to be changed to mollify the censors. In Bess Meredyth's script the heroine still lived recklessly and died by wrecking her car, but her husband (John Mack Brown) now committed suicide because of his embezzling, not VD. John Gilbert, for the first time secondary to Garbo in both billing and footage, co-starred under Clarence Brown's direction, with Douglas Fairbanks Jr, Hobart Bosworth and (here, with the stars) Lewis Stone and Dorothy Sebastian.

William Haines was going from strength to strength. Having run through baseball (Slide, Kelly, Slide), golf (Spring Fever) and football (West Point), he continued his sporting chronicle with polo in **The Smart Set**. The formula was kept intact: bumptious hero lacked team spirit, was thrown out, then restored just in time to win the USA–Great Britain match. Jack Conway directed the Byron Morgan story, and Alice Day (with Haines here), Jack Holt and Hobart Bosworth were featured.

Tim McCoy kept the action fans happy with five 1928 releases. **The Adventurer** with Dorothy Sebastian (here) and Charles Delaney; a South American revolt story directed by Viachetslav Tourjansky (who promptly returned to Europe) . . . **The Bushranger** with Marian Douglas, Russell Simpson and two

unnamed troopers (here); an Australian bandit story directed by Chet Withey. . . . **Beyond the Sierras** with Sylvia Beecher (right), Polly Moran (left) and Roy D'Arcy; a Californian bandit story directed by Nick Grinde. . . . **Riders of the Dark** with (left to right) D'Arcy, Bert Roach and Rex Lease; a Texas Ranger story also directed by Grinde. . . . **Wyoming**/ The Rock of Friendship with Miss Sebastian and William Fairbanks; an Army versus Indians story directed by W. S. Van Dyke.

Joan Crawford up and down: she and John Gilbert made a striking pair in **Four Walls**, an underworld drama adapted by Alice D. G. Miller from a recent Broadway winner by George Abbott and Dana Burnet. Gilbert played a gangster from New York's ghetto, jailed for manslaughter, released, then involved in the murder of his gang's leader. Carmel Myers, Vera Gordon and Robert Emmet O'Connor also responded effectively to William Nigh's strong direction. **Dream of Love** was supposed to be a big one for Joan but the fans wanted her as the whoopee girl of Our Dancing Daughters and the new movie flopped. It was based on the old French play Adrienne Lecouvreur whose plot, about a gypsy girl becoming a great actress and loving a prince, made a better opera than movie; script by Dorothy Farnum. Fred Niblo did it the old-fashioned way, as indicated by this scene with Warner Oland, Aileen Pringle and Nils Asther.

While the City Sleeps was a cops-and-robbers piece by A. P. Younger with a strong cast: Lon Chaney and Anita Page (here) and Carroll Nye, Wheeler Oakman, Mae Busch and Polly Moran. Jack Conway's customary brisk direction brought conviction to the drama of a flapper who learned too much about her gangster boyfriend's boss and went to detective Chaney for help. Business was good.

Lillian Gish and director Victor Seastrom had an artistic triumph in **The Wind**, but it was not a box-office success, and Lillian's contract was curtailed by mutual consent. The story was basically the old favourite about the gentle girl going out to the raw West and being assaulted by a villain. The difference in this film was the extraordinary effect of mounting terror and mental aberration conveyed by actress and director. Montagu Love (here) was the man she killed before being driven mad by her conscience and the relentless winds of the plains. Lars Hanson and Dorothy Cumming were other principals in Frances Marion's screenplay.

General Alexandroff discovers that Tania, the beautiful Russian spy, had stolen the Secret Papers in order to save her Austrian lover, so she is forced to shoot him. This sort of melodramatic nonsense did Garbo's artistic reputation no good, but **The Mysterious Lady** was a moneymaker nevertheless. Gustav von Seyffertitz shared this scene with the star, and Conrad Nagel was her leading man for the first time. Fred Niblo directed the screenplay by Bess Meredyth.

The Lew Cody–Aileen Pringle partnership was discontinued after **A Single Man**, a trivial comedy in which Cody was cured of his infatuation with a young girl and proposed marriage to his secretary while the girl departed with a swain of her own age. Harry Beaumont directed (left to right) Eddie Nugent, Marceline Day, Cody and Miss Pringle in the F. Hugh Herbert–George O'Hara version of H. H. Davies' 1914 play.

Donald Crisp, as Leif Ericsson in **The Viking**, sights the east coast of America after a stormy voyage from Norway. Crisp had an extraordinary career. Born in London and educated at Oxford, he went to the States in 1906 in his twenties and spent a year in opera. He later began half a century in pictures, first as an actor, then as a director of stars like Douglas Fairbanks and John Barrymore, then as an actor again until the late Fifties. Meanwhile, he became important in banking circles and was a key figure in several big film financial deals. He died in 1974 at the age of 93. The Viking was an expensive flop, distinguished only (aside from Crisp's moustache) in being the first movie filmed entirely in the improved Technicolor process. Roy William Neill directed Jack Cunningham's script, and Pauline Starke, LeRoy Mason and Anders Randolf were also in the cast.

Loretta Young started her 25-year movie career at the age of 15, in **Laugh, Clown, Laugh**. The David Belasco stage weepie had starred Lionel Barrymore; it came to the screen as an exercise for Lon Chaney's histrionics. He played a part he had done before–a circus clown in love with a girl (Miss Young) in love with a younger man–and played it well. The lover was Nils Asther. Herbert Brenon directed and Elizabeth Meehan scripted. The film was silent but its box-office success was aided by a song of the same title which topped the 1928 hit parade.

LAST OF THE SILENTS

1929

MGM-Loew's profits zoomed to $12,107,026, having risen gently to $6,737,205 in 1927 and $8,568,162 in 1928, and all the other companies (except Universal) were equally stimulated by the talkie boom.

Gary Cooper, Myrna Loy, Richard Arlen, Charles 'Buddy' Rogers, Lupe Velez and the entrancing Nancy Carroll were among the rising stars developed by Hollywood, but they were greatly outnumbered by famous newcomers from the stage: Ruth Chatterton, George Arliss, Helen Morgan, the Marx Brothers, Claudette Colbert, Rudy Vallee, Paul Muni, Barbara Stanwyck, Maurice Chevalier, Sophie Tucker, Walter Huston, Ann Harding, Chester Morris, Jeanette Mac-Donald, Fredric March, Ina Claire. But it was the old-timers who got the Academy Awards: Mary Pick-ford (*Coquette*) and Warner Baxter (*In Old Arizona*); director Frank Lloyd (*The Divine Lady*, *Weary River* and *Drag*). The talkie talk of Britain was Alfred Hitchcock's *Blackmail*.

King Vidor's prestige was so high in 1929 that he could pick his own subject, no matter how unpromising for the box office. With this carte blanche, *he went totally* noir *for* **Hallelujah!**, *written from his original by Wanda Tuchock and Richard Schayer. The drama of religion versus sin in the deep South was played entirely by unknown Negro performers, a MGM 'first' almost as revolutionary as the advent of sound. Vidor took advantage of that novelty too, adding dialogue and music to the scenes he had shot silent in Tennessee and completing interiors in one of Culver City's new sound stages. His skill and the fervent sincerity of the black cast, including Nina Mae McKinney, Daniel Haynes, and (here) Fanny Belle de Night, Victoria Spivey and Harry Gray, made* Hallelujah! *an emotional experience the critics praised unrestrainedly. Augmenting traditional songs was the first number Irving Berlin wrote for MGM, 'Waiting at the End of the Road'.*

Irving Thalberg took no chances with his wife's first talkie and gave her the title role in **The Trial of Mary Dugan**. *It was MGM's first straight all-dialogue picture and came immediately after the talk-song-and-dance Broadway Melody. This New York and London stage smash kept Norma Shearer listening tensely to courtroom testimony most of the time, then let her loose on a big emotional scene. Miss Shearer had never had stage experience, but she used a well-modulated voice and excellent diction to make the transition from silent stardom with immense success. Raymond Hackett (here) was her defence-lawyer brother, the role he created on Broadway. H. B. Warner, Lewis Stone, Lilyan Tashman, Olive Tell, Claude Allister and Mary Doran also scored in the Bayard Veiller thriller, directed by the author from his and Becky Gardiner's screenplay.*

The Duncan Sisters, long famous for their 'Topsy and Eva' act in vaudeville (they made a 1926 movie under that title) were starred in **It's a Great Life** as consolation for losing the Broadway Melody leads to Bessie Love and Anita Page. It had almost the same plot, several musical numbers (here, Vivian and Rosetta doing 'Following You') and some Technicolor– but to no avail. Their personalities tended to cloy on the screen. Others appearing under Sam Wood's direction in the Al Boasberg–Willard Mack screenplay were Lawrence Gray, Jed Prouty and Benny Rubin.

Bessie Love leads the boys and girls through the 'Everybody Tap' number in **Chasing Rainbows**. She and Charles King hoped they had another Broadway Melody in this backstage musical, but the market was already flooded with that triumph's imitators. Still, this Bess Meredyth story was among the best of them, with Marie Dressler, Polly Moran, Jack Benny and George K. Arthur giving it strong comedy voltage, and 'Happy Days Are Here Again' supplying a smash song. Charles Reisner directed.

Everybody but Garbo and the gateman seemed to be in **The Hollywood Revue**, the most popular in a cycle (Fox Movietone Follies, Paramount on Parade, etc.) of musicals filmed with no story–on purpose, that is. Pictured here are Marie Dressler, Bessie Love and Polly Moran in 'Singin' in the Rain', the biggest hit of its 17 songs; and George K. Arthur, Karl Dane and Jack Benny in a comedy turn. (Dimly seen above Benny's fiddle is Ann Dvorak, then a teenage chorus girl.) Marion Davies, Buster Keaton, Norma Shearer, John Gilbert, William Haines, Laurel and Hardy, Conrad Nagel, Anita Page, Charles King, Cliff Edwards, Joan Crawford and Lionel Barrymore also contributed, augmented by two singing groups and three dancing troupes. It was a sensational success. Director Charles Reisner shot a lot of it in the 7 pm-7 am 'graveyard shift' since most of the stars were working in other movies during the day. Harry Rapf produced.

In 1929 MGM bought the rights of Sidney Howard's play about illicit love, They Knew What They Wanted, and gave it to Victor Seastrom to direct as an all-talkie titled **A Lady to Love**. It was the quickest remake on record – a 1928 silent Paramount version starring Pola Negri had skirted film censorship by calling itself The Secret Hour. (RKO gave it a third go in 1940 with its original title.) Vilma Banky played the mail-order bride of vineyard owner Edward G. Robinson; Robert Ames was the hired hand she pressed too many grapes with. Edward G. went on to become the world's favourite gangster; Miss Banky retired. Her glamorous career, mostly co-starring with Valentino and Ronald Colman, was ended by an accent described by one critic as 'a strange mixture of Budapest and Chicago'.

The Rogue Song was the first all-Technicolor all-talkie, and Lionel Barrymore's fourth and last directing job at his home studio. (Columbia borrowed him to direct Barbara Stanwyck in Ten Cents a Dance before he returned to acting.) It was also the successful film début of opera star Lawrence Tibbett, who combined a splendid baritone with an ebullient personality. Vaguely based on the Franz Lehar operetta Gypsy Love, it was highly praised for everything except a strangely hit-less musical score. Supporting Tibbett were Judith Vosselli and Catherine Dale Owen (here), Stan Laurel and Oliver Hardy, Nance O'Neil, Ulrich Haupt, Florence Lake, Lionel Belmore, Kate Price. Script: Frances Marion and John Colton.

Bayard Veiller's spiritualist stage thriller **The Thirteenth Chair** wracked nerves nicely in Tod Browning's talkie, with Margaret Wycherly in her original role as the medium. Going into a trance every reel or so until the murderer was unmasked, she had Gretchen Holland, Bela Lugosi and Holmes Herbert (here) and Conrad Nagel, Leila Hyams, Helene Millard, Mary Forbes and Cyril Chadwick as seance table-grippers. Script: Elliott Clawson.

With Hearst keeping a beady eye on the studio to see that Marion Davies didn't get left behind in the talkie race, Thalberg hurried to give her a wartime musical, **Marianne**, directed by Robert Z. Leonard. Making her a French girl speaking broken English disguised the fact that Marion talked with a slight stammer. The movie was received with less than rapture, but it got by on the merits of six songs plus attractive performances by the star and Lawrence Gray (here) and Benny Rubin and Cliff Edwards, known on hit discs as Ukelele Ike. A separately made silent version had Oscar Shaw and Robert Ames as her leading men. Script: Dale Van Every.

The Woman Racket/Lights and Shadows offered a lacklustre story about a cop, a nightclub hostess and a gang killing, with old-timers Blanche Sweet and Tom Moore and (here) John Miljan, Robert Agnew and Sally Starr as Broadway denizens. Robert Ober and Albert Kelley co-directed for the first and last time; Albert LeVino adapted the play 'Night Hostess' by Philip and Frances Dunning.

Navy Blues, a rare try by Clarence Brown at handling comedy, turned out well. The yarn about a sailor on leave and a dance-hall girl (Anita Page) proved that William Haines had lost none of his zest by going the all-talking route. Karl Dane, J. C. Nugent and Edythe Chapman helped. Nugent and his son Elliott were among the film's many writers.

The biggest star problem that faced Mayer and Thalberg when talkies arrived was John Gilbert, their top male box-office attraction until 1929. Then his first all-dialogue release, **His Glorious Night**, opened with a dull thud. Somehow his voice didn't match his face, and his impassioned love scenes with Catherine Dale Owen drew giggles instead of gasps from the fans. Lionel Barrymore's direction of this Willard Mack adaptation of Molnar's play 'Olympia' didn't help; nor did the performances of Hedda Hopper, Gustav von Seyffertitz and Nance O'Neil.

S. S. Van Dine's Philo Vance was the American Sherlock Holmes of the Twenties, a cultured eccentric whose detections kept millions of breaths bated through book after book, film upon film. Paramount made three starring William Powell, then MGM took over with Basil Rathbone in **The Bishop Murder Case**. Nick Grinde and David Burton co-directed the all-talkie about a dear old professor who called in Vance to solve a murder mystery and turned out to be the killer. L to r: Rathbone, Alec B. Francis, Leila Hyams, Clarence Geldert. Also in Lenore Coffee's screenplay: Roland Young, George F. Marion, Carroll Nye, Delmer Daves.

Norma Shearer picked him for **Their Own Desire**, a sophisticated drama about a young pair having an affair complicated by her father having an affair with his mother. So Robert Montgomery became the actor all MGM's female stars wanted – and got – as leading man. The parents in this successful talkie were Helene Millard (his), Belle Bennett and Lewis Stone (hers). Director, E. Mason Hopper; script, Frances Marion and J. G. Forbes.

Tim McCoy made four more movies in 1929, then saddled his horse and went thataway out the MGM gates—forever. All silent in a talkie world, they were: **The Desert Rider** with Raquel Torres (above), Bert Roach, Edward Connelly, directed by Nick Grinde . . . **Morgan's Last Raid** with Dorothy Sebastian, Wheeler Oakman (top right), directed by Grinde . . . **The Overland Telegraph** with Lawford Davidson (bottom right), Dorothy Janis, Frank Rice, directed by John Waters . . . **Sioux Blood** with Chief Standing Bear (middle right), Robert Frazer, Marion Douglas, directed by Waters.

THE TALKIE CRAZE
1930

The talkie craze shielded Hollywood's major companies from the world's financial crisis, and they thrived: MGM-Loew's netted a new high, $15m, which it topped only in 1946. War pictures were in the money. Howard Hughes made the most, with *Hell's Angels*, by starring a sensational blonde, Jean Harlow, opposite Ben Lyon; James Whale filmed R. C. Sherriff's great play *Journey's End*; and best of all was Lewis Milestone's version of Erich Maria Remarque's *All Quiet on the Western Front* with Louis Wolheim and Lew Ayres, which won the Academy Award.

Marlene Dietrich skyrocketed in *The Blue Angel* and *Morocco*; Edward G. Robinson in *Little Caesar* started the gangster cycle; John Wayne arrived in *The Big Trail*, Spencer Tracy in *Up the River*, Leslie Howard in *Outward Bound*. Drifting out were Norma Talmadge, Alice Joyce, Milton Sills, Corinne Griffith, Thomas Meighan, Laura La Plante, Vilma Banky, Rod La Rocque, Billie Dove and, temporarily, Lillian Gish.

An actor who had last worked on the lot as an extra in The Merry Widow *in 1925 was given a short-term contract in 1930 and cast as a gangster in Joan Crawford's* **Dance, Fools, Dance**. ▽ *By late 1931 he was a star, having appeared in eight more pictures with an increasingly electrifying effect on the public. The Clark Gable era at MGM had begun its 24-year span. Joan had a strong movie in this, playing a girl who became a crime reporter when her family was ruined by the stock market crash. It had much censorship trouble with a scene, which today would probably be played nude, of boys and girls stripping to their underwear for a midnight swim. Harry Beaumont's cast included Earle Foxe (left), William Bakewell, Lester Vail, Cliff Edwards and Natalie Moorhead. Script: Richard Schayer, Aurania Rouverol.*

Because it was scheduled to be John Gilbert's first talkie, Thalberg stinted nothing on **Redemption**. *He gave him a role in which John Barrymore had triumphed on the stage, Dorothy Farnum and Edwin Justus Mayer's carefully scripted version of Tolstoy's 'The Living Corpse', a strong cast including Renee Adoree, Eleanor Boardman and Conrad Nagel, epic director Fred Niblo and a lavish production.*

Result: disaster. Gilbert was quickly shunted into His Glorious Night *while the studio worked out a salvage job on* Redemption. *Several scenes—like this suicide of the hero for the sake of his wife and friend who had married since his presumed death (left to right: Gilbert, Boardman, Nagel)—were remade and the movie was eventually released as the star's second talkie. Result: flop.*

While never a superstar, William Haines was a steady moneymaker for MGM. A returned college hero and his family's astonishment at his moneymaking schemes provided spirited fun in **The Girl Said No**, *directed by Sam Wood. Marie Dressler (a one-scene riot as a drunk millionairess), Leila Hyams and Francis X. Bushman Jr were the only cast members not in this scene. Left to right: William V. Mong, Phyllis Crane, William Janney, Clara Blandick, Haines, Polly Moran, Junior Coghlan. Sarah Y. Mason and Charles MacArthur scripted.*

In **Way Out West** *Haines played a carnival gambler forced to work on a ranch to repay the cowboys he'd fleeced. Fred Niblo, the Ben-Hur director, made it as his last under MGM contract. Left to right: Haines, Miss Moran, Miss Hyams, Charles Middleton, Francis X. Bushman Jr, Cliff Edwards. Script: Byron Morgan, Alfred Block, Joe Farnham, Ralph Spence.*

Remote Control *gave Haines another success. It should have been a mishmash, with four directors and seven writers working on it at various times, but it turned out rather well. Malcolm St Clair and Nick Grinde wound up with direction credit. Haines played a music salesman (with Eileen Percy) turned radio announcer, foiling a crook entertainer (John Miljan) who broadcast code instructions to his gang. Charles King, Mary Doran, J. C. Nugent, Eddie Nugent (no relation) and the ubiquitous Miss Moran were also involved.*

Romance, *Garbo's second talkie, confirmed her skill with dialogue, making you believe that the Italian soprano heroine could sound like a Swedish contralto. (Strange, considering her long USA residence, that Garbo always spoke with an English–Swedish rather than an American–Swedish accent.) The old Edward Sheldon play in which Doris Keane had an international success was in sharp contrast to* Anna Christie, *and returned Garbo to an ambience of glamorous, ill-starred love. Her rather inadequate leading man was Gavin Gordon (here) as the suitor of the opera star, mistress of a rich man (Lewis Stone). Elliott Nugent, Florence Lake, Clara Blandick and Henry Armetta were also in Clarence Brown's cast. Script: Bess Meredyth, Edwin Justus Mayer.*

Ramon Novarro's second talkie, **In Gay Madrid**, *was a letdown after* Devil May Care. *A song-interrupted comedy, its frail Bess Meredyth–Edwin Justus Mayer–Edward Fields script about the loves of a highspirited student was directed by Robert Z. Leonard. Left to right: William V. Mong, Novarro, Beryl Mercer, Dorothy Jordan.*

Lady of Scandal/The High Road *was Frederick Lonsdale's sister-under-the-typewriter-ribbon to Pinero's 'Trelawny of the Wells'. Ruth Chatterton played the actress whose fiancé (Ralph Forbes) took her to visit his aristocratic family (Fred Kerr, Nance O'Neil). After dallying with his cousin (Basil Rathbone, here) she gave both men up and returned to the stage. Stylishly directed by Sidney Franklin, but all a bit hoity-toity for the average fan. Script: Hans Kraly, Claudine West, Edwin Justus Mayer.*

Fifi d'Orsay, surely the most durable mamselle in show-biz history, was still rolling her eyes and Rs in a big Broadway musical of 1972, 'Follies'. In 1930 she romped through **Those Three French Girls** *with Reginald Denny and English stage veteran George Grossmith (here) and Yola d'Avril, Sandra Ravel, Cliff Edwards and Polly Moran. Direction, Harry Beaumont; story, Arthur Freed, Dale Van Every; script, Sylvia Thalberg, Frank Butler; dialogue, P. G. Wodehouse.*

MGM's own glamour stars were working or looked the other way when **Passion Flower** *went into production, so Kay Francis was borrowed from Paramount. The movie was one for the ladies, a typical Kathleen Norris romantic novel made into a typical Kay Francis movie. In this scene she was eloping with her chauffeur (Charles Bickford) when a letter from his wife (Kay Johnson) ended their idyll, and he left Kay F. hiding a broken heart under several yards of mink. William DeMille directed, with Lewis Stone and ZaSu Pitts featured in the Martin Flavin–Laurence Johnson–Edith Fitzgerald screenplay.*

An absolute winner was **The Divorcee**, *which reaped a fortune from the public, praise from the critics, and the 1929–30 best actress Oscar from the Academy for Norma Shearer. After this, her carefully planned and highly successful career ('Well, she sleeps with the boss', philosophized Joan Crawford) included many wayward wives, in sharp contrast to the offscreen Mrs Thalberg. Chester Morris (with her here), Robert Montgomery, Conrad Nagel and Florence Eldridge also sparkled in Robert Z. Leonard's production, written by Zelda Sears, Nick Grinde, John Meehan. All concerned worked wonders with not obviously ideal screen material, Ursula Parrott's novel* Ex-Wife *about a woman who shed her husband, emulated his sexual freedom, then returned to him.*

Somerset Maugham's 'The Circle', filmed silent in 1925, found its voice in **Strictly Unconventional**. *But by 1930 a teacup talkie needed strong star values to sustain it, and this one didn't have the most illustrious cast in the world. There was criticism of David Burton's stiff direction and the Sylvia Thalberg–Frank Butler treatment of the story about infidelity in two generations, with (left to right) Tyrrell Davis, Catherine Dale Owen, Paul Cavanagh and Mary Forbes; also cast were Lewis Stone, Alison Skipworth and Ernest Torrence.*

The apex of cuckoo supercolossalness was achieved by Cecil B. DeMille's **Madam Satan**, *a box-office disaster. A little pastry of a plot (by Jeanie Macpherson, Gladys Unger, Elsie Janis) about marital jealousy was covered by layer upon layer of spectacular icing until it became indigestible even to DeMillions for whom it was confected. Climax came in this scene, a costume party in a giant airship which was struck by lightning, obliging hundreds of guests to descend on New York by parachute. The stars were Kay Johnson and (here) Reginald Denny, Lillian Roth and Roland Young. Miss Roth's hectic life made a much better movie,* I'll Cry Tomorrow, *25 years later.*

Once he could do no wrong, but in 1930 John Gilbert was slightly off-key in every try. **Way for a Sailor** *attempted to make him a tough seafarer, but sank at the box-office. Sam Wood directed (left to right) Leila Hyams, Gilbert, and Wallace Beery whose hearty humours with a pet seal occupied much footage; also writer/actor Jim Tully and Polly Moran. Laurence Stallings, W. L. River, Charles MacArthur and Al Boasberg all had a go at the script.*

GABLE STARS
1931

The Depression deepened, and the movie-makers could not all go on prospering when millions of their customers were thrown out of work and faced actual hunger. Warner Bros, which had absorbed First National and many of the biggest music publishers during its three-year boom, reported an $8m loss. RKO-Radio, despite a blockbuster (and Academy Award winner) in *Cimarron* with Richard Dix and Irene Dunne, dipped $5½m into the red. So did Fox.

MGM and Paramount stayed solvent with $12m and $6m profits respectively, while Universal, which had lost $2½m in 1930, climbed back into the black with twin horrors: Boris Karloff in *Frankenstein* and Bela Lugosi in *Dracula*, starting a never-ending vogue.

James Cagney shocked in *Public Enemy*, and Phillips Holmes demonstrated how to drown your pregnant girlfriend so graphically in Dreiser's *An American Tragedy* that the British censor banned it.

Constance Bennett, Kay Francis, Miriam Hopkins and Sylvia Sidney became big names; Herbert Marshall, Tallulah Bankhead and Laurence Olivier took the London-to-Hollywood route.

The irresistible force meets the immovable object: Clark Gable woos Greta Garbo in **Susan Lenox, her Fall and Rise**/The Rise of ▷ Helga. *As this shot shows, Robert Z. Leonard directed with an eye for Freudian symbolism; the stars responded with emotion-charged performances. That MGM's two most potent personalities, paired for the first and last time, failed to set the screen on fire was blamed on a meandering script toiled upon by no fewer than 14 writers; Wanda Tuchock, Zelda Sears and Edith Fitzgerald got screen credit. In support were Jean Hersholt, Alan Hale, John Miljan, Hale Hamilton, Hilda Vaughn, Ian Keith, Cecil Cunningham, Theodore Von Eltz, Helene Millard, Russell Simpson. How did Gable reach his Garbo co-star prestige? See next pages.*

Ramon Novarro gave a polished performance as the prewar Austrian guardsman of Arthur Schnitzler's play **Daybreak**, with a delicately △ appealing leading lady in Helen Chandler (here) and adroit direction by Jacques Feyder. The strong cast also had Karen Morley, Kent Douglass, C. Aubrey Smith, Jean Hersholt, William Bakewell, Glenn Tryon and Clyde Cook. It was further enhanced by the newly developed supersensitive Eastman film which improved photographic values, especially in low-key lighting like this. All in vain: the crowds didn't want this movie. Script: Ruth Cummings, Zelda Sears, Cyril Hume.

France and Spain. Left to right: Irene Rich, Robert Montgomery, Miss Shearer and Neil Hamilton; also cast were Marjorie Rambeau, Hale Hamilton, Jed Prouty, Albert Conti and Conchita Montenegro.

Clark Gable had started 1931 as a bit player and he ended it as a star in **Hell Divers**, his eighth MGM assignment that year. Scenes like this, with Marie Prevost wrapping herself around him, threw millions of female moviegoers into tizzies of rapture. George Hill's production was a thriller in other respects, with magnificent aviation sequences, Wallace Beery excellent as a US Navy veteran, and Dorothy Jordan, Conrad Nagel, Cliff Edwards, Marjorie Rambeau and John Miljan. Script: Malcolm Stuart Boylan, Harvey Gates.

A come-hither title and an excellent cast gave strong box-office impetus to **Strangers May Kiss**, with which George Fitzmaurice, French-born director of many hits for Samuel Goldwyn, made his MGM début. Practically a reprise of The Divorcee for Norma Shearer, it was based by John Meehan on another Ursula Parrott story and had the star, elegantly gowned, toying with lovers across America,

1932

MGM-Loew's $8m profit seemed downright indecent in 1932 when movie profits generally were plummeting: Paramount made a $16m loss for the year, followed by bankruptcy; Fox topped that with a $17m loss, and Warner Bros. went $14m deeper into the red. Credit MGM's tremendous name power: Marie Dressler, Wallace Beery, Norma Shearer, Joan Crawford, Garbo, Clark Gable, Jean Harlow & Co. were at their zenith, and the multi-starred *Grand Hotel* was the film of the year.

With breadlines longer than the box-office queues, laughter was worth its decibels in gold; it was supplied by such clowns as Eddie Cantor, Joe E. Brown, Wheeler and Woolsey, Laurel and Hardy, Will Rogers and Jack Oakie. At Paramount, where Dietrich slunk through von Sternberg mists, Mae West arrived to prove that a sex queen could be funny on purpose. They needed laughs there; apart from their financial troubles Warner Bros had snatched three of their top stars: Ruth Chatterton, William Powell and Kay Francis. The latter two promptly scored with *One Way Passage*.

In Europe, too, light fare dominated: Gracie Fields, Jack Hulbert, Cicely Courtneidge, Jack Buchanan and Anna Neagle starred in Britain; France had Clair's *A Nous la Liberté*, and Germany enjoyed Charell's *Congress Dances* (but made more permanent impressions with Pabst's *Kameradschaft* and Sagan's *Maedchen in Uniform*). And the English censor spread mirth by insisting that *Merrily We Go to Hell* delete the title's last word; filling in the '——' drew some alarming guesses.

Lionel Barrymore was Mayer's favourite actor, and Thalberg shared his view that the great name of Barrymore lent prestige to any movie. So they grabbed brother John the minute his Warner contract ended, signed him to a $150,000-per-film pact and cast him as the gentleman thief **Arsene Lupin** *with Lionel as his detective nemesis. It was the brothers' first picture together, although each had interspersed stage roles with movies since the pre-Hollywood silent era. They struck histrionic sparks off each other and the picture was a hit. Jack Conway directed Karen Morley, John and Lionel (here) and Tully Marshall and John Miljan. Script: Carey Wilson, Leonore Coffee, Bayard Veiller.*

Jean Harlow cost MGM $60,000 when Howard Hughes sold her contract and she started earning it back in **The Beast of the City** *Walter Huston, also beginning an MGM contract, starred as the police chief. W. R. Burnett's racketeering melodrama, scripted by John Lee Mahin, began with a foreword by President Hoover and ended with police mowing down the vice gang. Left to right: Tully Marshall, J. Carrol Naish, Jean Hersholt, Harlow. Wallace Ford, Dorothy Peterson and John Miljan were also in the cast under Charles Brabin's direction.*

Clark Gable took his turn as Marion Davies' leading man in **Polly of the Circus**, *playing a clergyman who restored a fallen trapeze artiste to physical and moral health. Not even this mad caprice of casting could check Gable's career, but the resulting flop did nothing for Marion's. Alfred Santell did his sole MGM directing job on this movie, and the Carey Wilson–Laurence Johnson script updated Margaret Mayo's ancient play; in 1917 it had been filmed as the Goldwyn Company's first production, starring Mae Marsh. Also in the new version: C. Aubrey Smith, Raymond Hatton, Ruth Selwyn, Maude Eburne, Guinn Williams, Ray Milland.*

Prosperity *was the farewell appearance in tandem of Polly Moran and Marie Dressler. It had its hilarious moments, but the basic plot of a small town stricken by the Depression hit a bit too close to home for 1932 escapist entertainment. The huge Dressler following made it profitable, however, and Sam Wood's direction gave full scope to her extraordinary acting range. Anita Page, Norman Foster, Henry Armetta, John Miljan and Jacquie Lyn were also in the Eve Greene–Zelda Sears screenplay, from an original by Sylvia Thalberg and Frank Butler. Much of it was remade after a dismal preview.*

Tallulah Bankhead was lent to MGM by Paramount for **Faithless**. *Her flamboyant personality and uninhibited performances on and off the stage had kept Londoners on a vicarious spree for eight years until Paramount brought her back to the States in 1931. They starred her in five films, and she returned to the stage after this MGM job. The camera unaccountably dimmed her lustre and her crowd magnetism. Robert Montgomery partnered Tallulah in this drama of the rich impoverished by the Wall Street crash, scripted by Carey Wilson from a Mildred Cram novel. Harry Beaumont directed, with Hugh Herbert and Louise Closser Hale featured.*

Thalberg shook the industry by throwing five of the studio's biggest stars into a single picture: **Grand Hotel**. *It was a gamble which paid off ▷ richly at the box-office, and won the best film Academy Award. Vicki Baum's successful novel and play, scripted by William Drake, gave equal prominence to Garbo and John Barrymore and to Joan Crawford, Wallace Beery and Lionel Barrymore (here). That's the order in which they were billed, after much tact had been applied to stellar egos, but the chief plaudits went to Joan as Beery's hotel stenographer and Lionel as his clerk on a dying spree. Garbo was miscast as a mercurial ballerina and for once her acting seemed forced. Smoothly directed by Edmund Goulding, they were supported by Lewis Stone, Jean Hersholt, Ferdinand Gottschalk, Rafaela Ottiano, Purnell Pratt, Frank Conroy, Tully Marshall.*

King Vidor returned to MGM in 1933 to film **The Stranger's Return** from a novel by Phil Stong, whose State Fair had just registered a major hit. The new one didn't, although Vidor captured the atmosphere of rural life with refreshing simplicity, and inspired fine work by Miriam Hopkins, Franchot Tone and Beulah Bondi (here) and Lionel Barrymore, as Miriam's grandfather dismayed by her affair with a married farmer. In support were Stuart Erwin, Irene Hervey and Grant Mitchell. Brown Holmes collaborated with Stong on the screenplay, produced by Lucien Hubbard.

MGM continued to sail out of the 1933 doldrums with **Tugboat Annie**, a perfect example of what Mayer (and most of the public) considered to be ideal entertainment: the hokum of husband-and-wife slapstick brawling and mother-and-son sentiment, given the warmth of life by its makers' skill. Not least that of its co-stars, Wallace Beery and Marie Dressler, aided by Robert Young (here) as their son, Maureen O'Sullivan, Willard Robertson and Frankie Darro. Mervyn LeRoy returned to direct them in Norman Reilly Raine's story, adapted by Zelda Sears and Eve Greene; producer, Harry Rapf. Its receipts were colossal.

A quickie by MGM standards, **The Solitaire Man** was distinguished by the first Culver City assignments of two expert performers: Herbert Marshall and Mary Boland. Although the Samuel and Bella Spewack play about double-crossing crooks was set in a cramped Paris–London airplane cabin, its tension, heightened by scenarist James K. McGuinness and director Jack Conway, gave it the illusion of action. Left to right: Lionel Atwill, May Robson, Marshall, Elizabeth Allan, Miss Boland; also present were Lucille Gleason, Ralph Forbes and Robert McWade.

Many critics ranked **Sons of the Desert**/Fraternally Yours as Laurel and Hardy's best full-lengther, both for their comedy and its broad satire on American conventions. Hal Roach threw in another of his shorts stars, Charley Chase (centre), and Stan and Oliver were henpecked by Mae Busch and Dorothy Christy. William Seiter directed the Frank Craven–Byron Morgan screenplay.

Musicals were back in fashion by late 1933, and Marion Davies had a fairly good one in **Going Hollywood**. Its box-office appeal was guaranteed by co-star Bing Crosby, then at his crooning zenith. His acting ability not yet able to stand strain, he was cast as a crooner, with Marion (centre) as his greatest fan. Donald Ogden Stewart's screenplay, from an original by Frances Marion, was produced by Walter Wanger and directed by Raoul Walsh, with Fifi d'Orsay (right) and Stuart Erwin and Ned Sparks. Of its six songs, 'Temptation' became the big hit.

What had been almost completed years before as a revue, The March of Time, finally saw light as **Broadway to Hollywood**/Ring Up the Curtain with all but a smidgin of the revue jettisoned, but with a dramatic story developed from the original show-business-through-the-years idea. It turned out very well, giving strong opportunities to Frank Morgan, Jackie Cooper and Alice Brady (here) and Madge Evans, Jimmy Durante, Eddie Quillan, May Robson, Una Merkel, Russell Hardie, Nelson Eddy (début – one song). Mickey Rooney, who had been in movies since the age of four, made his MGM bow at 10. Produced by Harry Rapf, the film was a fitting farewell by its writer and director, Willard Mack, who died soon after.

The 'B' pictures churned out at Culver City in 1933 maintained a praiseworthy standard. Shot in a couple of weeks without any of the studio's superstars, dramas like these kept release schedules filled and audiences satisfied. Madge Evans. Richard Dix (the veteran star's only MGM movie), Clarence Wilson in **Day of**

Reckoning; written by Eve Gordon, directed by Charles Brabin, with Conway Tearle, Una Merkel, Stuart Erwin . . . Irene Hervey, Ben Lyon, Otto Kruger in **The Women in His Life**; written by F. Hugh Herbert, directed by George B. Seitz, with Una Merkel, Nat Pendleton, Isabel Jewell . . . Alice Brady, Maureen O'Sullivan in **Stage Mother**; written by Bradford Ropes, John Meehan; directed by Brabin, with Franchot Tone, Phillips Holmes, Ted Healy, C. Henry Gordon. Lucien Hubbard produced the first two, Hunt Stromberg the third.

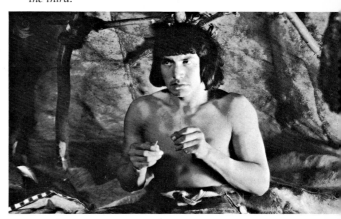

The Academy gave film editor Conrad Nervig an Oscar for his work on **Eskimo**/Mala the Magnificent. Director was W. S. Van Dyke. That glutton for punishment made yet another arduous location trip for the movie, this time into the Arctic. He sailed in a whaling schooner loaded with movie technicians and equipment to the northernmost inhabited settlement in Alaska, where the ship was frozen-in for the 1932–3 winter. Their guide was Peter Freuchen, author of the book on which John Lee Mahin based his script. Clyde DeVinna got some stunning photographic effects. The native cast spoke in the Eskimo tongue, translated on film by subtitles. Mala, seen here, played the lead so winningly that producer Hunt Stromberg gave him an MGM contract. Released late in 1933 after a year in production, it got a warm reception, but some of the paybox returns had a touch of frostbite.

OF NEW YORK

Joan Crawford (right) had one of her biggest hits and the studio a record-breaker in ◁ **Dancing Lady**, a strong backstage story with musical trimmings on a lavish scale. Scripted by Allen Rivkin, Zelda Sears and P. J. Wolfson from James Warner Bellah's novel, it took her from a raided burlesque show with Winnie Lightner (left) to Broadway stardom with Fred Astaire. Their 'Rhythm of the Day' number (Fred's only appearance for his screen début) was written for the movie by Rodgers & Hart, but the one that lasted was Lane & Adamson's 'Everything I Have is Yours'. Clark Gable, overshadowed for once, co-starred, with Franchot Tone, May Robson, Ted Healy and his 3 Stooges, Grant Mitchell, Sterling Holloway, Nelson Eddy (one song) and Robert Benchley. Robert Z. Leonard directed, David O. Selznick produced.

Louis Mayer had called in his son-in-law, Selznick, to strengthen the top production brass while Thalberg was on sick leave. Selznick obliged with a flourish, out-starring Grand Hotel with an astonishing cast for **Dinner at Eight**, and bringing director George Cukor over from RKO where they had turned out a succession of hits. The picture made a massive profit. The order of billing was: Marie Dressler, John Barrymore, Wallace Beery, Jean Harlow, Lionel Barrymore, Lee Tracy, Edmund Lowe, Billie Burke, Madge Evans, Jean Hersholt, Karen Morley, Phillips Holmes, May Robson, Louise Closser Hale, Grant Mitchell, Elizabeth Patterson . . . and then some. Here: Miss Burke as hostess of the dinner (which began as the film ended) and Beery and Miss Harlow as guests whose bickering was a comedy highlight.

◁ John Barrymore was outstanding as an alcoholic, suicidal actor, in the neatly jigsawed stories of the Herman Mankiewicz–Frances Marion–Donald Ogden Stewart script from the Edna Ferber–George Kaufman play.

The Secret of Madame Blanche was another dip into the Madame X–Madelon Claudet corn-bag. Irene Dunne and Douglas Walton (with Jean Parker, left) played mother and son who didn't know they were, until he committed murder, whereupon she took the blame. . . . It had the lot, including a Nineties' music hall, World War I, a big courtroom scene, and a tear-tapping performance by Irene. Charles Brabin directed the Frances Goodrich–Albert Hackett screenplay, with Phillips Holmes, Lionel Atwill, Una Merkel, C. Henry Gordon and Mitchell Lewis.

Has Phillips Holmes just murdered Mae Clarke? No–it's a frame-up! **Penthouse**/Crooks in Clover was a crime drama spiced with wit, and pointed the way for director W. S.

Van Dyke, producer Hunt Stromberg, scripters Frances Goodrich and Albert Hackett and co-star Myrna Loy to their triumphant Thin Man a year later. C. Henry Gordon (here) was the gangster heavy and Warner Baxter the lawyer hero, supported by Nat Pendleton, Charles Butterworth, Martha Sleeper, George E. Stone, Robert Emmet O'Connor and Raymond Hatton.

Laugh at yourself, Hollywood, and the world laughs with you. Jean Harlow, playing from experience, demonstrated how an actress can be glamourized and publicity-pressured into an

△ idol in **Bombshell**/Blonde Bombshell, an uproarious satire on the dream factories and their star-building methods. Lee Tracy (left) was her high-powered press agent and Louise Beavers her maid; others contributing were Frank Morgan, Franchot Tone, Pat O'Brien, Una Merkel, Ivan Lebedeff, Ted Healy, C. Aubrey Smith, Mary Forbes and Isabel Jewell. Director Victor Fleming and scenarists John Lee Mahin and Jules Furthman helped make the Harlow–Tracy partnership a dazzler. Hunt Stromberg produced.

Marie Dressler's last appearance was in **Christopher Bean** with Lionel Barrymore. She died, aged 65, six months after its release. Her films are not revived, so it's hard to realize

today what a powerful hold this large, unlovely woman had on the moviegoing masses. She played both drama and comedy with immense verve. If it sometimes swept her into over-acting, nobody cared: the warmth of her personality was irresistible. Sidney Howard's stage hit 'The Late Christopher Bean' (from René Fauchois' 'Prenez Garde à la Peinture') revolved upon a deceased character and, strangely enough, was also the last screenplay written by Laurence Johnson (with Sylvia Thalberg) before his death. Sam Wood directed and Harry Rapf produced this comedy of an avaricious family whose housekeeper was the custodian of a posthumously famous artist's paintings. Beulah Bondi, George Coulouris, Helen Mack, Russell Hardie, H. B. Warner and Jean Hersholt supported.

Paul Osborn's play 'The Vinegar Tree' was fashioned by Bella and Samuel Spewack into an Alice Brady vehicle, **Should Ladies Behave?**, which was better than its title. The domestic comedy of three women infatuated with one man was smoothly directed by Harry Beaumont for producer Lawrence Weingarten and featured Conway Tearle and Lionel Barrymore, here with Miss Brady, aided by Katherine Alexander, Mary Carlisle, William Janney and Halliwell Hobbes. But the star's eccentric mannerisms were meeting audience resistance outside the city centres. MGM had bought Noël Coward's 'The Vortex' for her next, but censorship problems proved insoluble and she left the contract list.

1933

Helen Hayes was splendid in **Another Language**, adapted by Herman Mankiewicz, Gertrude Purcell and Donald Ogden Stewart from Rose Franken's play about domestic conflict, but she was challenged for critics' honours by Louise Closser Hale as her dominating mother-in-law. Sadly, Miss Hale's first leading role immediately preceded her death. This scene, in which the new bride realizes that she and her husband's family speak different languages, shows (left to right) Margaret Hamilton, Minor Watson, Miss Hale, Henry Travers, Robert Montgomery, Miss Hayes and Maidel Turner. Edward H. Griffith directed for the first time at MGM.

What! No Beer? was a sorry MGM swansong for Buster Keaton and allowed co-star Jimmy Durante to play first fiddle. Buster's drinking problem was now acute, and when he was able to work he had little enthusiasm for the picture. Neither had the public, although the Carey Wilson–Jack Cluett script about the partial repeal of Prohibition had its comic moments. Edward Sedgwick directed, with Roscoe Ates, Phyllis Barry, John Miljan, Henry Armetta and Edward Brophy.

The long and painful decline of John Gilbert from topmost star to second-feature hero ended with **Fast Workers**, which concluded his contract. Ironically, its routine script about skyscraper construction men came from Laurence Stallings, writer of his 1925 triumph, The Big Parade. Karl Brown and Ralph Wheelwright collaborated. Willard Mack and Mae Clarke (with Gilbert, here), Robert Armstrong and Sterling Holloway were featured; Tod Browning directed.

1933 went out with one star rising and another falling in **Cat and the Fiddle**. Jeanette MacDonald, who had scored in some Paramount frolics, was beginning her MGM career and Ramon Novarro had only two more films to go in his. The 1931 stage musical about bohemians in Brussels was adapted by the Spewacks for producer Bernard Hyman and directed by William K. Howard, with Charles Butterworth (right) and Frank Morgan, Vivienne Segal, Jean Hersholt, Henry Armetta, Joseph Cawthorn, Frank Conroy.

The fifth and last film to star both Barrymore brothers was **Night Flight**. With Clark Gable, Helen Hayes, Robert Montgomery, Myrna Loy and William Gargan also cast, it was intended as another all-star blockbuster but didn't measure up to Grand Hotel or Dinner at Eight at the box-office. Glamour was neglected in favour of gritty drama in the story, adapted from Antoine de Saint-Exupery's book by Oliver H. P. Garrett, about a South American airline run by John B. with ruthless disregard for his pilots' safety. Clarence Brown directed the David O. Selznick production.

Rouben Mamoulian had Garbo's movements timed to a metronome like a ballet for the lyrical 'I am memorizing this room' scene in **Queen Christina**. After making As You Desire ▷ Me Garbo had taken a year off, mostly in Sweden, leaving the world (and not least MGM) in suspense about her possible retirement. A new and lucrative contract, with script, director, photographer and cast approval rights, brought her back. The romanticized story of Sweden's 17th-century queen became the star vehicle in excelsis; it was still getting profitable bookings 40 years later. Script was by Garbo's friend Salka Viertel (with S. N. Behrman and H. M. Harwood), direction by Mamoulian, photography by her favourite William Daniels; her leading man was John Gilbert (replacing newcomer Laurence Olivier because she wanted to restore her old co-star's prestige), and production was by Walter Wanger. All was as Garbo desired it, and she responded with her finest performance to date. Lewis Stone, Ian Keith, C. Aubrey Smith, Akim Tamiroff and Reginald Owen supported reverently.

GREAT HITS, GREAT PROFITS
1934

Weekly attendances rose 10m as the eight major companies (MGM, Paramount, Fox, Warner Bros., United Artists, Universal, RKO-Radio, Columbia) sighed with relief and upped their output to 361 features. Of these, MGM had the lion's share of hits and by far the highest net with $7½m (Warner Bros. had its fourth successive year in the red, the aggregate loss reaching $30m).

Little Columbia scooped the major Academy Awards with *It Happened One Night* and W. C. Fields made his funniest film, *It's a Gift*. Two blondes were the star sensations of the year, both via loan-outs from their studios. After dozens of supporting roles at Warners, Bette Davis came back a star from RKO's *Of Human Bondage*, while Paramount's *Little Miss Marker* gave Fox a goldmine in Shirley Temple. The latter jumped straight into the top ten money-magnets (elected annually by the exhibitors via the Motion Picture Herald), joining Will Rogers, Clark Gable, Janet Gaynor, Wallace Beery, Mae West, Joan Crawford, Bing Crosby, Marie Dressler and Norma Shearer.

One of MGM's most brilliantly successful years got off to a modestly profitable start with **The Mystery of Mr X**. *Director Edgar Selwyn, producer Lawrence Weingarten and their crew could take a bow for its authenticity. One English critic wrote: 'I have never yet seen a London policeman who looked like a London policeman in a British film. The Metro policemen, however, looked amazingly like the real thing.' Robert Montgomery played the thief and chief suspect who tracked down the actual Mr X, a maniacal killer of cops. In support were Lewis Stone, Henry Stephenson, Elizabeth Allan, Ralph Forbes, Alec B. Francis and (here) Forrester Harvey. Philip Mac-Donald adapted his novel with Monckton Hoffe and Howard Emmett Rogers.*

1934 brought Norma Shearer's first appearance for a year. Thalberg had recovered his health sufficiently to return to the studio, but as producer of a limited number of films rather than as overseer of its entire output. After toying with the idea of his wife doing a remake of The Green Hat, *he settled on* **Riptide** *as his unit's first. It was one of those talkative plots about adultery among the rich, and no great shakes as a movie. But the fans were glad to have Miss Shearer back, and Thalberg had better to come. Edmund Goulding wrote it and directed (left to right) Herbert Marshall,*

Miss Shearer, Robert Montgomery, Mrs Patrick Campbell (once London's most dazzling star, making her Hollywood debut at 69) and Lilyan Tashman (screen veteran at 35, who died just after this film); also Ralph Forbes, Skeets Gallagher, George K. Arthur and Halliwell Hobbes.

Jean Harlow and Patsy Kelly were a couple of gals on the make in **The Girl from Missouri**/ 100% Pure *and Franchot Tone was ready to be made by Jean. The ostensible virgin with cash-register eyes was a character very like the one she'd played in* Red-Headed Woman *but with a lot more Anita Loos humour. Many of the laughs were got by Patsy, a recruit from Hal Roach shorts, whose slam-bang delivery of dialogue enlivened scores of movies until she returned to Broadway in the seventies. Jack Conway directed the Bernard Hyman production, which featured Lionel Barrymore, Lewis Stone, Hale Hamilton, Alan Mowbray, Clara Blandick and Nat Pendleton.*

Thalberg relit the dazzling catherine wheels of musical comedy spun by director Ernst Lubitsch, Maurice Chevalier and Jeanette MacDonald in Paramount's Love Parade *and* One Hour with You *for the 1934 version of* **The Merry Widow**. *Gone were the orgiastic ▷ abandon and insinuated depravity of 1925's von Stroheim; now the widow had Jeanette's gentility, the prince had Chevalier's naughty-but-niceness, and if Lubitsch's closed bedroom doors implied a roll on the chaise-longue – well, it was all in fun. It also had Lehar's music, plus new lyrics by Lorenz Hart, plus a witty Ernst Vajda–Samson Raphaelson script, plus MGM's unparamountable opulence enhanced by Oliver Marsh's photography. (Cedric Gibbons' and Frederic Hope's art direction was Academy Awarded.) Edward Everett Horton, Una Merkel, George Barbier, Minna Gombell, Herman Bing and Donald Meek supported. Mayer and Thalberg had been trying to get its co-stars for years; they held on to MacDonald, but Chevalier's first Hollywood period was ending.*

A much less ambitious musical, **Student Tour**, *was whipped out by producer Monta Bell and director Charles Reisner in half the time and at one-tenth the cost of* The Merry Widow. *It looked it. The script by Ralph Spence and Philip Dunne about collegiates on a cruise yielded a few amusing scenes for Jimmy Durante and Charles Butterworth, but little for heroine Maxine Doyle or (left to right) Herman Brix (later Bruce Bennett), Monte Blue, Mary Loos, Phil Regan, Florine Mc-Kinney, Fay McKenzie, Bobby Gordon, Douglas Fowley and (pre-fame) Betty Grable. Nelson Eddy made another one-song appearance.*

Meanwhile still another kind of musical was hatching up the road at Hal Roach's studio. **Babes in Toyland** *was something for the kiddies, and enough of them took ma and pa along to make it a moneyspinner. That was thanks to Laurel and Hardy, at the peak of their fame; their gags were woven into Glen MacDonough's yarn about nursery rhyme characters. Gus Meins and Charles Rogers directed this version of Victor Herbert's operetta, with Stan, Harry Kleinbach, Ollie (here) and Charlotte Henry, Felix Knight and Johnny Downs.*

Early in 1934 Mayer gave Marie Dressler's morale a boost with a new contract, although he knew her illness was fatal and the studio needed a replacement for some of her scripts. He had recently let Columbia have May Robson for Frank Capra's Lady for a Day *and the movie had shot her to stardom. So* **You Can't Buy Everything** *became a Robson vehicle. The Dudley Nichols–Lamar Trotti original was based on the true story of Hetty Green, the miserly woman who amassed millions on Wall Street. Zelda Sears' and Eve Greene's script, directed by Charles Reisner, softened the character with a strong injection of mother-love. William Bakewell (here with May), Jean Parker and Tad Alexander played the young generation and Lewis Stone, Reginald Mason, Walter Walker and Claude Gillingwater the old. Lucien Hubbard produced, with medium paybox results.*

Robert Young's straightforward sincerity made him one of the best liked–and hardest worked –of actors during his dozen MGM years. In 1934 he did several loan-outs and four respectable 'Bs' on the home lot: as a Louisiana
▽ *bayou boy with Jean Parker in* **Lazy River***, directed by George B. Seitz, scripted and produced by Lucien Hubbard, with Ted Healy, C. Henry Gordon, Nat Pendleton, Maude Eburne . . . as an American expatriate with*
▽ *Una Merkel in* **Paris Interlude***, directed by Edwin L. Marin, produced by Hubbard, adapted by Wells Root from an S. J. and Laura Perelman play, with Madge Evans, Otto Kruger, George Meeker, Edward Brophy . . . as a baseball professional with Madge Evans and Joseph Sauers in* **Death on the Diamond***,* ▽ *directed by Edward Sedgwick, produced by Hubbard, story by Cortland Fitzsimmons, with Pendleton, Healy, Gordon, Paul Kelly, Mickey Rooney . . . as a football star with Stuart Erwin and Preston Foster in* **The Band** ▽ **Plays On***, directed by Russell Mack, produced by Marin, with Betty Furness, Leo Carrillo, Russell Hardie, Healy, and seven writer credits.*

In **Sadie McKee** *Joan Crawford, not for the first time or the last, played a poor girl forced to choose between a rich man (Edward Arnold, brilliant as a happy alcoholic) and true love (Gene Raymond, who crooned the theme song 'All I Do Is Dream of You'). Clarence Brown's direction and a good cast brought dramatic vitality to this negligible bit of magazine fiction by Vina Delmar, adapted by John Meehan and produced by Lawrence Weingarten. Others involved were Franchot Tone, Joan's second husband in more or less private life, Jean Dixon (here with Joan and Gene) and Esther Ralston, Leo Carrillo, Akim Tamiroff and Zelda Sears.*

Jean Parker, Charles Bickford and Mady Christians in **A Wicked Woman***. Eleventh in the cast list was Robert Taylor, an MGM discovery making his feature début there after a highly-praised short,* Buried Loot*, and a minor loan-out. Miss Christians, a Viennese charmer, played the title role in this story of a mother who, having killed her sadistic husband while defending her children, kept her guilty secret for ten years. Ann Austin's story, scripted by Zelda Sears and Florence Ryerson, could have been a dank weepie without her. Although an actress of note in Europe, she went on to grace other Hollywood movies without reaching deserved stardom. Also cast: Betty Furness, William Henry, Jackie Searle, Miss Sears (her last role and screenplay) and Sterling Holloway. Harry Rapf produced, Charles Brabin directed.*

Every prolific director has made at least one he'd like to forget. **Laughing Boy** *was W. S. Van Dyke's. A glumly dramatic tale by Oliver La Farge, noted writer about Red Indian life, was converted to a sort of screenplay by John Colton and John Lee Mahin, and produced by Hunt Stromberg, apparently while thinking of something else. Mexican stars Ramon Novarro in the mis-title role, and Lupe Velez as his*

wigwam warmer, tried in vain to act like Indians. Audiences had plenty of seats to put their coats on.

Lupe Velez had a happier time in **Hollywood Party** *as her temperamental self, wearing an off-the-hip number and clowning with Laurel and Hardy. Producer Harry Rapf had half the stars and directors on the lot taking a whack at this musical mishmash, but it boiled down to these three plus Jimmy Durante, Charles Butterworth, Jack Pearl, Ted Healy, June Clyde and, best of all, a Mickey Mouse cartoon sequence from Walt Disney. Richard Boleslawski got such director credit as there was. Script was by MGM's publicity chief Howard Dietz, a celebrated revue librettist in his spare time, and Arthur Kober.*

Gladys George, a Broadway star, started a brief spell of Hollywood fame in **Straight is the Way***, but Karen Morley was leading lady of this minor gangster piece, a remake of the Gilbert–Crawford silent* Four Walls*. Producer, Lucien Hubbard; director, Paul Sloane; script, Bernard Schubert. Left to right: May Robson, Franchot Tone, Miss George. Also cast: Jack La Rue, Nat Pendleton, C. Henry Gordon and William Bakewell.*

The pedigree of **Biography of a Bachelor Girl** *was impeccable: producer, Thalberg; director, E. H. Griffith, who had made star Ann Harding's best movies; author, S. N. Behrman, from his Broadway hit, 'Biography', about a painter with a past who stirred up an entertaining fuss by writing her memoirs; script, Anita Loos, Horace Jackson; camera, James Wong Howe; cast, Miss Harding and Edward Arnold (here) and Robert Montgomery, Edward Everett Horton, Una Merkel. Box-office: spotty.*

While MGM paid lip-service to the industry's 1934 campaign against double features, it continued delivering 'Bs' to meet stubborn public demand. Two good little programmers were: **Murder in the Private Car**/Murder on the Runaway Train, *a non-stop chase item with Russell Hardie and Charles Ruggles, and Mary Carlisle, Una Merkel and Porter Hall, produced by Lucien Hubbard, directed by Harry Beaumont, script by Ralph Spence, Edgar Allan Woolf, Al Boasberg, Harvey Thew . . .* **Have a Heart**, *a comedy about a street vendor, with Jean Parker and James Dunn, and Una Merkel, Stuart Erwin and Willard Robertson, produced by John Considine Jr, directed by David Butler, script by Florence Ryerson and Woolf.*

After Queen Christina, *the Garbo classic,* **The Painted Veil** *came as something of a letdown. The Somerset Maugham story, as adapted by John Meehan, Salka Viertel and Edith Fitzgerald, harked back to Garbo's silent movies, with Greta torn between worthy husband and passionate lover. In fact its plot hardly differed from that of* Wild Orchids, *but now Herbert Marshall, here, played the w.h. and George Brent the p.l., while China replaced Java as the exotic locale. Richard Boleslawski directed, Hunt Stromberg produced; Katherine Alexander, Warner Oland, Jean Hersholt, Beulah Bondi, Cecilia Parker and Forrester Harvey were featured.*

Besides grooming new stars, MGM knew how to revive old ones, as in the case of William Powell. After many years of stardom at Paramount, then Warners, he was fading until cast in **Manhattan Melodrama** as the DA who had to prosecute his boyhood friend, gangster Clark Gable, and charmed the latter's mistress, Myrna Loy, away from him. It was a walloping hit. All three stars, producer David O. Selznick, director W. S. Van Dyke, author Arthur Caesar (Academy Award, best original) and scenarists Joseph Mankiewicz and Oliver H. P. Garrett were highly praised for a potent crime drama, laced with unforced fun as in this scene with Herman Bing, Loy and Powell. Leo Carrillo Isabel Jewell, Nat Pendleton and Mickey Rooney (playing Gable as a lad) were also cast.

The tyke on the left pinched this scene in **Hide-Out** from Robert Montgomery and Edward Arnold so easily you might have thought he was Hollywood's biggest star. It took Mickey Rooney a few more years to become that. The versatile W. S. Van Dyke made a real audience-pleaser from this Frances Goodrich–Albert Hackett script about a New York racketeer forced to take cover in the country, and taught to like it by the farmer's daughter. Maureen O'Sullivan, C. Henry Gordon, Elizabeth Patterson, Edward Brophy, Herman Bing and Henry Armetta were also in the Hunt Stromberg production.

Marion Davies, Marjorie Gateson, and Gary Cooper carrying Jean Parker in **Operator 13**/Spy 13, Marion's last film for MGM. It was a complicated Civil War story by Robert W. Chambers, lavishly produced by Lucien Hubbard, which hardly earned back its cost. Richard Boleslawski directed from a Harvey Thew–Zelda Sears–Eve Green script, with Mae Clarke, Douglass Dumbrille, Ted Healy, Ned Sparks, Henry B. Walthall and the four Mills Brothers (singing 'Sleepy Head'). Marion played a Northern spy assigned to liquidate Southern officer Cooper; you guessed it, they fell in love. Offscreen, Marion fell out of love with MGM when Thalberg, backed by

Mayer, scorned her startling request to star in The Barretts of Wimpole Street and Marie Antoinette, *both earmarked for Norma Shearer. Later in 1934 Marion and Hearst moved her famous bungalow and his Cosmopolitan Productions over to Warners. Miss Shearer's name wasn't mentioned in Hearst newspapers for quite a while.*

'You geev Pancho beeg kees, eh?' growled Wallace Beery to Fay Wray, who rejected the invitation and got horsewhipped for her trouble in **Viva Villa!**, a David O. Selznick near-epic, and one of the year's big winners. Howard Hawks started directing it in Mexico and Jack Conway finished it in Hollywood, getting sole credit. Between these two events there was many a foul-up. For instance, both Mexican government co-operation and Lee Tracy's contract were abruptly cancelled after the star made an intoxicated appearance on his Mexico City hotel balcony and watered a military parade passing below. Retakes with Stuart Erwin in his role ensued. Meanwhile, Beery was giving a rousing performance as the revolutionary bandit in a rip-roaring series of action scenes contrived by Ben Hecht from fact, legend and the movie stockpile. Leo Carrillo, H. B. Warner, Joseph Schildkraut, Donald Cook, George E. Stone, Katherine DeMille (Cecil's adopted daughter) and thousands of extras were in the cast.

You can find many an oldster whose all-time favourite team is William Powell, Myrna Loy and Asta. Bill and Myrna were so easy, natural and affectionately insulting together that a large section of the public believed they were △ married in life, as in **The Thin Man**. Nothing quite like this relationship had been screened before; critics and customers were totally captivated. The never failing producer-director-writers team of Hunt Stromberg, W. S. Van Dyke and Frances Goodrich–Albert Hackett filmed Dashiell Hammett's vivid detective novel, with Maureen O'Sullivan, Nat Pendleton, Minna Gombell, Porter Hall, Henry Wadsworth, William Henry, Harold Huber, Cesar Romero, Natalie Moorhead and Edward Brophy. Edward Ellis played the thin man, a murder victim.

Men in White gave Clark Gable (here with Russell Hardie) the chance to score with quietly forceful acting instead of a personality display. And its success gave MGM a penchant for hospital doctor stories, manifest even unto the television era. Richard Boleslawski directed, with Myrna Loy as Gable's society fiancée, Elizabeth Allan as his adoring nurse, Jean Hersholt as the inevitable veteran surgeon guiding him, and Otto Kruger, C. Henry Gordon, Wallace Ford, Henry B. Walthall and Samuel S. Hinds. Monta Bell produced Waldemar Young's adaptation of Sidney Kingsley's play.

Spencer Tracy had been working none too happily at Fox since leaving Broadway in 1930, and was swapped with Robert Young for one picture in 1934. It was **The Show-Off**, George Kelly's durable comedy, filmed twice by Paramount and bought by MGM for Lee Tracy (no relation). Strangely enough, Spencer's axing from Fox the following year, which cleared the way for his MGM contract, was for the same reason that Lee had been dropped by Mayer: riotous behaviour. Meanwhile Spencer did a good job as the lovable liar in Lucien Hubbard's production, adapted by Herman Mankiewicz and directed by

SENSATIONAL YEARS
HARLOW AND MARX
1935

*Robert Taylor got top billing for the first time in **Times Square Lady**, a melodrama about crooked gamblers, directed by George B. Seitz for the Lucien Hubbard 'B' hive. Opposite the screen's new Adonis were Helen Twelvetrees (here) and Virginia Bruce, supported by Nat Pendleton, Isabel Jewell, Jack La Rue and Pinky Tomlin, who wrote and sang its hit song, 'The Object of My Affection'. Screenplay by Albert Cohen and Robert Shannon from their original.*

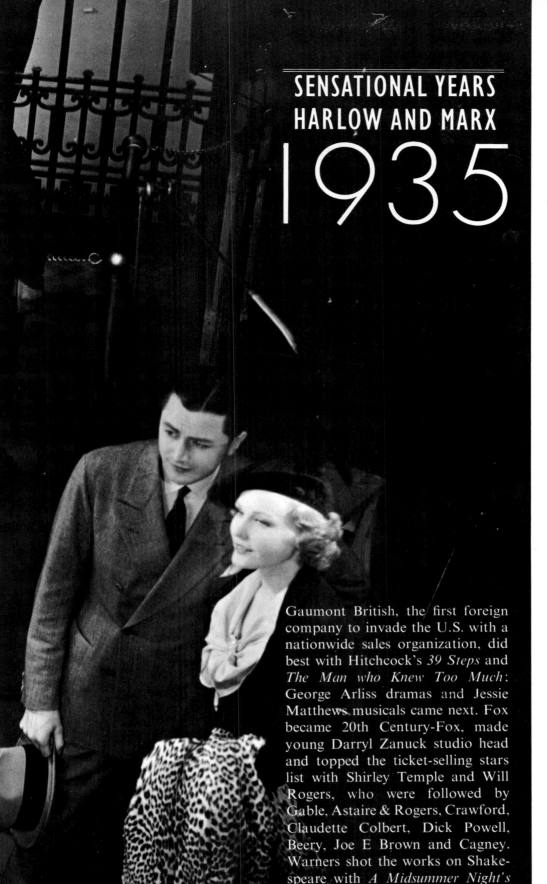

Gaumont British, the first foreign company to invade the U.S. with a nationwide sales organization, did best with Hitchcock's *39 Steps* and *The Man who Knew Too Much*: George Arliss dramas and Jessie Matthews musicals came next. Fox became 20th Century-Fox, made young Darryl Zanuck studio head and topped the ticket-selling stars list with Shirley Temple and Will Rogers, who were followed by Gable, Astaire & Rogers, Crawford, Claudette Colbert, Dick Powell, Beery, Joe E Brown and Cagney. Warners shot the works on Shakespeare with *A Midsummer Night's Dream* but made more money with new star Errol Flynn in *Captain Blood*. *Mutiny on the Bounty*, Bette Davis in *Dangerous* and Victor McLaglen in *The Informer* won Academy Awards. Paramount emerged from bankruptcy with a $3m profit (MGM netted $7½m again), reflecting the better times. Weekly world attendances rose 15% to 220m, 80m of them in the U.S.A.

George B. Seitz, one of Hollywood's most prolific directors since his Pearl White serial days, had a busy MGM year. Having launched Robert Taylor starwards in Only Eight Hours *and* Times Square Lady, *he made four good programmers in a few weeks each. Here, Seitz directing Robert Young and Madge Evans in* **Calm Yourself**, *a fast comedy starring Betty* ◁ Opposite *Furness, Nat Pendleton, Hardie Albright, Ralph Morgan; script by Arthur Kober from an Edward Hope story . . . Basil Rathbone and Aline MacMahon in* **Kind Lady**, *Bernard* △ Top Left *Schubert's adaptation of the Edward Chodorov play based on Hugh Walpole's thriller 'The Silver Casket', with Dudley Digges, Mary Carlisle, Frank Albertson, Doris Lloyd, Donald Meek . . . Maureen O'Sullivan, Joel McCrea and Adrienne Ames in* **Woman Wanted**, *a chase* △ Top Right *melodrama with Lewis Stone, Louis Calhern, Edgar Kennedy, Robert Greig and a Leonard Fields – David Silverstein script from a Wilson Collison story . . . Joseph Calleia repeating his vicious Public Hero No. 1 villainy in* **Exclusive** △ Above **Story**, *Michael Fessier's adaptation of Martin Mooney's newspaper-versus-gangster drama with Franchot Tone, Miss Evans, Stuart Erwin, Robert Barrat, J. Carrol Naish, Margaret Irving. Lucien Hubbard produced all but the third, a Philip Goldstone production.*

Director Roy Del Ruth and producer John Considine Jr had one of 1935's biggest successes in **Broadway Melody of 1936** ('So new it's a year ahead!'). The original Broadway Melody song, now sung by Harry Stockwell, ushered in the movie which was otherwise no sequel to the screen's first musical. It showed what enormous technical strides had been taken in seven years of putting song, dance and stage spectacle on film. It also had fast and funny 'book' scenes by Sid Silvers, Jack McGowan and Harry Conn (from Moss Hart's original). One of those developed into the 'Sing Before Breakfast' number (here), with Eleanor Powell and Vilma and Buddy Ebsen; note the photo-montage background for the Manhattan rooftop set. Miss Powell, a whirlwind tapdancer from Broadway with toothy charm, became an instant star with this movie, which also began a long career for Ebsen; sister Vilma soon retired. Jack Benny was top-billed, sharing comedy honours with Una Merkel and scenarist Silvers; Robert Taylor and June Knight provided romance, and Frances Langford belted out the Freed–Brown songs, including 'Broadway Rhythm' and 'You Are My Lucky Star'.

The tried and true team—Oliver Hardy, Stan Laurel and indignant stooge Jimmy Finlayson, directed by James Horne, produced by Hal Roach—had a winner in **Bonnie Scotland**. The starring pair now appeared more remuneratively in features than in shorts and this one rolled up the biggest world-wide gross of them all. The script was by Frank Butler and Jeff Moffitt but, as usual, a prime creative contributor was Laurel; he was therefore always more highly paid than Hardy, who was solely an actor. June Lang, William Janney, Daphne Pollard and David Torrence had supporting spots.

Laurel and Hardy had completed a seventh full-length feature for Hal Roach (not to mention 64 shorts) by the end of 1935. It was Michael Balfe's operetta **The Bohemian Girl**, adapted by Alfred Bunn, and directed by James Horne and Charles Rogers to give maximum scope to the Stan and Ollie comedy routines. Dramatic and/or musical interludes by Mae Busch and Antonio Moreno, veterans of the silents (with them here) and Thelma Todd, Mitchell Lewis, Felix Knight and Jacqueline Wells were given

by-the-way treatment. Jimmy Finlayson was the stars' butt again, and they were still sure-fire ticket-sellers.

Ah, sweet mystery of showbiz! Producer Hunt Stromberg put together a soprano who acted as if every nuance had to reach the top gallery of an opera house, a baritone who didn't act at all, and an ancient (1910) operetta—and, presto, out came a smash hit establishing the screen's most successful singing team of all time. Jeanette MacDonald and Nelson Eddy in **Naughty Marietta** had cinema audiences literally applauding their Victor Herbert–Rida Johnson Young songs, 'I'm Falling in Love with Someone', 'Italian Street Song', 'Ah, Sweet Mystery of Life', etc. They were so well recorded that Douglas Shearer won an Oscar. Frank Morgan (with them here) and Elsa Lanchester, Douglass Dumbrille, Walter Kingsford, Greta Meyer, Joseph Cawthorn, Cecilia Parker and Akim Tamiroff also enacted the John Lee Mahin–Frances Goodrich and Albert Hackett screenplay, directed with W. S. Van Dyke's customary verve.

West Point of the Air was a successful, crowd-satisfying 1935 companion-piece to the 1928 Flying Fleet, dealing with flight training in the US Army instead of in the Navy. Wallace Beery (second from left, with Maureen O'Sullivan, Robert Young, Richard Tucker and Rosalind Russell) camera-hogged his way through the part of trainee Young's old-sweat father, supported also by Lewis Stone, James Gleason and, as Young's classmates, Russell Hardie, Robert Taylor and Henry Wadsworth. Richard Rosson directed, former director Monta Bell produced, and later producer James K. McGuinness wrote it with John Monk Saunders.

The Flame Within *was a rare solo effort in a studio given to credit-splitting: Edmund Goulding wrote the script from his own original, produced and directed it. This drama of a lady psychiatrist getting too involved with a neurotic young couple (Louis Hayward, Maureen O'Sullivan) broke no records, but it drew praise from the critics for its emotional tension, well conveyed by (left to right) Henry Stephenson, Ann Harding and Herbert Marshall.*

A Night at the Opera *was a smashing success,* ▽ *reversing the financial decline of the Marx Brothers' preceding pictures. Irving Thalberg knew what he was doing when he got the Paramount clowns to move over (dropping 'straight' brother Zeppo en route) to MGM, where they were given more opulent production and more elaborate gags, tested in a pre-filming stage tour, than ever before – although some Marx buffs deplored their yielding footage to romantic subplot and musical numbers. Sam Wood directed the George*

Kaufman–Morrie Ryskind script that bristled with laugh lines for Groucho. Left to right: the monumental Margaret Dumont, singers Kitty Carlisle and Allan Jones (their hit song was 'Alone'), Chico, Groucho, Robert Emmet O'Connor, Harpo, Purnell Pratt. Walter Woolf King and Sig Ruman completed the cast.

Rosalind Russell was emerging into leading ladyship when Philo Vance gumshoed back to solve another murder in a family of neurotics, in **The Casino Murder Case.** *Left to right: Paul Lukas, the new Philo; perennial butler Eric Blore; nurse Claudelle Kaye; Donald Cook (the last one you'd ever suspect); Miss Russell; serious cop Purnell Pratt; frightened maid Louise Fazenda; comic cop Ted Healy. Lukas seemed a bit heavy for Philo and the Florence Ryerson–Edgar Allan Woolf script wasn't among the best of the S. S. Van Dine series. Edwin Marin directed, Lucien Hubbard produced, with Alison Skipworth, Arthur Byron, Isabel Jewell, Leslie Fenton and Leo G. Carroll.*

1935

Public Hero Number One *harked back to the heyday of Warners' gangster cycle, and actually outclassed most of the Cagney–Robinson toughies in pace, suspense and savagery. Business was virile too. Lucien Hubbard entrusted newcomer J. Walter Ruben with direction of the Wells Root script about lawman Chester Morris (left) posing as a criminal and joining cellmate Joseph Calleia in a jail break to learn his gang's secrets. Morris had his most violently effective role since* The Big House *and Calleia, a stage actor, made a stunning movie début as a cold killer. Lionel Barrymore and Jean Arthur also starred, with Paul Kelly and Lewis Stone featured.*

Escapade, *a remake of a German hit – Maskerade – emerged only a year after its 1934 original. It was tailored for William Powell and Myrna Loy by producer Bernard Hyman and scenarist Herman Mankiewicz who adapted Walter Reisch's light comedy of a philandering artist in pre-war Vienna. But Myrna, having compared her MGM salary with what MGM charged other companies for her services, took a slow boat to England and awaited results. One unexpected result was a quick script rewrite for a new European discovery, Luise Rainer (here with Powell) who proceeded to waltz away with the picture. She won extraordinary raves from the critics, and Leo had a new star. Robert Z. Leonard directed, with Virginia Bruce, Mady Christians, Frank Morgan, Reginald Owen, Laura Hope Crews and Henry Travers.*

Another Myrna Loy part which made another new star while she was on strike went to Rosalind Russell in **Rendezvous**. *Signed by MGM when acting on Broadway, Rosalind had an attractively forceful style, cultivated in increasingly important roles until this one put*

her on top. William Powell played a World War I code-breaker. William K. Howard directed the ingenious screenplay devised by Bella and Samuel Spewack, P. J. Wolfson and George Oppenheimer from Major H. O. Yardley's non-fiction 'The American Black Chamber'. Binnie Barnes, Lionel Atwill, Cesar Romero, Henry Stephenson and Samuel S. Hinds were featured in the Lawrence Weingarten production.

During his brief Hollywood sojourn Hugh Walpole was kept busy by David O. Selznick. After working on (and in) David Copperfield he collaborated with Lenore Coffee on a script from the fourth of his Herries novels. The American title **Vanessa, Her Love Story** *(Vanessa in Britain) was a tip-off to the movie's emphasis on the purple romance in the book. It was a loser. William K. Howard directed (left to right) Robert Montgomery, miscast as a swaggering adventurer; Helen Hayes in the name role, which made her flee back to Broadway; and Otto Kruger as her mad husband. Also cast: May Robson, Lewis Stone, Henry Stephenson, Violet Kemble-Cooper, Donald Crisp, Jessie Ralph and George K. Arthur.*

Shakespearean actress Constance Collier, who coached MGM stars in drama and diction, brought her own formidable talents to the leading role of **Shadow of Doubt**, *an Arthur Somers Roche thriller adapted by Wells Root. George B. Seitz directed this effective 'B' for the Lucien Hubbard unit, with Ricardo Cortez and Virginia Bruce (here, with Miss Collier) and Isabel Jewell, Arthur Byron, Betty Furness, Regis Toomey and Edward Brophy.*

Always on the verge of becoming another Gable, Chester Morris found himself back in the 'Bs' after his Public Hero No. 1 hit. **Pursuit** *was a chase piece by Wells Root from L. G. Blochman's novel about an aviator and a female detective (Sally Eilers) hired to get a disputed child (Scotty Beckett) out of the country. Dorothy Peterson, C. Henry Gordon, Henry Travers and Minor Watson supported; Edwin L. Marin directed and Lucien Hubbard produced.*

Myrna Loy and Leo kissed and made up with a fat new contract, and within weeks of her return she had completed **Whipsaw** *with Spencer Tracy. Myrna was in a jewel-robbing gang, he was a detective, and they clashed to good box-office effect in the Howard Emmett Rogers adaptation of J. E. Grant's story, produced by Harry Rapf and directed at a fast clip by Sam Wood. Harvey Stephens, William Harrigan, Robert Warwick, Halliwell Hobbes, John Qualen and Irene Franklin supported.*

Peter Lorre's peeled-egg countenance made its Hollywood début in **Mad Love**/The Hands of Orlac, *frightening as many moviegoers as it had in* M, *the German shocker that won him worldwide attention. The new film, based on a French story by Maurice Renard, also stemmed from Germany; it had been made silent in the Twenties with Werner Krauss in Lorre's role of a surgeon who grafted a murderer's hands on an accidentally maimed pianist. Colin Clive played the latter (Conrad Veidt in the original) with Frances Drake, Ted Healy, Sara Haden, Edward Brophy, Keye Luke and Isabel Jewell in support. The Guy Endore–John Balderston–P. J. Wolfson script dragged in some awkward comedy relief. John Considine Jr produced this last directorial effort of Karl Freund, who returned to cinematography.*

1935 *Three stars at their zenith were box-office insurance for* **China Seas**, *which hardly needed it. Thalberg's meticulous production of a good story, loaded with spectacular action sequences and zestfully directed by Tay Garnett, would have been a hit anyhow. With Wallace Beery as a modern pirate, Jean Harlow given pithy lines to snap and a loose-top-tight-bottom gown to fill, and Clark Gable in command of the ship and the screen, it became a record-breaker. Others on board were Rosalind Russell rather over-doing an English milady, Robert Benchley as a very funny drunk, Lewis Stone, Dudley Digges, C. Aubrey Smith, William Henry, Lillian Bond, Edward Brophy, Donald Meek, Emily Fitzroy and Akim Tamiroff. Screenplay by James K. McGuinness and Jules Furthman from Crosbie Garstin's novel.*

Mayer was taking no chances with the Tarzan
◁ *goldmine and* **Tarzan Escapes** *was put back
into production for virtually a complete remake
after a so-so audience reaction at a preview
early in 1936. Retakes were standard procedure at MGM, but this was the first wholesale job since* Prosperity *in 1932. It yielded
rich box office ore. Johnny Weissmuller,
Maureen O'Sullivan and Cheeta the chimp ran,
leaped and swam through marvellously impossible jungle adventures in the Cyril Hume
script, directed by Richard Thorpe. Film
editor Sam Zimbalist got his first crack at producing, and John Buckler, Benita Hume,
William Henry, Herbert Mundin and E. E.
Clive were featured.*

*Romantic scenes with Chester Morris and
Irene Hervey relieved the grim realism of* **The
Three Godfathers** *in the third of four movie
versions of Peter B. Kyne's story. (Offscreen,
Irene became the wife of one singing star, Allan
Jones, and the mother of another, Jack Jones.)
Lewis Stone and Walter Brennan joined Morris
to play the trio of fugitive gunmen who paused
in their desert trek to rescue the newborn baby
they found in a covered wagon with its dying
mother. Joseph Mankiewicz produced and
Richard Boleslawski directed, getting full
dramatic value from the E. E. Paramore–
Manuel Seff script. Also cast: Dorothy Tree,
Willard Robertson, Sidney Toler.*

*'Hollywood is worried by star shortage. One
company, MGM, has corralled most of the
moneymaking names.' ('Daily Express',
London, September 1936). Shedding a crocodile tear for his rivals, Leo tossed four top
names into a comedy script so good it would
have clicked with unknowns in the leads. With
William Powell, Myrna Loy, Spencer Tracy
(here) and Jean Harlow,* **Libeled Lady** *became
a brilliant triumph. The Maurine Watkins–
Howard Emmett Rogers–George Oppenheimer
script, about an heiress slapping a $5m. libel
suit on a newspaper, glittered with wit, and
Jack Conway directed for overlapping laughs.
It got them, also huge receipts. Walter Connolly, Cora Witherspoon, E. E. Clive and
Charley Grapewin were prominent in the
Lawrence Weingarten production.*

The most sensational profit-maker of 1936 was
San Francisco, *which unexpectedly nosed past*
The Great Ziegfeld *in the popularity stakes to
become one of MGM's all-time winners. Star
power was an important factor; Clark Gable,
Jeanette MacDonald and Spencer Tracy were
at their best in roles tailormade by Anita Loos,
whose husband John Emerson co-produced with
Bernard Hyman. It was also strong musically;
Jeanette's songs ranged from a 'Faust' aria to a
hit ballad 'Would You?' and included a title
song so rousing that San Francisco has made it
the city's anthem ever since. Robert Hopkins'
story, set in the rowdy Barbary Coast district in
1906, had sure appeal. But the big knockout
punch was the earthquake sequence, rocking
and roaring for ten minutes of newsreel-like
realism. Arnold Gillespie's special effects,
Oliver T. Marsh's photography and Douglas
Shearer's theatre-shaking sound recording
created an illusion which was for many years
unsurpassed among movies' technical achievements. Much of the credit for the picture's
stunning impact went to director W. S. Van
Dyke, whose cast included Jack Holt, Jessie
Ralph, Ted Healy, Shirley Ross, Margaret
Irving and Harold Huber.*

Cynics who had expected Thalberg's version of
Romeo and Juliet *to be just an expensive
indulgence for his wife were confounded. His
infinite capacity for taking pains–not to
mention retaking–resulted in a production of
visual and verbal beauty, praised by the great
majority of critics. The picture was so lavishly
produced that it showed a bookkeeping loss of
almost $1m., but MGM got its money's worth
in praise and prestige. Surprisingly, the most
highly lauded performance was Norma
Shearer's Juliet. With no stage, let alone
Shakespearean, experience, she had studied
and rehearsed for months under Constance
Collier and other tutors, then gave the part an
air of spontaneity and a radiance all her own.
She had indispensable aid from George Cukor's
direction and the ardent Romeo of Leslie
Howard (seen here with her between scenes).
Both stars were really too old for their roles, but
it didn't hurt, the rest of the cast being scaled up
in age accordingly. John Barrymore could have
played Mercutio with his eyes shut, and almost
did; he and Basil Rathbone, C. Aubrey Smith,
Ralph Forbes, Reginald Denny, Conway
Tearle, Henry Kolker, Robert Warwick and
Violet Kemble-Cooper were impressive; Edna
May Oliver and Andy Devine struck discordant
notes. Talbot Jennings' screenplay clarified
without distorting.*

Audiences responded faintly when three of Robert Louis Stevenson's 'Suicide Club' stories were knocked into one by E. E. Paramore and Manuel Seff for new MGM producer Louis D. Lighton's **Trouble for Two**/The Suicide Club. It was a nice try, but the essentially modern Robert Montgomery and Rosalind Russell seemed unhappily cast as 1880 Ruritanians. J. Walter Ruben's direction was also on the fish-out-of-water side. Supporting cast: Frank Morgan (centre), Louis Hayward, Reginald Owen, E. E. Clive, Walter Kingsford, Tom Moore, Pedro de Cordoba, Robert Greig and (the stars as children) David Jack Holt, Virginia Weidler.

The Lucien Hubbard–Edwin Marin producer-director team manufactured double-feature fodder with boundless energy in 1936. Four more were: Joseph Calleia, Robert Young, ▽ Florence Rice in **Sworn Enemy**, with Lewis Stone, Nat Pendleton, Harvey Stephens, Leslie Fenton; crime drama by Richard Wormser, script by Wells Root . . . H. B. Warner, Katherine Alexander, Leo Carrillo, Benita Hume in **Moonlight Murder**, with Chester ▽

Morris, Madge Evans, Frank McHugh, Grant Mitchell, J. Carrol Naish, Duncan Renaldo; whodunit in an opera company, by Florence Ryerson, Edgar Allan Woolf . . . James Stewart, Ted Healy, Wendy Barrie in **Speed**, △ with Una Merkel, Ralph Morgan; script by Michael Fessier from a racing car yarn by Lawrence Bachmann (future head of the MGM British studio), Milton Krims . . . . Edward Brophy, Stuart Erwin, Edmund Gwenn, Florence Rice, Robert Armstrong in **The All-** ▽ **American Chump**/The Country Bumpkin, with Harvey Stephens, E. E. Clive; con-man comedy by Lawrence Kimble.

The delectable Ann Sothern made her MGM début in **Dangerous Number**, preceding her long contract by a couple of years. With Cora Witherspoon as her nutty ex-burlesque-queen mother, she played an actress whose caprices maddened staid husband Robert Young. Richard Thorpe directed the Lou Ostrow production from a script by Carey Wilson. Reginald Owen, Dean Jagger, Marla Shelton and Franklin Pangborn were featured.

Wife Versus Secretary showed what thoroughly professional writing, production and acting can do for a trite theme. The story, a typical Faith Baldwin magazine piece, was polished by Norman Krasna, Alice Duer Miller and John Lee Mahin, director Clarence Brown and producer Hunt Stromberg until it shone like the silver that poured into the box offices. A major reason for this success was the cast: a restrained and charming Jean Harlow as the secretary; Clark Gable, vital in almost every frame of the film; and May Robson as his mother, igniting the jealousy of his wife, Myrna Loy, who was at her subtle best. James Stewart, George Barbier, Hobart Cavanaugh, Gilbert Emery and Tom Dugan supported.

Robert Taylor was now so big that the London 'Observer' declared: '1936 will go on record as the year of Edward VIII, the Spanish war and Robert Taylor.' He and Barbara Stanwyck married some time after making **His Brother's Wife** with Joseph Calleia. On-screen the Taylor–Stanwyck romance was far from smooth, as scripted by Leon Gordon and John Meehan. He was a medical researcher, she a nightclub hostess; he went out to the tropics to investigate spotted fever; she, miffed, married his brother; by the last reel she had spotted

fever, he had her, and W. S. Van Dyke had another in his seemingly endless series of hits. Jean Hersholt, John Eldredge, Samuel S. Hinds, Jed Prouty and Pedro de Cordoba were also in the Lawrence Weingarten production.

Three phases of Hollywood fame are represented in this shot from **Piccadilly Jim**. Robert Montgomery and Madge Evans (right) were the stars, Aileen Pringle was an ex-star playing a small part, and the unbilled Dennis O'Keefe was emerging from the extra ranks into future stardom. The P. G. Wodehouse story, adapted by Charles Brackett and Edwin Knopf, was smartly directed by Robert Z. Leonard and performed by expert farceurs, including Frank Morgan, Eric Blore, Billie Burke, Robert Benchley, Ralph Forbes, Cora Witherspoon, Grant Mitchell, Billy Bevan and E. E. Clive. Harry Rapf produced.

A wafer-thin story served to give Robert Taylor and Janet Gaynor, in her first MGM appearance, a hit in Hunt Stromberg's **Small Town Girl**. Janet, the Fox studio's biggest attraction until Shirley Temple came along, played a rural miss picked up by playboy Taylor and married during his drunken spree. His rich fiancée demanded an annulment, whereupon he found that even while sober he preferred Janet, so have you read any good scripts lately? William Wellman directed, John Lee Mahin and Edith Fitzgerald scripted from a Ben Ames Williams novel. Also cast: Binnie Barnes, Lewis Stone, Andy Devine, Elizabeth Patterson, James Stewart, Frank Craven and Charley Grapewin.

△ **Suzy** had practically everything; Jean Harlow and Cary Grant (here) as American showgirl and French flying ace, Franchot Tone with Irish brogue, Benita Hume as bewitching spy, the 1914 Derby, World War I, spectacular air battles and a hit theme song, 'Did I Remember?'. George Fitzmaurice got it all into 99 minutes for producer Louis D. Lighton, who had jig-sawed the scripts of Dorothy Parker, Alan Campbell, Horace Jackson and Lenore Coffee. Also cast: Lewis Stone, Inez Courtney, Reginald Mason, Theodore Von Eltz and Una O'Connor.

Producer Joseph Mankiewicz threw bushels of MGM dollars, top director Clarence Brown and one of the year's most dazzling casts into **The Gorgeous Hussy** but public response was disappointing. The teaming of Joan Crawford and Robert Taylor had been its initial attraction but the Ainsworth Morgan–Stephen M. Avery screenplay from Samuel Hopkins Adams' novel focused more interest on Lionel Barry-more and Beulah Bondi (here with Joan and Melvyn Douglas) who gave vivid performances as President Andrew Jackson and his back-woods wife. Spotlighting historical and political events had a cooling effect on the Crawford–Taylor fans. Franchot Tone, James Stewart, Alison Skipworth, Louis Calhern, Sidney Toler, Melville Cooper, Gene Lockhart and Clara Blandick had other principal roles.

Mayer took a great interest in juvenile players and made MGM the most successful studio in developing child stars. Three of them were cun-ningly given equal importance in the John Lee Mahin–Richard Schayer script for **The Devil is a Sissy**/The Devil Takes the Count: Mickey

Rooney as a slum kid, Freddie Bartholomew as rich Ian Hunter's son, and Jackie Cooper as a middle-class boy were thrown together in a New York school. Cooper had been a star for half a decade; Bartholomew was a big draw since David Copperfield; Rooney, then the least famous of the three, was to become the industry's number one box-office attraction for years on end. This Frank Davis production was given the golden directorial touch of W. S. Van Dyke, with Katherine Alexander, Peggy Conk-lin, Grant Mitchell, Etienne Girardot, Gene and Kathleen Lockhart and Andrew Tombes (as the cop) in the cast.

Joan Crawford and producer Mankiewicz snapped out of the solemnity of Gorgeous Hussy for her next, **Love on the Run**. She was back in Clark Gable's arms, when he wasn't at her heels in one long, carefree, sexy chase, and the fans were happy again. W. S. Van Dyke's direction was a breeze, and the smooth farcing of Franchot Tone (as Gable's rival reporter, also pursuing Joan), Reginald Owen, Mona Barrie, Ivan Lebedeff and William Demarest helped to make the John Lee Mahin–Manuel Seff–Gladys Hurlbut screenplay a popular hit.

Camille: tragedy on the screen, tragedy at the studio. Before its completion, its producer, Irving Thalberg, died in September 1936 at the age of 37 and at the peak of his creative power. His associate and best friend, Bernard Hyman, finished the picture, with George Cukor con-tinuing his superlative direction. Aware of their film's excellence and in tribute to Thal-berg, an unprecedented MGM contingent attended its California premiere, including Schenck, Mayer and–rarest of public appear-ances–Garbo. The applause of that audience has continued ever since; it is one of the most frequently revived movies, and some consider Garbo's performance to be the finest on film. Certainly it was her best. The range of feeling expressed by the subtle play of her features and voice, from the flirtatious gaiety of the early sequences (here, with Robert Taylor respect-fully passionate as Armand, Laura Hope Crews and Rex O'Malley) to the feverish ex-haustion of her dying, was screen acting of the highest order. In the best scene of all she and Henry Daniell, as her protector, bait each other with the knowledge that her new lover is wait-ing outside her door; their barbed dialogue, his piano playing and her sardonic laughter rise to a brilliant crescendo. Daniell delighted the critics in the role Thalberg originally intended for John Barrymore, who was indisposed;

brother Lionel was present, though, to play Taylor's father in heavy-handed style. Jessie Ralph as the motherly maid and Lenore Ulric as the rival strumpet won praise, and minor roles were filled by Elizabeth Allan, Russell Hardie, E. E. Clive and Douglas Walton. The screenplay by Zoe Akins, Frances Marion and James Hilton oiled the creaks out of the old Dumas story, and William Daniels surpassed himself in photographing the star.

Thalberg had **The Good Earth** in preparation and production for three years before his death on the eve of its completion. It was twice marked by tragedy: George Hill, first chosen to direct, had shot background footage in China when he died in 1934, a suicide. Sidney Franklin eventually directed it, and very well too, with Bernard Hyman supervising after the producer's death. Although they looked un-Chinese and sounded Teutonic, Paul Muni and Luise Rainer won raves for their superlative work as the peasants of Pearl Buck's novel, which was movingly adapted by Talbot Jen-nings, Tess Slesinger and Claudine West. Miss Rainer got the 1937 best actress Academy Award, setting a precedent by winning for two successive years; the election of this per-formance over Garbo's Camille raised some eyebrows. The stars' artistry in the intimate scenes was matched by exterior production effects: storm, looting, famine and, above all, a terrifying locust plague (faked by Arnold Gillespie's magic department) were staged with tremendous sweep, and photographed in sepia by the masterly Karl Freund. Thalberg's associate producer was, as usual, Albert Lewin, and the cast included Walter Connolly, Tilly Losch, Keye Luke, Jessie Ralph, Charley Grapewin and Harold Huber. In a dignified dedication the picture bore the name of Thal-berg, who had never given himself screen credit. Others that he left unfinished were Maytime, A Day at the Races and Marie Antoinette; a share of the income of these and his previous productions continues to augment the fortune he left his wife and children.

1937

Hollywood output rose to 778 features, the most since 1928. Europe offered stiffer competition with hits like *Elephant Boy*, *Mayerling*, *King Solomon's Mines*. Paul Muni followed *Pasteur* with another biography, *Life of Emile Zola* which won the Academy Award, while critics applauded Ronald Colman in *Lost Horizon* and Irene Dunne and Cary Grant in *The Awful Truth*.

United Artists had a good year starring Fredric March with Janet Gaynor in *A Star is Born* and with Carole Lombard in *Nothing Sacred*; Sylvia Sidney with Joel McCrea in *Dead End* and with Henry Fonda in *You Only Live Once*; and remakes of *Prisoner of Zenda* and *Stella Dallas*. Paramount had a comedy classic: Jean Arthur and Edward Arnold in *Easy Living*. But MGM again won the box-office race by miles, netting $14½m. Universal found a mortgage lifter in Deanna Durbin, who mysteriously never made the exhibitors' top ten list. They did elect Fox's dimpled skater Sonja Henie, and Jane Withers, bad-girl foil to Shirley Temple, who topped the list again, followed by Gable, Taylor, Bing Crosby, William Powell, Astaire & Rogers, Cooper and Myrna Loy.

They don't make movies like **Rosalie** *any more, and they never will again. It would take a goldmine and a couple of oil wells to finance just this one number: it went on for what seemed like hours, covered 60 acres of the MGM lot, and used 27 cameras to film more than 2,000 people dancing, singing or just standing there, to the tune of Cole Porter's title song. William Anthony McGuire, who learned extravagance from his ex-employer, master spendthrift Flo Ziegfeld, produced it; he also wrote the peanut of a story hidden under all the spectacle and music. The latter included one of Porter's loveliest songs, 'In The Still of The Night', sung by Nelson Eddy who co-starred with Eleanor Powell (that's her in the middle). Frank Morgan played the Ruritanian king he originated in the 1928 Ziegfeld show, whose Romberg and Gershwin numbers were dropped in favour of the new Porter score. Ray Bolger, Edna May Oliver, Ilona Massey (debut), Reginald Owen, Billy Gilbert, Janet Beecher, George Zucco and Virginia Grey also performed for director Robert Z. Leonard.*

debut at 72, was outstanding as his victim. She, Kathleen Harrison, Merle Tottenham and Matthew Boulton re-created their stage roles, while Rosalind Russell scored as the sensitive girl fascinated by the murderer. Alan Marshal, E. E. Clive and Beryl Mercer supported. Richard Thorpe's direction of the John Van Druten screenplay for producer Hunt Stromberg kept suspense taut.

Teamed for the seventh time, William Powell and Myrna Loy were again in easy command of that most difficult art, the playing of comedy. **Double Wedding***, a giddy romp encompassing sophisticated dialogue and visual slapstick, was adapted by Jo Swerling from a Ferenc Molnar play. Richard Thorpe's direction ensured laugh-getting performances also from the secondary romantic pair, John Beal and Florence Rice, and character actors Sidney Toler, Edgar Kennedy, Jessie Ralph, Katherine Alexander and Barnett Parker. Joseph Mankiewicz produced this profit-producer.*

A 15-year-old bombshell exploded when **Broadway Melody of 1938** *(made in '37) spotlighted the MGM feature debut of Judy Garland, seen here with Buddy Ebsen in the finale. Earlier in the footage she had sung 'You Made Me Love You' to a photo of Clark Gable, snatching the movie from Robert Taylor, Eleanor Powell, George Murphy, Sophie Tucker, Binnie Barnes and Ebsen, all billed above her. Judy previously made a short with another juvenile singer, Deanna Durbin, and Mayer hit the ceiling when he discovered that Deanna's option had lapsed and that Universal had signed her for starring roles. 'We'll make Judy an even bigger star!' thundered the Czar and, sure enough, they eventually did. This Melody, like Born to Dance, was a lucrative hit produced by Jack Cummings, written by Sid Silvers and Jack McGowan, and directed by Roy Del Ruth; but instead of a Cole Porter score it had off-form Freed & Brown songs. Robert Benchley, Raymond Walburn, Charley Grapewin, Barnett Parker, Billy Gilbert, Broadway comedian Willie Howard and singer Igor Gorin rounded out the cast.*

The Bride Wore Red *was made by Dorothy Arzner, Hollywood's only woman director for many years. Robert Young and Franchot Tone were on Joan Crawford adoration duty for the picture and Joseph Mankiewicz again produced a Molnar work, following* Double Wedding *with this heavier piece, adapted from the playwright's 'The Girl from Trieste' by Bradbury Foote and Tess Slesinger, about a waterfront café singer posing as a society belle. It was not one of the highlights of Miss Crawford's career. Also cast: Reginald Owen, Billie Burke, George Zucco, Lynne Carver, Mary Phillips, Dickie Moore.*

Against Mayer's predictions of failure, Robert Montgomery, tiring of his debonair playboy image before his fans did, insisted on making **Night Must Fall***. It was anything but a failure; the psychotic killer of Emlyn Williams' sinister play became an equally nerve-tingling movie character and opened up a whole new field for the star. Dame May Whitty, making her film*

Mama Steps Out *was built around Alice Brady's stock screen character of dizzy matron; producers had forgotten that her greatest New York stage triumph had been the tragic 'Strange Interlude'. Left to right: Betty Furness, Ivan Lebedeff, Guy Kibbee, Heather Thatcher, Miss Brady and Gregory Gaye in this farce about new-rich Americans on the Riviera. John Emerson produced the screenplay by his wife, Anita Loos, and George B. Seitz directed. Stanley Morner, playing opposite Miss Furness, sang his last two songs for MGM before becoming Dennis Morgan for Warner Bros.*

Don Marquis' play 'The Old Soak' provided Wallace Beery with an effective vehicle for his good-natured-slob act. **The Good Old Soak**, *adapted by A. E. Thomas, was produced by Harry Rapf, one of the company's old originals and now its most prolific producer. The script involved bootlegging, a stock market swindle and small-town family problems. Under J. Walter Ruben's direction, Beery's support included Ted Healy and Una Merkel (here), Eric Linden, Betty Furness, Janet Beecher, Robert McWade and Margaret Hamilton.*

Paradise for Three/Romance for Three *brought the fascinating Mary Astor, who had been playing leads for 15 years, to the MGM contract list. The George Oppenheimer–Harry Ruskin script, from Erich Kaestner's novel 'Three Men in the Snow', sparkled, and Edward Buzzell in his directorial bow for Leo made every laugh line count. Frank Morgan (right) scored in the central role, with Robert Young (centre) and Edna May Oliver, Florence Rice, Reginald Owen, Henry Hull, Herman Bing, Sig Ruman and Walter Kingsford helping to keep the love-in-the-Alps fun bubbling. Sam Zimbalist produced.*

Live, Love and Learn *was a fairly successful item in the 'crazy comedy' vogue of the Thirties. Robert Montgomery and Rosalind Russell co-starred as a struggling artist and his rich wife, with the priceless Maude Eburne (centre) as their Greenwich Village landlady. George Fitzmaurice directed and producer Harry Rapf gave it a strong cast, including Robert Benchley, Monty Woolley, Helen Vinson, Mickey Rooney, E. E. Clive, June Clayworth, Charles Judels, Ann Rutherford and Zeffie Tilbury. Helen Grace Carlisle's story was adapted by Charles Brackett, Cyril Hume and Richard Maibaum.*

Wallace Beery did his Viva Villa *stuff again as an outlaw in* **The Bad Man of Brimstone**. *By stretching the long arm of coincidence to snapping point, the Richard Maibaum–Cyril Hume script from a J. Walter Ruben–Maurice Rapf original managed to work in Beery's other forte, father-love, with Dennis O'Keefe as his longlost son. Harry Rapf produced with Ruben directing. Left to right: Robert Gleckler, Cliff Edwards, Joseph Calleia, Beery, Bruce Cabot, Arthur Hohl. Also cast: Virginia Bruce, Lewis Stone, Guy Kibbee, Noah Beery (acting with his brother for the first time since 1916), Scotty Beckett, Guinn Williams, John Qualen, Charley Grapewin, John Wray, Robert Barrat and Beery's co-star in the old Paramount comedies, Raymond Hatton.*

Simulating teenage enthusiasm with commendable zeal, Robert Young (30), Tom Brown (24) and James Stewart (29) played Annapolis midshipmen in **Navy Blue and Gold** *so well that audiences forgot they'd seen it all many times before. It was a winner. George Bruce incorporated the usual* esprit de corps, *dormitory horseplay and big football match in his script. Smartly paced by Sam Wood and produced by Sam Zimbalist, it also featured Lionel Barrymore, Billie Burke, Paul Kelly, Florence Rice, Frank Albertson, Samuel S. Hinds and Barnett Parker.*

Thoroughbreds Don't Cry *was the first picture to give Judy Garland top billing and the beginning of the Rooney–Garland team. Left to right: Sophie Tucker, Mickey Rooney, Ronald Sinclair (New Zealand-born, English-accented Freddie Bartholomew type) and Judy. Miss Tucker's slam-bang stage personality seemed to lose some of its gusto on the screen, and in this movie it was pretty well swamped by the three talented juveniles. The Harry Rapf production, ably directed by Alfred E. Green, was a racetrack story by J. Walter Ruben and Eleanor Griffin, scripted by Lawrence Hazard. Also cast: C. Aubrey Smith, Helen Troy, Frankie Darro, Elisha Cook Jr, Henry Kolker, Forrester Harvey, Charles D. Brown.*

Man-Proof startled Myrna Loy fans by casting 'the perfect wife' as a predatory bachelor girl who kept stalking her prey (Walter Pidgeon) even after he'd married her rival (Rosalind Russell, right). She had to make do with Franchot Tone eventually. Unusually in this era, the comedy had no farcical elements. Rita Johnson, Nana Bryant, Ruth Hussey, Leonard Penn, John Miljan and Oscar O'Shea were also in the Louis D. Lighton production. Richard Thorpe directed the Vincent Lawrence –Waldemar Young–George Oppenheimer screenplay based on Fanny Heaslip Lea's novel 'The Four Marys'.

Kelly the Second having clicked, Hal Roach rolled out two more Patsy Kelly starrers in quick succession. Lyda Roberti, from Broadway musicals, teamed with her in **Nobody's Baby**, a maternity hospital farce by Harold Law, Hal Yates and Pat C. Flick, with Lynne Overman, Robert Armstrong and Don Alvarado, directed by Gus Meins. It had several songs, as did **Pick a Star**, a Hollywood comedy with most of the Roach talent, plus Mischa Auer stealing the picture as a temperamental star. Edward Sedgwick directed the Richard Flournoy–A. V. Jones–Tom Dugan story, with (left to right) Auer, Rosina Lawrence, Charles Halton, Patsy and Jack Haley. They were augmented by Lyda Roberti, Dugan, Jimmy Finlayson, and Laurel and Hardy as themselves.

Married Before Breakfast was something of a surprise package, a wild little comedy by Everett Freeman and George Oppenheimer which scored on novel situations and an air of spontaneity. Left to right: Irene Franklin, Hugh Marlowe, Florence Rice, Robert Young. Edwin Marin directed (his 17th picture in four years) for producer Sam Zimbalist, with June Clayworth, Barnett Parker and Warren Hymer also supporting Young and Miss Rice.

Restive under the yoke joining her cinematically to Nelson Eddy, Jeanette MacDonald asked Mayer for a solo vehicle and got it: **The Firefly**. Ironically, her new leading man, Allan Jones, had what turned out to be the big song success of the film, 'The Donkey Serenade', while Jeanette did some graceful dancing and much coy emoting as a Spanish spy during the Napoleonic war of 1808–12. The picture grossed close to Maytime. Rudolf Friml's 'Sympathy', 'Giannina Mia' and 'Love is Like a Firefly' came from the original 1912 stage show; the 'Donkey' song was developed from one of his piano pieces. Warren William, Douglass Dumbrille, Leonard Penn, Henry Daniell and George Zucco were involved in the hammy plot which had been assigned inexplicably to writers like Ogden Nash, Frances Goodrich and Albert Hackett; the latter pair fled MGM after this chore. Hunt Stromberg produced the overlong, overacted charade, working again with director Robert Z. Leonard.

Racehorse owner Allan Jones and sheriff Robert Middlemass were getting on with the plot of **A Day at the Races**, but who cared? Every audience eye was on jockey Harpo and tipster Chico Marx. Groucho, in the immortal role of Hugo Z. Hackenbush, horse doctor, was off somewhere wooing Margaret Dumont. The Marxes tested the new gags in 140 stage performances in various cities before filming; the final result was almost as funny as A Night at the Opera and equally profitable. Maureen O'Sullivan, Sig Ruman, Douglass Dumbrille and Esther Muir were also in the Lawrence Weingarten production, directed by Sam Wood from a Robert Pirosh–George Seaton–George Oppenheimer script.

Mayer unknowingly laid the foundation for the most profitable series in Hollywood's history when he put most of the Ah, Wilderness cast into **A Family Affair** in another vain effort to recapture the former's magic. Based on a

modest Broadway success by Aurania Rouverol called 'Skidding', it was a story of Judge Hardy and his small-town family, played by (left to right) Lionel Barrymore, Julie Haydon, Cecilia Parker, Sara Haden, Eric Linden, Spring Byington and, not in this scene, Mickey Rooney. It was a Lucien Hubbard–George B. Seitz 'B' and drew a surprising number of requests from exhibitors for more like it. So its sets were kept standing and its scenarist, Kay Van Riper, was assigned to write a sequel (which eliminated the Haydon and Linden characters). The Hardy Family saga was on its way.

For the only time in Garbo's starring career, her male opposite had a more interesting role than her own in **Conquest**/Marie Walewska. ▷ Napoleon, played by Charles Boyer, was the flame around which his Polish mistress fluttered in the Samuel Hoffenstein–Salka Viertel–S. N. Behrman script; their doomed affair was superbly acted by both stars under Clarence Brown's direction. But it lacked the bravura scenes that had made Camille so special; although looking utterly beautiful in Karl Freund's photography, Garbo seemed somewhat exhausted, as if still recovering from that extraordinary previous performance, and she departed for a year's rest in 1938. Conquest, expensively mounted by Bernard Hyman, did not earn its cost in America but was strong overseas. Supporting cast: Alan Marshal, Reginald Owen, Henry Stephenson, Dame May Whitty, Leif Erickson, C. Henry Gordon, Vladimir Sokoloff, George Zucco, Maria Ouspenskaya, Scotty Beckett. As Garbo's last dramatic vehicle, this is often included in the retrospectives that have kept her genius visible to new generations.

The Garland career was really rolling as 1937 neared its end. Toplining **Everybody Sing**, Judy did a blackface number that demonstrated her flair for comedy as well as her already famous talent for putting over a song. This Harry Rapf production had a funny script by Florence Ryerson and Edgar Allan Woolf about a mad theatrical family (Reginald Owen, Billie Burke, Lynne Carver) whose servants (Allan Jones, Fanny Brice) put on a Broadway show with the younger daughter (Judy). Edwin Marin directed them and Monty Woolley, Reginald Gardiner, Helen Troy, Henry Armetta and Mary Forbes.

AND GARLAND SINGS
1938

The industry was going into another slump: most companies reported less than half the previous year's profits, with MGM-Loew's again the envy of all at $10m. Simultaneously the US Government started an anti-trust suit against the film combines to divorce theatres from studios and sales. It bedevilled the majors for years, threatening the very basis of their operation. Hollywood spent millions on publicizing the slogan 'Movies Are Your Best Entertainment', then halted it when people noticed its initials spelled 'MAYBE'.

Important releases included Walt Disney's *Snow White and the Seven Dwarfs*, new star William Holden in *Golden Boy*, Wendy Hiller in *Pygmalion*, Tyrone Power, Alice Faye and Don Ameche in *Alexander's Ragtime Band* and *In Old Chicago*.

Bette Davis won her second Oscar for *Jezebel*, Frank Capra his third for *You Can't Take It With You*. Tyrone Power, Miss Faye, Mickey Rooney and Spencer Tracy entered the Top Ten; Bing Crosby, William Powell, Gary Cooper, Fred Astaire and Ginger Rogers moved out of the list.

The second Hardy Family movie, **You're Only Young Once**, *had the cast which was to become famous: Lewis Stone and Fay Holden (an English actress oddly becoming the typical American Ma) replaced Lionel Barrymore and Spring Byington as Judge and Mrs Hardy; Mickey Rooney and Cecilia Parker carried on as their children; so did Sara Haden as Aunt Milly. Director George B. Seitz and scenarist Kay Van Riper repeated their Family Affair success. Lucien Hubbard had left the studio and the series, supervised by J. J. Cohn, continued without a producer credit. Also cast: Frank Craven, Ann Rutherford (a regular henceforth), Ted Pearson, Eleanor Lynn, Charles Judels.*

Mickey Rooney took over the 'Hardy' spotlight in **Judge Hardy's Children**, *and held it forever after. Here he's teaching Jacqueline Laurent a dance craze of the Thirties, the Big Apple, during the family's visit to Washington. The public was now really 'Hardy'-hooked. Director-writer team George B. Seitz and Kay Van Riper, and players Lewis Stone, Cecilia Parker, Fay Holden and Ann Rutherford continued, assisted by Robert Whitney, Ruth Hussey, Jonathan Hale, Janet Beecher, Leonard Penn, and Betty Ross Clark who temporarily replaced Sara Haden.*

The 'Hardy' series zoomed into the box-office stratosphere when its fourth instalment, **Love Finds Andy Hardy**, *outgrossed 1938 releases that cost ten times as much. The front-and-centre positioning of Mickey Rooney's role in both title and script (by William Ludwig) and the injection of Judy Garland into the cast turned the trick. The love that found Andy was a cute teenager called Lana Turner, just given a trial contract by studio executives who thought she had 'something'. Whatever it was, it lasted for 18 years at MGM. Mayer became the Hardys' foremost fan, scrutinizing every detail during production. Although there was still no screen credit for a producer, Carey Wilson, MGM stalwart since the 1924 merger, was always prominently involved. George B. Seitz again directed regulars Stone, Holden, Parker, Rutherford; and Gene Reynolds, Mary Howard, Raymond Hatton, Betty Ross Clark, Don Castle and Marie Blake.*

Rich Man, Poor Girl, *the 1938 remake of 1929's* The Idle Rich, *was chiefly notable for bringing Lew Ayres into the MGM fold for a lengthy spell; his last work there had been his 'discovery' appearance opposite Garbo in* The Kiss *nine years before. Left to right: Ruth Hussey, Robert Young, Don Castle, Ayres, Sarah Padden, Guy Kibbee and Lana Turner. A new producer-director team, Edward Chodorov and Reinhold Schunzel, filmed the Joseph Fields–Jerome Chodorov screenplay, with Rita Johnson, Gordon Jones and Virginia Grey cast.*

Hokum? Corn? Commercial soul-wallop? Whatever it was, **Boys Town** *delivered it with such superb professionalism that not even the toughest critics were able to resist it. The public didn't even try; they flocked in by the million, making the John Considine Jr production one of MGM's biggest winners. Spencer Tracy was a winner too, getting his second Oscar for his portrayal of Father Flanagan. The latter and his home for delinquent boys existed in real life, although the Dore Schary–John Meehan script–also Oscared–used a fictional story centred on Mickey Rooney (here with Tracy and Bobs Watson) as a roughneck refusing to reform. Norman Taurog, who had directed Jackie Cooper to boy-stardom in 1931, began an MGM long-termer with this, guiding a horde of youngsters plus adults Henry Hull, Leslie Fenton, Addison Richards, Edward Norris, Minor Watson, Jonathan Hale, Victor Kilian.*

Janet Gaynor, winner of the first Academy Award for an actress (1928), was coming to the end of a happy career with **Three Loves Has Nancy**. She married Adrian, whose designs for MGM stars influenced women's fashions throughout the Thirties. This movie was a crowd-pleasing comedy about a small-town girl, a novelist (Robert Montgomery) and a publisher (Franchot Tone, here) in a New York ménage à trois–quite platonic, you understand. Grady Sutton played her third love, with Claire Dodd, Guy Kibbee, Reginald Owen, Cora Witherspoon, Emma Dunn, Charley Grapewin and Lester Matthews also cast. Richard Thorpe directed the Norman Krasna production. Script: Samuel and Bella Spewack, George Oppenheimer, David Hertz.

Seeking a more rugged image for the almost too handsome Robert Taylor, the studio cast him as a prizefighter in **The Crowd Roars**. It worked, thanks to Richard Thorpe's vigorous direction of a hardboiled screenplay by Thomas Lennon, George Bruce and George Oppenheimer from Bruce's original, and to Taylor's always serious application to his profession. The box office roared. Here in the foreground: trainer Lionel Stander, boxer Taylor, father and manager Frank Morgan, promoter Charles D. Brown. Also in the Sam Zimbalist production were Edward Arnold, Maureen O'Sullivan, William Gargan, Jane Wyman, Nat Pendleton, Gene Reynolds and Isabel Jewell . . . Tough guy

Taylor put up his dukes again for a run-in with Beery in **Stand Up and Fight**, a rousing melodrama of stagecoach-versus-railroad pioneering days. Producer Mervyn LeRoy got into his box-office stride with this one, directed by busy W. S. Van Dyke. Notable in support of Bob and Wally were heroine Florence Rice, black actor Clinton Rosemond, heavies Charles Bickford and Barton MacLane, Helen Broderick for laughs, and John Qualen, Charley Grapewin, Jonathan Hale, Robert Gleckler. Script by James Cain, Jane Murfin and Harvey Ferguson from a Forbes Parkhill original.

Only the horse looked bored when everybody went **Out West With the Hardys**. Title told all, but the series was now so important that three writers had to work on it: Kay Van Riper, William Ludwig, Agnes Christine Johnston. George B. Seitz directed (left to right) Sara Haden, back for good as Aunt Milly, Nana Bryant, Cecilia Parker, Fay Holden, Ralph Morgan, Virginia Weidler, Mickey Rooney and Lewis Stone. Also cast were Ann Rutherford, Don Castle, Gordon Jones, Tom Neal, Anthony Allan.

Maureen O'Sullivan, Lew Ayres and Burgess Meredith were the rather mature college kids frolicking through **Spring Madness**. A pleasant featherweight, it was unique among varsity movies in having no football or other athletic climax. The Philip Barry play 'Spring Dance' was adapted by producer Edward Chodorov with newcomer S. Sylvan Simon directing. Ruth Hussey, Ann Morriss, Frank Albertson, Joyce Compton, Jacqueline Wells, Truman Bradley, Marjorie Gateson and Sterling Holloway rounded out the cast.

MGM departed from policy to distribute the independently-produced **Flirting with Fate**. It just happened to have been made by David Loew, son of Marcus and twin brother of Arthur, MGM foreign sales chief. A so-so farce set in South America, it starred Joe E. Brown, previously Warners' top comedian, with Steffi Duna (left), Leo Carrillo (right) and Wynne Gibson, Beverly Roberts, Charles Judels, Leonid Kinskey, Irene Franklin and George Humbert. Frank McDonald directed the Joseph March–Ethel LaBlanche–Charles Melson–Harry Clork screenplay.

Franciska Gaal, whose face and style brought back memories of Mary Pickford, was imported from Budapest for three Hollywood movies; **The Girl Downstairs** was the last. Naive to a degree as the slavey who won man-about-town Franchot Tone from her rich employer, Rita Johnson, she couldn't make a hit of the flimsy Harold Goldman–Felix Jackson–Karl Noti script, directed by Norman Taurog and produced by Harry Rapf. Tone came off best in a cast that included Walter Connolly, Reginald Owen, Reginald Gardiner, Franklin Pangborn, Robert Coote and Barnett Parker.

Laurel and Hardy again. In **Swiss Miss** they played a couple of mousetrap salesmen with no customers who took jobs in a Tyrolean hotel–which immediately became disaster-prone. Singers Della Lind from Vienna and Walter Woolf King from Broadway supported the zanies, who had comic competition from Eric Blore in the Hal Roach production directed by John Blystone. The James Parrott–Felix Adler–Charles Melson script stemmed from an original by Jean Negulesco and Charles Rogers . . . **Block-Heads**, the last of the Laurel and Hardy features made by Roach for MGM, was trimmed to a fast 55 minutes. Patricia Ellis and Billy Gilbert (here with the stars) joined in their knockabout fun with élan, as did Minna Gombell and Jimmy Finlayson. Some of their gags were supplied by that great clown of the silents, Harry Langdon; other contributors were Adler, Rogers, Parrott and Arnold Belgard. Blystone directed.

Made for Christmas 1938, and given frequent annual revivals, **A Christmas Carol** radiated Dickensian warmth to the last chortle and holly berry. Reginald Owen and Terry Kilburn (foreground) were just right as Scrooge and Tiny Tim; Owen replaced Lionel Barrymore, whose lameness prevented his filming the radio characterization he broadcast every Christmas. Gene Lockhart, Barry Mackay and Lynne Carver (rear) and Leo G. Carroll, Kathleen Lockhart, Ann Rutherford, Ronald Sinclair and Lionel Braham supported. Producer, Joseph Mankiewicz; scenarist, Hugo Butler; director, Edwin Marin.

1938

Dorothy Parker was observed one day leaning out of her window in the writers' building, shouting 'Let me out–I'm as sane as you are!'. She and husband Alan Campbell were embroiled in the script of **Sweethearts**, assigned on the theory that Jeanette MacDonald and Nelson Eddy could stand some acid of wit added to their usual sugary recipe. The ancient Victor Herbert operetta seemed an unlikely subject for the experiment, but it came out as an updated, well-Parkerized comedy of a temperamental theatre couple, brightly acted and splendidly sung by its stars. Another daring move was shooting it all in Technicolor–a first at MGM since 1929's The Mysterious Island. Here: Florence Rice, Miss MacDonald, Eddy, Frank Morgan. Also cast: Ray Bolger, Mischa Auer, Herman Bing, George Barbier, Raymond Walburn, Gene and Kathleen Lockhart, Terry Kilburn. Another moneyspinner from the Hunt Stromberg–W. S. Van Dyke producing–directing mint.

The second MGM-British effort was even more successful than A Yank at Oxford. **The Citadel**, A. J. Cronin's best-seller about a young doctor temporarily forsaking his ideals for money made a strong vehicle for Robert Donat (left), lifted Rosalind Russell's career another notch and brought director King Vidor (right) back to the Metro fold after five years away. Victor Saville, who produced, drew upon the London theatre's acting riches for the cast: Ralph Richardson, Rex Harrison, Emlyn Williams, Mary Clare, Cecil Parker, Penelope

Dudley-Ward, Francis L. Sullivan, Nora Swinburne, Felix Aylmer, Athene Seyler, Edward Chapman. Williams also collaborated with Ian Dalrymple, Frank Wead and Elizabeth Hill (Vidor's wife) on the screenplay.

A diverting trilogy began with **Fast Company**, filmed from Marco Page's whodunit about a rare-book buff, his wife and their amateur detecting. Made to mollify exhibitors who complained of the long wait between 'Thin Man' movies, it was followed by two more with the same characters–oddly enough, played by different stars each time. The originals were Melvyn Douglas and Florence Rice, with Claire Dodd (here with Douglas) as the blonde menace, and Louis Calhern, Shepperd Strudwick, Nat Pendleton, Douglass Dumbrille, George Zucco, Horace MacMahon, Thurston Hall, Minor Watson and Mary Howard. Edward Buzzell directed and Frederick Stephani produced from Page's script. Page became a staff writer under his real name, Harry Kurnitz.

Emotions erupted in **Woman Against Woman** and **The Shining Hour**. The first had Wife No. 1 (Mary Astor) versus Wife No. 2 (Virginia Bruce) slugging it out for the love of Herbert Marshall. Edward Chodorov's screenplay, from Margaret Banning's 'Enemy Territory', was one for the ladies to catch between lunch and the hairdresser. Chodorov produced it himself, with Broadway's Robert Sinclair making his bow as a movie director, and Janet Beecher, Marjorie Rambeau, Betty Ross Clark, Zeffie Tilbury, Sarah Padden, Dorothy Christy and moppet Juanita Quigley in the cast . . . Joan Crawford, Melvyn Douglas, Margaret Sullavan, Robert Young, Fay Bainter were in **The Shining Hour**, Keith Winter's stage success fattened up with additional action by scenarists Ogden Nash and Jane Murfin. Miss Crawford played a nightclub dancer taken by husband Douglas to his Wisconsin farm, where emotional involvements

with his sister-in-law, Miss Sullavan, brother Young and sister Miss Bainter gave all the acting talents concerned a good work-out. Allyn Joslyn, Frank Albertson, Hattie McDaniel and Oscar O'Shea supported them in Joseph Mankiewicz's production, directed by Frank Borzage.

THE WAR BOOM
1942

The war boom was booming and profits went into orbit: Paramount $13m, MGM–Loew's $12m, Fox $10½m, Warner Bros $8½m, Universal $3m, Columbia $1½m. The first Hollywood star to be killed on active service was Phillips Holmes of the Canadian Air Force; Carole Lombard died during a War Bond tour. Noël Coward's *In Which We Serve*, one of many impressive war pictures being turned out by British studios, won the New York Critics Award. James Cagney in *Yankee Doodle Dandy* got one of the few Academy Awards not won by *Mrs Miniver*. Humphrey Bogart and Ingrid Bergman memorably mooned at each other in *Casablanca*; Fred Astaire and Rita Hayworth glided together in *You Were Never Lovelier*; Tyrone Power and Joan Fontaine wrung tears in *This Above All*; Rosalind Russell reaped laughs in *My Sister Eileen*. *Kings Row* and Welles' *Magnificent Ambersons* gripped. Alan Ladd, Susan Hayward, Paul Henreid, Gene Tierney were new stars.

Two melodramas set in France had the most complicated plots of 1942. In **Reunion in France***/Mademoiselle France John Wayne was a chauffeur arrested by Nazi officers Henry Daniell and Moroni Olsen. Had Joan Crawford betrayed him? Or he her? Who cared? Enough customers to make a nice profit on this web of wartime intrigue woven by Jan Lustig, Marc Connolly and Marvin Borowski from a Ladislaus Bus–Fekete story. Jules Dassin directed the Joseph Mankiewicz production, with Philip Dorn, Reginald Owen, John Carradine, Ann Ayars, Albert Bassermann, Howard da Silva, J. Edward Bromberg, Morris Ankrum,*

flanked by ZaSu Pitts and Aline MacMahon. The comedy about village spinsters adopting a baby was extracted by Annalee Whitmore and Thomas Seller from Mary Roberts Rinehart's 'Tish' stories (originally bought for Marie Dressler) and scripted by the prolific Harry Ruskin. Susan Peters proved a find in the romantic lead; others on hand were Lee Bowman, Guy Kibbee, Richard Quine, Virginia Grey, Ruby Dandridge, Al Shean and Gerald Oliver Smith. S. Sylvan Simon directed for that hapless producer who, sick of being kidded about his billing as O. O. Dull, now changed it to Orville Dull (!).

MGM reached its peak as self-appointed publicist for Britain with a Hollywood movie, **Mrs Miniver***; Churchill said its propaganda was worth many battleships. It was supposed to portray a typical English couple in World War II. It didn't: the Minivers were nobler and nicer than any typical couple anywhere, and well over the average income line. But what a marvellously effective movie it was, and what a sensation it caused! It swept the board in public and exhibitor polls as 1942's most popular picture, won cheers from even the crustiest critics and seven Oscars from the Academy: best film, best actress (Greer Garson), best director (William Wyler), best supporting actress (Teresa Wright), best script (Arthur Wimperis, George Froeschel, James Hilton, Claudine West), best photography (Joseph Ruttenberg) and best producer (Thalberg Memorial Award to Sidney Franklin). Shown here are Miss Garson and Walter Pidgeon as Mrs Miniver and her husband in their air-raid shelter, one of the film's more authentic sets. Also cast: Dame May Whitty, Reginald Owen, Henry Travers, Richard Ney, Tom Conway, Helmut Dantine, Christopher Severn, Brenda Forbes, Henry Wilcoxon, Clare Sanders, Rhys Williams.*

Odette Myrtil cast . . . William Powell was an American in pre-war Paris, with Margaret Wycherly here, in **Crossroads***, a John Kafka–Howard Emmett Rogers story scripted by Guy Trosper, produced by Edwin Knopf, directed by Jack Conway. Hedy Lamarr played Powell's wife; Claire Trevor and Basil Rathbone the baddies who enmeshed them in a blackmail plot; also cast were Felix Bressart, Sig Ruman, H. B. Warner, Philip Merivale, Vladimir Sokoloff.*

Three fine old troupers gave the folks a good show in **Tish***: Marjorie Main in the title role,*

In **Random Harvest** *Ronald Colman and Greer Garson were guided by Mervyn LeRoy through the wonderful land of Amnesia, whose paths were paved with gold for moviemakers. This James Hilton romance had (a) Colman as a soldier with no identity, Garson as a music-hall girl; and (b) by a double-twist of the lost memory bit, Colman restored to health and wealth but with a blank spot for (a). and Greer as his wife, not telling him about (a) until (b) had run long enough to make a second feature unnecessary. It's easy to smile now at such contrivances, but* Miniver *producer Sidney Franklin and writers Hilton, Claudine West, George Froeschel and Arthur Wimperis had a way with them, numbing resistance at the time. The movie was a gigantic box-office hit, restoring Colman to the top echelon of stardom and clinching Miss Garson's MGM queendom. Also cast were Philip Dorn, Susan Peters, Henry Travers, Reginald Owen, Bramwell Fletcher, Rhys Williams, Una O'Connor, Margaret Wycherly, Alan Napier, Arthur Margetson, Melville Cooper, Aubrey Mather, Jill Esmond, Marta Linden, Ann Richards, Norma Varden, Ivan Simpson, Elisabeth Risdon.*

For once, MGM went to other studios to get drawing power for its first 1942 musical, **Rio Rita**. *Originally a Ziegfeld show on Broadway, it was bought from RKO Radio, who made a smash film version in 1929. For star strength, Abbott and Costello were borrowed from Universal, where they were the hottest property of the Forties. Gladys Lehman and Richard Connell wrote, and S. Sylvan Simon directed, the Pandro Berman production in routine fashion. Left to right: Kathryn Grayson and John Carroll, singing leads who occasionally managed to nudge the comedians out of camera range; Lou Costello, Joan Valerie, Bud Abbott. Also cast: Tom Conway, Patricia Dane, Barry Nelson and Eros Volusia.*

1942

Two breadwinning 'Bs' produced by J. Walter Ruben during his last year: **Mokey** with Bobby Blake, Donna Reed, Dan Dailey, about a kid getting used to his stepmother; script, Wells Root and Jan Fortune; director, Root; also cast, Matt Moore, Cliff Clark, Cordell Hickman, Etta McDaniel, Mary Field . . . **Maisie Gets Her Man**/She Got Her Man, with Ann Sothern, Red Skelton, took the durable heroine back into show biz; script, Betty Reinhardt and Mary McCall Jr; director, Roy Del Ruth; also cast: Allen Jenkins, Leo Gorcey, Donald Meek, Frank Jenks, Lloyd Corrigan, Walter Catlett, Rags Ragland, Fritz Feld.

Somewhere I'll Find You clicked on the strength ▷ of its Clark Gable–Lana Turner star lure, and contributed richly to the company's $12m. profit ($135m. gross, highest to date) in 1942. Gable and Robert Sterling, with Charles Dingle (left), played brothers, war correspondents, making a play for Lana; they had an offscreen parallel too, both joining the US Army Air Corps after this picture. MGM's male star list was getting thinned out by the war, a situation soon to be eased by finds like the one playing an unbilled bit in this: Van Johnson. The Marguerite Roberts screenplay, adapted by Walter Reisch from Charles Hoffman's original, was average war and sex stuff, slickly directed by Wesley Ruggles and produced by Pandro Berman. Also cast: Reginald Owen, Patricia Dane, Lee Patrick. Production was interrupted for a few weeks when Gable suffered severe shock after the aircrash death of his wife, Carole Lombard.

For Me and My Gal was a nostalgic romp ▷ along the memory lane of pre-War I vaudeville life. A smash for producer Arthur Freed and director Busby Berkeley, it set Judy Garland on a new pinnacle of stardom and established Gene Kelly (bought from David O. Selznick who signed but didn't use him after his Broadway hit in Pal Joey) as an unusual screen personality with exciting dancing talent. Left to right: Horace (later Stephen) McNally, Keenan Wynn, Kelly and Judy. George Murphy and Marta Eggerth, the Polish singer also making a Hollywood debut, were other contributors to the musical highlights which were topped by the title song ('The Bells are Ringing . . .'); Ben Blue, Richard Quine and Lucille Norman supported. Script by Fred Finklehoffe, Sid Silvers and Richard Sherman, from Howard Emmett Rogers' original.

Fingers at the Window starred Lew Ayres, and was his last film until 1946. He suddenly changed from an asset to an embarrassment before its release. Early in 1942, when patriotism meant belligerence and male stars from Gable on down were becoming real-life heroes, Ayres announced he was a conscientious objector. Shock waves spread from Mayer's office to fans in the smallest fleapits and back again. (Defending him, Nicholas Schenck stated solemnly that Ayres had been a vegetarian for years!) But second thoughts acknowledged that it took guts to stick to his I-won't-kill principles. In truth, there was a lot of the real Ayres in Dr Kildare and vice versa, and the parallel continued when the army sent him overseas for Medical Corps duty. Fingers, a neat thriller written by Lawrence Bachmann and Rose Caylor, was produced by Irving Asher and directed by Charles Lederer, with Laraine Day and Basil Rathbone (here) and Walter Kingsford, Miles Mander, Russell Gleason.

Another star in the old MGM constellation dropped out when Norma Shearer finished **Her Cardboard Lover**. This completed her six-picture contract, signed after Thalberg's death, and she called it a career. Like Garbo, she stopped with fame and beauty unfaded; again like Garbo, she had never made a movie for any studio but MGM through the years, silent and sound, of her stardom. A less happy parallel: her last was also a frothy, George Cukor-

directed brew that went flat at the box-office. Why, with the company's vast library to choose from, she elected to film Jacques Deval's old play for a third time (Marion Davies, 1928; Buster Keaton, 1932) was known only to Norma and God. Robert Taylor co-starred in the title role, with George Sanders, Frank McHugh, Elizabeth Patterson, Chill Wills. Producer, J. Walter Ruben; script, Deval, John Collier, Anthony Veiller, William H. Wright.

The Jeanette MacDonald–Nelson Eddy musicals, always costly, had showed signs of diminishing returns, so the company let Eddy go after starring them in **I Married an Angel**. Hunt Stromberg, producer of some of the studio's top 'A's since the silent era, also departed to go independent via United Artists. This show was notable too for having become a stage hit during the nine years it was on and off the Metro schedule. In 1933 Mayer, determined to get a reluctant Miss MacDonald to sign a long-termer, bought a Hungarian piece by Vaszary Janos for her and assigned Rodgers & Hart to write the songs. She accepted, but before work could start the then rigid Purity Code slapped a ban on the saucy story. Five years later it became a stage musical on Broadway. In 1942 the Anita Loos script about an angel luring a playboy from his terrestrial cuties broke no censorship rules. No records either. The co-stars were supported by Anne Jeffreys, Janis Carter, Marion Rosamond, Mona Maris, and Inez Cooper (here with Eddy) and Edward Everett Horton, Binnie Barnes, Reginald Owen and Douglass Dumbrille. W. S. Van Dyke directed.

Frankly imitative, **A Yank at Eton** had little of the warmth of A Yank at Oxford and got a comparatively mild reception. Mickey Rooney was the ebullient Yank playing havoc with the Old School conventions, represented by Freddie Bartholomew, now a lanky 18-year-old. Mickey had reached 20 and continued the longest boyhood in screen history; Freddie made a few more movies, later prospered in advertising. Tina Thayer (with them here) and Ian Hunter, Edmund Gwenn, Alan Mowbray, Marta Linden, Alan Napier, and juveniles Juanita Quigley, Peter Lawford, Raymond Severn and Terry Kilburn had roles in the George Oppenheimer–Lionel Houser–Thomas Phipps screenplay, directed by Norman Taurog and produced by John Considine Jr.

A prettier thing than Jean Rogers never won leading-ladyhood, which is what MGM gave her in two 'Bs'. With Mona Maris (right) in **Pacific Rendezvous**, a remake of Rendezvous, set one war later; script, Harry Kurnitz, P. J.

Wolfson, George Oppenheimer; director, George Sidney; producer, B. F. Zeidman; also cast, Lee Bowman, Carl Esmond, Paul Cavanagh, Blanche Yurka, William Post Jr, Arthur Shields, Frederick Worlock, Curt Bois, William Tannen, Addison Richards, Russell Hicks . . . With William Lundigan, Guy Kibbee, Dan Dailey in **Sunday Punch**, a comedy about a girl in a boarding house full of boxers; script, Fay and Michael Kanin; director, David Miller; producer, Irving Starr; also cast, J. Carrol Naish, Connie Gilchrist, Sam Levene, Leo Gorcey, Rags Ragland, Douglass Newland, Anthony Caruso.

A new leading man arrived for two 1942 actioners: James Craig, frequently referred to decades later in the pages of Gore Vidal's 'Myra Breckenridge'. In **The Omaha Trail** he helped haul a locomotive across the old West, with occasional pauses to woo Pamela Blake. Jesse Lasky Jr based his story on historical records, collaborating with Hugo Butler on the script; Edward Buzzell directed; Jack Chertok

produced; Dean Jagger, Edward Ellis, Chill Wills, Donald Meek, Howard da Silva and Henry Morgan were also cast. Left: **Northwest Rangers** had Craig as a crook caught by his boyhood pal, now a Mountie. David Lang and Gordon Kahn re-scripted Arthur Caesar's Manhattan Melodrama with Craig and William Lundigan (right, with Jack Holt) in the 1934 Gable and Powell roles. Joseph Newman, a new MGM shorts graduate, directed; Samuel Marx produced; Patricia Dane, John Carradine, Keenan Wynn, Grant Withers and Darryl Hickman supported.

Cairo wound up Jeanette MacDonald's MGM contract: she would be back, but her heyday was over. She and Ethel Waters (here) were two of America's most famous singers but you'd never have guessed it from this movie, which mired them in a feeble espionage comedy by John McClain (from an 'idea' by Ladislaus Fodor). Ethel played a maid, obligatory for black actresses then; others involved were Robert Young, Reginald Owen, Lionel Atwill, Grant Mitchell, Eduardo Ciannelli, Mitchell Lewis, Dooley Wilson, Larry Nunn, Dennis Hoey, Mona Barrie, Rhys Williams, Cecil Cunningham. W. S. Van Dyke directed; no producer was credited.

1942

Franchot Tone returned to play **Pilot No. 5** in an unsuccessful but out-of-the-rut war drama by David Hertz, with Marsha Hunt and Gene Kelly sub-starred. The hero was chosen from five United Nations pilots to fly a suicide mission against Jap invaders in Java; during his absence his comrades (Kelly, Van Johnson, Alan Baxter, Dick Simmons) discussed his chequered past. George Sidney directed, B. P. Fineman produced in the Schary unit. Also cast: Steve Geray, Howard Freeman, Frank Puglia, William Tannen.

▽ **Journey for Margaret** ranked close to Miniver as a well-made heart-tugger about wartime Britain; it drew unanimous praise and massive audiences. Better yet, it created a new star in five-year-old Margaret O'Brien as the London blitz orphan adopted by an American reporter and his wife. Margaret, recruited from the crowd in Babes on Broadway, had an emotional range beyond that of most adult actresses and could turn it on like no other child before or since. It was cleverly controlled by W. S. Van Dyke in the last of his many successful efforts for MGM since 1926: he died in 1942, aged 53. The David Hertz–William Ludwig script came from war reporter W. H. White's fact-based best-seller; B. P. Fineman produced for the Schary unit. Left to right: Laraine Day, William Severn, Robert Young, Margaret; also cast were Fay Bainter, Nigel Bruce, Elisabeth Risdon, Doris Lloyd, Halliwell Hobbes, Heather Thatcher, Jill Esmond, G. P. Huntley Jr.

In **Keeper of the Flame** Spencer Tracy and ▷ Katharine Hepburn switched to drama and scored just as strongly as in their first co-starrer. George Cukor directed the tense I. A. R. Wylie story of a journalist probing a widow's secrets about her famous husband's life and death. Script by Donald Ogden Stewart; production by Victor Saville (associate Leon Gordon). Also cast: Richard Whorf, Margaret Wycherly, Forrest Tucker, Frank Craven, Audrey Christie, Horace McNally, Percy Kilbride, Darryl Hickman, Donald Meek and Howard da Silva.

Whatever became of tap-dancing? Eleanor Powell brought it to such heights of speed and grace, maybe its other exponents got discouraged. Her numbers in **Ship Ahoy** were electrifying, and while she got her breath back Red Skelton and Bert Lahr kept its large audiences amused. Harry Clork's script, climaxed by the star sending a morse code message in taps, sufficed to hold the music and gags together, and Jack Cummings' production had glitter. Edward Buzzell directed a cast also including Virginia O'Brien, William Post Jr, John Emery, Stuart Crawford, Bernard Nedell and Tommy Dorsey's band. This last had an unbilled vocalist, a skinny kid with a nice voice, named Frank Sinatra.

Worst Idea of The Year prize went to **Tarzan's New York Adventure**, which took one of the movies' great fantasy figures out of his never-never jungle into the harsh reality of Manhattan. With clothes on, the legendary superman was just another tall actor. Mayer had carefully preserved the Tarzan illusion around Johnny Weissmuller by vetoing his appearance in any other role, so this was only his sixth film in ten years under contract. In the same period Maureen O'Sullivan had made 35 pictures but she, like Johnny, now checked out. (She was off the screen for six years while she and husband John Farrow increased their family to seven children.) The Myles Connolly–William Lipman script had them flying to New York to rescue their kidnapped son (Johnny Sheffield) with Cheeta the chimp tagging along for

Red Skelton, Ann Rutherford, Jean Rogers and Rags Ragland in **Whistling in Brooklyn**, *Skelton's third annual appearance as the addle-pated sleuth introduced in* Whistling in the Dark. *It hit its laugh target, but the series was not continued. S. Sylvan Simon, George Haight and Nat Perrin repeated as director/ producer/writer. Also cast: Ray Collins, Henry O'Neill, William Frawley, Sam Levene, Arthur Space, Robert Emmet O'Connor, Steve Geray, Howard Freeman.*

Lost Angel *proved that Mayer hadn't lost his star-developing skill. Margaret O'Brien's* Journey for Margaret *performance brought orders from his throneroom that an ideal story must be tailored for her, if it took a year (it did). After many rejects, Isobel Lennart's script from an idea by Angna Enters clicked: a surefire yarn about a foundling, reared by scientists to be a mental prodigy, then shown the joys of normal childhood by a kindly reporter—James Craig, here with the star. Well-directed by Roy Rowland and acting with the authority of a pint-sized Garbo, Margaret carried it to great popularity. Robert Sisk produced another hit for Schary's 'B'-plus crew, casting Marsha Hunt, Philip Merivale, Henry O'Neill, Donald Meek, Keenan Wynn, Alan Napier, Sara Haden, Kathleen Lockhart, Howard Freeman, Elisabeth Risdon, Bobby Blake.*

Bathing Beauty *was built around Esther Williams; of the 1944 total of 155 performers under MGM contract, she was one of ten promoted from featured players to the 'official' star list. (The others: Laraine Day, Kathryn Grayson, Van Johnson, Gene Kelly, George Murphy, Margaret O'Brien, Susan Peters, Ginny Simms, Robert Walker.) Red Skelton was co-starred for box-office insurance, and the expensive edifice was topped by a John Murray Anderson water ballet that out-Busbyed Berkeley. Other numbers promoted the current vogue for Latin American rhythms: 'Tico-Tico' played by swing organist Ethel Smith, 'Echo of a Serenade' sung by baritone Carlos Ramirez, several more by Xavier Cugat's orchestra with Lina Romay, and Harry James' band did their North American stuff. A tiny story about a girls' school emerged from the massed typewriters of Kenneth Earl, M. M. Musselman, Curtis Kenyon, Joseph Schrank, Dorothy Kingsley, Allen Boretz and Frank Waldman, giving jobs to Basil Rathbone, Bill Goodwin, Jean Porter, Nana Bryant, Donald Meek, Ann Codee, Francis Pierlot and a Marxless Margaret Dumont. George Sidney directed, Jack Cummings produced in Technicolor, and Metro made a juicy profit.*

Robert Young wound up his long stay at MGM with **The Canterville Ghost**, *a comedy of GIs billeted in a haunted castle, based more or less on Oscar Wilde's story by scenarist Edwin Blum. Charles Laughton (here with Young and Margaret O'Brien) capered frantically as the 300-year-old spook in a vain effort to stop Margaret's theft of the movie, while English atmosphere was supplied by Reginald Owen, Elisabeth Risdon, Peter Lawford, Una O'Connor and Lumsden Hare. William Gargan, Rags Ragland, Frank Faylen, Mike Mazurki and Bobby Readick played Young's buddies. Jules Dassin directed for laughs, which it didn't get enough of. Arthur Field produced.*

1944

National Velvet had been on Pandro Berman's ▷
must-do list since he tried to buy it for Katharine
Hepburn at RKO in 1935, but Paramount
grabbed the Enid Bagnold best-seller, couldn't
cast it, and sold it to MGM in 1937. By 1941
Berman and Velvet were under the same roof;
three years later a hit was born. Also a star:
Elizabeth Taylor was hardly a jockey type, but
she played the horse-loving title character with
such 'burning eagerness tempered with sweet,
fragile charm' ('N.Y. World Telegram') that
not even a splendidly restrained Mickey
Rooney, in his last film before army service,
could steal scenes. Donald Crisp and Anne
Revere, who won an Oscar (as did film editor
Robert Kern), here with Liz; and Angela
Lansbury, Juanita Quigley, Jackie Jenkins,
Reginald Owen, Arthur Treacher, Norma
Varden, Terry Kilburn and Arthur Shields also
reflected the warmth of Clarence Brown's
direction of the Theodore Reeves–Helen
Deutsch screenplay. And it had a thundering
Grand National climax – the best movie horse-
race ever.

Two more young hopefuls decorated **Three
Men in White**: Marilyn Maxwell and Ava
Gardner, with Lionel Barrymore wheelchairing
the Blair Hospital corridors for the 13th time.
Keye Luke and the ubiquitous Van Johnson
continued their rivalry for Dr Gillespie's
approval in a rather tired screenplay by Martin
Berkeley and Harry Ruskin, directed by Willis
Goldbeck. Rags Ragland was in for comedy
with the series standbys Alma Kruger, Walter
Kingsford, Nell Craig and George Reed.

Nominally a 'Dr Gillespie' movie, **Between
Two Women** (not the same-named 1937 story)
came out like a Van Johnson vehicle, what with
the tall redhead topping popularity polls all
over the map. Old Doc Barrymore had to take
sub-billing along with Gloria DeHaven (here
with Van), Keenan Wynn, Marilyn Maxwell,
Alma Kruger, Marie Blake, Keye Luke, Nell
Craig, Walter Kingsford and Leon Ames.
Harry Ruskin and Willis Goldbeck repeated as
writer and director, respectively, of this 14th of

the Kildare–Gillespie scalpel-slingers. Years
later in a TV series the same characters, played
by Richard Chamberlain and Raymond Massey,
earned MGM another mint.

Producer George Haight worked with one of
the MGM old-timers on **Maisie Goes to Reno**/
You Can't Do That to Me when Harry Beau-
mont, director of the original Broadway
Melody, came out of retirement to pilot Ann
Sothern through her annual 'Maisie' spree.
This one was a divorce and blackmail plot
devised by Harry Ruby and James O'Hanlon,
given the light touch by scripter Mary McCall
Jr and its always entertaining star. She had two
leading men, John Hodiak and Tom Drake,
supported by Paul Cavanagh and Marta
Linden (with her here) Ava Gardner, Bernard
Nedell, Chick Chandler, Donald Meek.

Long absent from the studio while she became
mother of the daughter who landed them both
in a murder scandal 15 years later, Lana Turner
returned in **Marriage Is a Private Affair** to have
a movie baby by John Hodiak. The slick
triangle story (James Craig in the third
corner), based by David Hertz and Lenore
Coffee on Judith Kelly's novel, kept Ray June's
camera focused lovingly on Lana for practically
two hours' running time. Its longueurs failed to
cool her popularity with the masses. Robert Z.
Leonard directed; Pandro Berman produced,
casting Frances Gifford, Hugh Marlowe,
Natalie Schafer (first film), Keenan Wynn,
Paul Cavanagh, Tom Drake, Morris Ankrum,
Nana Bryant, Virginia Brissac, Addison
Richards, Herbert Rudley.

A CLASSIC YEARLING
1946

World-wide cinema attendances were estimated at 235m a week: 90m in the US, 30m in Britain, 8m in France. Paramount's fantastic profit was $39m and Fox's and Warner Bros' $22m each. Thanks to a cuisine liberally sprinkled with such cornflakes as musicals, moppets and animals, the biggest MGM–Loew's profits ever were served up ($18m), although the gross income was down from 1945.

The Jolson Story made millions for Columbia and Jolson; not so for his old studio Warner Bros, which produced two other biographies: Cary Grant as Cole Porter in *Night and Day*, Ida Lupino and Olivia de Havilland as Brontë sisters in *Devotion*. Columbia made a mint with Rita Hayworth in *Gilda*. Ingrid Bergman, and Bing Crosby broke into the Top Ten list. The other eight strongest US magnets were Van Johnson, Gary Cooper, Bob Hope, Humphrey Bogart, Greer Garson, Margaret O'Brien, Betty Grable, Roy Rogers.

*There was a big public for **Courage of Lassie**, in which Lassie (née Pal), supported by Elizabeth Taylor and Frank Morgan, played a dog named Bill, making the title a misnomer. Its simple story was by Lionel Houser, its lush Technicolor photography by Leonard Smith. Tom Drake, Selena Royle, Harry Davenport, Catherine McLeod, Mitchell Lewis, Jane Green, George Cleveland, Minor Watson, Morris Ankrum and Donald Curtis were also in the Robert Sisk production, directed by Fred Wilcox.*

James Craig, a glutton for punishment, coped with Metro's scene-stealing youngsters singly and in bunches. Survivor of two Margaret O'Briens and one Jackie 'Butch' Jenkins, he took on two more with Butch in rapid succession. **Boys' Ranch** *was 'Son of Boys Town' in a Western setting, with Sharon McManus (here with Craig and Butch) and Skippy Homeier, Darryl Hickman, Dorothy Patrick,*

Ray Collins, Geraldine Wall, Minor Watson, Arthur Space, Robert Emmet O'Connor, Moroni Olsen. Roy Rowland directed and Robert Sisk produced the William Ludwig screenplay . . . **Little Mr Jim** *reunited Craig and Butch with Frances Gifford of Our Vines Have Tender Grapes; also cast were Henry O'Neill, Spring Byington, Luana Patten, Sharon McManus again, Morris Ankrum and silent star Laura La Plante. The thin story of army post families was scripted by George Bruce, directed by Fred Zinnemann, produced by Orville Dull.*

Meanwhile, The O'Brien herself was leaving no wither unwrung in **Three Wise Fools**, *aided by Thomas Mitchell and more Irish whimsy than you could shake a shillelagh at. Austin Strong's old play, first filmed by Goldwyn in 1923, was a bit icky for 1946, even as re-scripted by John McDermott and James O'Hanlon. Edward Buzzell directed and producer William Wright gave it a strong cast: Lionel Barrymore, Edward Arnold and Lewis Stone in the title roles; Jane Darwell, Harry Davenport, Cyd Charisse, Warner Anderson, Charles Dingle, Ray Collins, Henry O'Neill.*

Dean Stockwell plus pup too much competition? Wallace Beery dozes off in **The Mighty McGurk**. *William Lipman, Grant Garrett and*

Harry Clork wrote a compendium of several old Beery movies (particularly *The Champ*) for this one, set in the Bowery, 1900. Edward Arnold, Aline MacMahon, Cameron Mitchell, Dorothy Patrick, Aubrey Mather, Morris Ankrum and Clinton Sundberg took direction from John Waters; writer Nat Perrin turned producer for the occasion.

One of the year's best 'Bs', **Gallant Bess** brought one of MGM's oldest names, producer Harry Rapf, back to the credits; and a new process, Cinecolor, made the many exteriors look good. The movie also made a minor star of young Marshall Thompson, here with George Tobias, Clem Bevans, and the irresistible mare of the title. Jeanne Bartlett's story and script about an army horse taken home by a soldier got warm direction from Andrew Marton. Donald Curtis, Jim Davis, Chill Wills, and Wally Cassell supported the leads.

Another boy, another pet–but **The Yearling** ▷ *was at the other end of the budget scale, and among the most memorable of all MGM pictures. Claude Jarman Jr won a special Academy Award for his touching performance as the son of a poor farming couple (Gregory Peck, Jane Wyman). Oscars too to cameramen Charles Rosher, Leonard Smith and Technicolor specialist Arthur Arling; art directors Cedric Gibbons, Paul Groesse and Edwin B. Willis. Critics lauded Clarence Brown's direction of the Paul Osborn screenplay from Marjorie Kinnan Rawlings' novel, and the public responded abundantly. For producer Sidney Franklin it was a happy ending to a five-year headache that had started in 1941 when the film was shooting in Florida with a different cast headed by Spencer Tracy. Then swarms of insects hindered production, Tracy and director Victor Fleming had rows, King Vidor took over, boy and fawn grew too fast; finally Mayer ordered it shelved. In the new cast: Chill Wills, Margaret Wycherly, Clem Bevans, Forrest Tucker, Henry Travers, June Lockhart.*

Fred Zinnemann again directed Butch Jenkins in the moppet's third and best 1946 movie. Scripted by Morton Thompson from part of his book 'Joe the Wounded Tennis Player', **My Brother Talks to Horses** *(great guy for titles, Morton) told an amusing tale of a kid whose gift for animal conversation proved lucrative when it came to racehorses. Peter Lawford, Charles Ruggles, Edward Arnold, Beverly Tyler, Spring Byington, O. Z. Whitehead were cast in the Samuel Marx production.*

Fiesta *turned the spotlight on two young talents with decades of fame ahead: Ricardo Montalban and Cyd Charisse, whose dancing, together with the Technicolor photography of Mexican exteriors and a musical suite by Aaron Copland, were its chief assets. Esther Williams starred as a lady matador in the heavygoing script by George Bruce and Lester Cole, directed by Richard Thorpe, produced by Jack Cummings. Also cast: Mary Astor, John Carroll, Akim Tamiroff, Hugo Haas, Fortunio Bonanova, Frank Puglia, Alan Napier.*

◁ **Song of Love** *was a cut above the 'Ah, here comes Beethoven!' school of Hollywood biographies but the careful Clarence Brown production still lacked reality, settling for theatrical effect. Katharine Hepburn, Robert Walker and Henry Daniell played Clara Schumann, Brahms and Liszt. Miss Hepburn and Daniell had the requisite temperament and Paul Henreid, co-starred as Schumann, suffered nicely, but Walker was miscast. You could enjoy it with your eyes shut: glorious music, with William Steinberg conducting and Artur Rubinstein ghosting the stars' pianistics. The Ivan Tors–Irmgard von Cube–Allen Vincent–Robert Ardrey script from a play by Bernard Schubert and Mario Silva gave roles to Leo G. Carroll, Else Janssen, Gigi Perreau, Roman Bohnen, Ludwig Stossel, Tala Birell, Kurt Katch, Henry Stephenson.*

Hollywood's longest 1947 shooting schedule (five months) resulted when Gregory La Cava started **Living in a Big Way** *with Gene Kelly and Marie 'The Body' McDonald on the strength of a synopsis, written by himself, about postwar adjustment to a hasty marriage. He developed the script on the set, even letting the cast ad lib dialogue at times. The result was tedium, relieved only by two Kelly numbers which Gene choreographed with Stanley Donen, a new name on film credits. Producer, Pandro Berman; also cast, Phyllis Thaxter, Charles Winninger, Spring Byington, John Warburton, Clinton Sundberg, Jean Adair, Bill Phillips, Bernadene Hayes.*

William Powell and Myrna Loy played Nick and Nora Charles for the sixth and last time in **Song of the Thin Man,** *again making the difficult art of light comedy acting look easy. They'd co-starred in 13 films in 13 years. Leon Ames and Patricia Morison (left), Keenan Wynn, Philip Reed, Gloria Grahame, Dean Stockwell (as Nick Jr), Ralph Morgan, Don Taylor, Jayne Meadows, Warner Anderson, Connie Gilchrist, Bruce Cowling and Marie Windsor supported them in the Steve Fisher–Nat Perrin screenplay, from a whodunit by Stanley Roberts. Perrin produced, Edward Buzzell directed, exhibitors prospered.*

Two long and remarkably profitable series ended in 1947 with the final instalments of 'Maisie' and 'Dr Gillespie'. Above: **Undercover Maisie**/Undercover Girl, *Ann Sothern's tenth as the deliciously hardboiled blonde, had her wooed by Mark Daniels and Barry Nelson (left and right) while working for the police. Thelma Robinson wrote and Harry Beaumont directed the George Haight production, with Leon Ames, Clinton Sundberg, Dick Simmons, Gloria Holden, Douglas Fowley, Morris Ankrum, Nella Walker and Charles D. Brown cast . . .* **Dark Delusion**/Cynthia's Secret *featured Lucille Bremer as a neurotic patient and James Craig as yet another Dr Kildare replacement. Lionel Barrymore played Gillespie for the 15th time. Others directed by Willis Goldbeck in the Jack Andrews–Harry Ruskin screenplay were Edward Arnold, Jayne Meadows, Warner Anderson, Keye Luke, Alma Kruger, Henry Stephenson, Lester Matthews, Geraldine Wall. As with the 'Hardy' swansong, a producer was screen credited for the first time: Carey Wilson.*

Gladys George, Leon Ames, Dorothy Patrick and Wallace Beery in **Alias a Gentleman,** *mild stuff about an ex-con going straight. Director, Harry Beaumont; producer, Nat Perrin; script, William Lipman (who could write Beery scenes without looking by this time) from Peter Ruric's original; cast, Tom Drake, Warner Anderson, John Qualen, Sheldon Leonard, Trevor Bardette.*

Robert Taylor goes berserk under the care of asylum doctor Audrey Totter in **High Wall.** *He'd murdered his wife, or was it Herbert Marshall whodunit? Pretty tense stuff, made on a tight budget by two who learned how at Warners: director Curtis Bernhardt and producer Robert Lord. The Sydney Boehm–Lester Cole script from an Alan Clark–Bradbury Foote original gave roles to Dorothy Patrick, H. B. Warner, Warner Anderson, Elisabeth Risdon, Moroni Olsen, John Ridgely, Morris Ankrum, Vince Barnett.*

Following The Show-Off *Red Skelton tried another remake of another time-tested comedy,* **Merton of the Movies**. *Paramount had filmed the George Kaufman–Marc Connelly play in 1924 with Glenn Hunter and in 1932 with Stuart Erwin (as* Make Me a Star*). In the new script by George Wells and Lou Breslow, Gloria Grahame played the Hollywood siren who attempted to besmirch Red's honour; Virginia O'Brien, Leon Ames, Hugo Haas, Alan Mowbray, Charles D. Brown and Douglas Fowley were other denizens of the old-time studios. Albert Lewis produced, and Robert Alton directed for the first time: he started his MGM career doing the rhumba with Garbo in* Two-Faced Woman, *then choreographed many big musicals.*

Tenth Avenue Angel, *starring Margaret O'Brien, was one of several projects that ran into trouble in 1946–7. It went through script and cast changes, re-takes and cutting, finally emerging 18 months after it started, and after the release of Margaret's next,* Unfinished Dance. *She played a little angel of the New York tenements, infecting everyone but the audience with her faith and joy. Harry Ruskin and Eleanore Griffin pieced together a story by Angna Enters and a sketch by Craig Rice; Roy Rowland directed, Ralph Wheelwright produced. Cast included George Murphy, Warner Anderson, Phyllis Thaxter and Margaret (above); also Angela Lansbury, Barry Nelson, Rhys Williams, Connie Gilchrist, Tom Trout.*

Richard Hart, a recruit from the New York stage, started at the top with the lead opposite Greer Garson in **Desire Me**. *He replaced Robert Montgomery, whose walk-out soon after its start in February 1946 was only one of the snags for MGM that didn't end with its September 1947 release. Script troubles bedevilled producer Arthur Hornblow Jr and director George Cukor; Garson, who needed a hit after* Adventure, *was unhappy; retakes and re-editing culminated in Cukor disowning it, so it became the company's only major*

movie carrying no director credit. Casey Robinson adapted Leonhard Frank's novel– 'Karl and Anna', filmed by Paramount, also unsuccessfully, as The Homecoming *in 1925– about a soldier (Robert Mitchum), presumed dead, coming home to find his comrade-in-arms now in the arms of his wife. Scripters Zoe Akins and Marguerite Roberts tried in vain to make this hoary situation look fresh. Morris Ankrum and George Zucco had the only other significant roles.*

High Barbaree *was an example of the bland escapism overdone by Hollywood. Its authors' names, Charles Nordhoff and James Norman Hall, revived memories of their* Mutiny on the Bounty *but such adventurous scenes as this one with Van Johnson and Cameron Mitchell were outnumbered by long sugary sequences depicting the deathless love of Johnson and June Allyson, directed by the usually trenchant Jack Conway. Everett Riskin produced the Anne Chapin–Whitfield Cook–Cyril Hume screenplay casting Thomas Mitchell, Marilyn Maxwell, Claude Jarman Jr, Henry Hull, Geraldine Wall, Paul Harvey.*

Green Dolphin Street *was scripted by Samson Raphaelson from Elizabeth Goudge's book, the first winner of the annual $200,000 MGM Novel Award, a new way of buying rights before publication; later winners were never filmed. It had everything, i.e. too much for a single movie: a glorious wallow in family conflict, triangle romance, Maori uprising in old New Zealand, earthquake, tidal wave, pathos and bathos. It got the double-'A' works from producer Carey Wilson, director Victor Saville, the technicians (Oscars won by Arnold Gillespie and Warren Newcombe for visual effects, Douglas Shearer and Michael Steinore for sound effects), and a costly cast including Richard Hart, Lana Turner, Van Heflin and Gigi Perreau (here); also Donna Reed, Frank Morgan, Gladys Cooper, Reginald Owen, Edmund Gwenn, Dame May Whitty, Linda Christian, Moyna MacGill. Returns were excellent. Hart, a potential star, died at 35.*

Another MGM fling at the Arts: ballet in **The Unfinished Dance** *with Margaret O'Brien as student and Cyd Charisse as ballerina. Broadway comedian Danny Thomas and former showgirl Karin Booth had other leads in the backstage screenplay by Myles Connolly (from Paul Morand's 'Mort du Cygne'), supported by Esther Dale, Thurston Hall, Ann Codee, Ruth Brady, Gregory Gaye. The Technicolor cameras of Robert Surtees did a fine job for the old producer-director team, Joe Pasternak and Henry Koster, but box-office results were spotty.*

Mayer, aware that adolescence was the exit sign for most child stars, nurtured Elizabeth Taylor's career by buying a Broadway play about an adolescent, **Cynthia**/The Rich, Full Life, *and entrusting her to the direction of Robert Z. Leonard, glorifier of MGM females from Mae Murray on. Liz did her share by growing from lovely child to gorgeous teenager. Mary Astor and James Lydon (here as her mother and first date) supported her along with George Murphy, S. Z. Sakall, Spring Byington, Gene Lockhart, Scotty Beckett, Kathleen Howard, Morris Ankrum, Shirley Johns, Harlan Briggs and silent star Anna Q. Nilsson. Edwin Knopf produced the Harold Buchman–Charles Kaufman adaptation of Vina Delmar's play.*

Rustic charm spread through **The Romance of Rosy Ridge** *like molasses. That icky title put off some customers, but enough relished Van Johnson's performance as a wandering minstrel in post-Civil War Missouri, a rousing fight sequence, Roy Rowland's sympathetic direction, and the debut of a piquant discovery (by Norma Shearer), Janet Leigh, Lester Cole scripted Mackinlay Kantor's novel for producer Jack Cummings. Left to right: Dean Stockwell, Selena Royle, Miss Leigh, Thomas Mitchell, Johnson; also cast were Marshall Thompson, Guy Kibbee, Charles Dingle, Elisabeth Risdon, Jim Davis.*

pictures as *Pinky, Home of The Brave, All the King's Men* and *The Snake Pit* dealing with racial prejudice, political corruption and the treatment of the insane. But comics and cowboys were the money magnets, the most popular stars being Bob Hope, Bing Crosby, Abbott and Costello, John Wayne and Gary Cooper. Former MGM hit-maker Joseph L. Mankiewicz won Oscars for writing and directing Fox's *A Letter to Three Wives*.

In Britain, Sir Laurence Olivier continued to collect awards for his *Hamlet*, but J. Arthur Rank said he'd close his studios unless entertainment tax was abolished.

rs of Metro-Goldwyn-Mayer

1949

At the start of 1949 post-production was completed on **Edward, My Son** which had inaugurated MGM's big new studios at Borehamwood near London in 1948. Spencer Tracy as the ruthless self-made millionaire and Deborah Kerr as his neglected, alcoholic wife starred in Donald Ogden Stewart's screenplay of the Robert Morley—Noel Langley stage hit. Mayer sent over two of his best men for it, director George Cukor and producer Edwin Knopf, but the result fell short of hopes. Critics said Tracy was not ideally cast, and the play's trick of never showing the title character who motivated the drama seemed an irritating gimmick on screen. Cast included: Ian Hunter (left), James Donald, Leueen MacGrath, Mervyn Johns, Felix Aylmer, Walter Fitzgerald.

Gene Kelly enjoyed tackling a straight dramatic part once in a while, and was surprisingly good at it. In **Black Hand**, set in early 1900s New York, he fought the bloodthirsty secret society that became infamous as the Mafia. Here he vows vengeance for the death of his parents, Peter Brocco and Eleanora Mendelssohn, to Marc Lawrence. Richard Thorpe got the full charge of excitement out of Luther Davis' script, replete with knifings and dynamitings, from Leo Townsend's original. William Wright produced, casting J. Carrol Naish, Teresa Celli, Frank Puglia, Barry Kelley, Bert Freed, Phyllis Morris.

Long announced by Enterprise as a vehicle for Ginger Rogers, who had script approval and didn't approve, **Caught** left its viewers as depressed as Robert Ryan and Barbara Bel Geddes in this scene. It bogged Barbara down

in the travails of that much-dramatized character, the richest girl in the world. Chief interest was stirred by the Hollywood debut of No 1 British star James Mason; also cast were Natalie Schafer, Ruth Brady, Bernadene Hayes, Curt Bois. Max Ophuls and Wolfgang Reinhardt directed and produced, with less than Teutonic efficiency, the Arthur Laurents screenplay from Libbie Block's Wild Calendar.

James Stewart returned to MGM for **The Stratton Story**. His underplaying and Sam Wood's firm direction kept the goo out of a sad story, based on fact by Douglas Morrow (who won the Oscar for best original) and Guy Trosper, about a baseball star losing his leg. Left to right: Agnes Moorehead, Stewart, June Allyson, baby William Basset and Robert Gist. Frank Morgan, Bill Williams, Bruce Cowling and Cliff Clark were in the Jack Cummings production which was well reviewed and a big moneymaker, especially in the US.

Finale for a team that made movie history: Fred Astaire and Ginger Rogers in the last number they did together, 'Manhattan Downbeat' in **The Barkleys of Broadway.** The ten years since their last movie at RKO had slowed them not at all, and this Arthur Freed production got a hearty welcome. Ginger was a late replacement for Judy Garland, whose breakdowns were becoming a serious studio problem. The conventional backstage, battling stars story by Betty Comden and Adolph Green was directed by Charles Walters (the numbers by Robert Alton), with Oscar Levant, Billie Burke, Jacques François, Gale Robbins, George Zucco, Clinton Sundberg, Inez Cooper.

Margaret O'Brien, growing fast at 12, bowed out with **The Secret Garden** and retired for several years. Later, the talent remained but movie stardom had fled. With her here are Brian Roper, Dean Stockwell and Herbert Marshall, in a cast including Gladys Cooper,

Elsa Lanchester, Reginald Owen, Aubrey Mather, Lowell Gilmore, George Zucco, Billy Bevan, Dennis Hoey, Isobel Elsom, Matthew Boulton, Norma Varden. The gentle period piece, first filmed by Paramount in 1919, ten years after Frances Hodgson Burnett wrote it, fared mildly at 1949 box-offices. Script, Robert Ardrey; director, Fred Wilcox; producer, Clarence Brown.

Yet another farewell, sadder still: Wallace Beery died soon after making **Big Jack**, his 252nd movie in 36 years. He was ailing during its production and seemed aware that he was playing the bold bandit once too often. Gene Fowler, Marvin Borowsky and Osso Van Eyss wrote it from a Robert Thoeren original and Gottfried Reinhardt produced. Richard Thorpe directed Richard Conte, Beery, Marjorie Main and Edward Arnold (left to right) and Vanessa Brown, Charles Dingle, Clinton Sundberg, Clem Bevans and Bill Phillips.

Several new films were dubbed Silver Jubilee Productions in MGM's 25th anniversary year and some of them didn't click. **The Great Sinner** had a million-dollar cast: Walter Huston, Melvyn Douglas, Gregory Peck and Ava Gardner (here) and Ethel Barrymore, Frank Morgan, Agnes Moorehead; but director Robert Siodmak and producer Gottfried Reinhardt added heavily Germanic treatment to an already doom-laden Russian story, making for a gloomy evening. Ladislas Fodor, Rene Fulop—Miller and Christopher Isherwood adapted Dostoievsky's 'The Gambler' so thoroughly that he didn't even get author credit.

Galsworthy wasn't let off lightly either. **That Forsyte Woman**/The Forsyte Saga, with Greer Garson gracious as Irene and Errol Flynn surprisingly effective as Soames, had a doggedly stagey air. American accents of the other principals—Walter Pidgeon, Robert Young, Janet Leigh, Harry Davenport (who died in 1949 after 77 years as an actor)—invalidated the Englishness demanded of the story, which scripters Jan Lustig, Ivan Tors, James B. Williams and Arthur Wimperis restricted to Book One of the Saga. But director Compton Bennett in his Hollywood debut made his dramatic points and the film was generally popular. Leon Gordon produced it in Technicolor; with Aubrey Mather, Lumsden Hare, Gerald Oliver Smith, Halliwell Hobbes and Matt Moore. MGM had scheduled it 16 years earlier as a David Selznick production starring the three Barrymores.

Judy Garland was back in good (if overweight) form in **In the Good Old Summertime**, and Buster Keaton made his last appearance at his old studio. This was The Shop Around the Corner with Budapest taken out and several songs put in for Judy; a charming show and a moneymaker. Left to right: Spring Byington, S. Z. Sakall, Clinton Sundberg, Judy, Keaton and Van Johnson. Robert Z. Leonard directed and Albert Hackett, Frances Goodrich and Ivan Tors revamped the original script for Joe Pasternak.

The Jack Cummings musical hit **Neptune's Daughter** won an Academy Award for best song, Frank Loesser's 'Baby, It's Cold Outwide', sung by Esther Williams and Ricardo Montalban, then reprised by Betty Garrett and Red Skelton. Here Miss Williams is congratulated by Keenan Wynn and Miss Garrett on winning a swim trophy in the film. Edward Buzzell directed Dorothy Kingsley's breezy screenplay, with Xavier Cugat and band, Ted de Corsia and Mike Mazurki in the cast.

Dore Schary had a penchant for hard, fast thrillers done with documentary realism and minimum expense. Two such winners in 1949: Van Johnson in **Scene of the Crime**, handcuffed

to corpse William Haade, and Ricardo Montalban in **Border Incident**, struggling with Howard da Silva. Producer credit for the first was given to Harry Rapf, but the old MGM exec had died while preparing it. Charles Schnee wrote and Roy Rowland directed, with Arlene Dahl, Gloria DeHaven, Tom Drake, Leon Ames, Donald Woods, John McIntire, Norman Lloyd, Jerome Cowan, Tom Powers, Anthony Caruso, Robert Gist, Tom Helmore . . . The second, John C. Higgins' story of Mexican farmworkers smuggled over the US border, was directed and produced by Anthony Mann and Nicholas Nayfack, with George Murphy, Teresa Celli, James Mitchell, Arnold Moss, Charles McGraw, Sig Ruman, John Ridgely.

Left to right: Angela Lansbury, Walter Pidgeon, Peter Lawford and Ethel Barrymore wondered what to do about Janet Leigh, a refugee in the British-occupied zone of Vienna. in **The Red Danube**. Bruce Marshall's novel got the full MGM works in casting and production from Carey Wilson, but the public didn't seem to care. Francis L. Sullivan, Alan Napier, Robert Coote and Melville Cooper were directed by George Sidney in the sluggish Gina Kaus–Arthur Wimperis screenplay.

The release of **Malaya**/East of the Rising Sun was delayed until after Spencer Tracy's next, while producer Edwin Knopf tried to pep it up in the cutting room. Mechanically written by Frank Fenton (original, Manchester Boddy) and directed likewise by Richard Thorpe, this melodrama was unworthy of its cast: James Stewart, Tracy, Valentina Cortese and Sydney Greenstreet (here) and Lionel Barrymore, John Hodiak, Gilbert Roland, Tom Helmore and Roland Winters.

Battleground was a remarkable case of MGM history repeating itself. When Thalberg planned to make The Big Parade Mayer said no one wanted a war drama in 1925. Now Schary, the 'new Thalberg', had brought a pet project over from RKO, where Howard Hughes had vetoed it, and Mayer said no one wanted a war drama in 1949. Both movies turned out to be outstanding hits and each started a rift between Mayer, who naturally disliked being proved wrong, and his No. 2. Battleground had force in its script by Robert Pirosh (Academy Award) and realism in its direction by William Wellman. Even the glamour boys among its actors looked and sounded like GI's enduring the Battle of the Bulge. Left to right, John Hodiak, Denise Darcel, Van Johnson; also cast were Ricardo Montalban, George Murphy, Marshall Thompson, Don Taylor, Richard Jaeckel, Jerome Courtland, Leon Ames, Douglas Fowley, Bruce Cowling, James Whitmore, James Arness, Thomas Breen, Scotty Beckett. Paul Vogel's camerawork won it a second Oscar.

Don't try to get away! Richard Basehart, William Conrad, Barry Sullivan, Audrey Totter and Cyd Charisse in **Tension**, an ingenious, tightly-plotted murder story by John Klorer. Scripter Allen Rivkin and director John Berry kept the title as their watchword throughout. Producer, Robert Sisk. Also cast: Lloyd Gough, Tom d'Andrea, Tito Renaldo.

Below: Geraldine Brooks, Edmund Gwenn, Lassie and Reginald Owen in **Challenge to Lassie**, for which the star (not the original, but a look-alike owned by the same trainer) had to learn sheep-herding. Adapted by William Ludwig from 'Greyfriars Bobby', the Robert Sisk production in Technicolor was directed by Richard Thorpe. Donald Crisp, Alan Webb, Henry Stephenson, Alan Napier, Sara Allgood, Arthur Sheilds, Edmond Breon and Lumsden Hare rolled Scottish Rs.

1949 *A baseball story,* **Take Me Out to the Ball Game** *(Everybody's Cheering in Britain, where the game is box-office poison) scored an entertainment home-run everywhere. Like all MGM musicals now, it was in Technicolor. With two of the world's best song-and-dance men, Frank Sinatra and Gene Kelly, how could*

it miss? Just to make sure, Arthur Freed added Esther Williams, Betty Garrett and Jules Munshin and turned them all loose on that old master of musicals, Busby Berkeley. Kelly and Stanley Donen got co-author credit for what resembled a rewrite of the 1930 flop, They Learned About Women; Harry Tugend and George Wells scripted.

But the musical that won all the critics' and customers' awards was **On the Town**, starring Betty Garrett, Frank Sinatra, Ann Miller, Jules Munshin, Vera-Ellen and Gene Kelly (left to right, above; the last two also at left). A ballet by Jerome Robbins inspired this show's triumphant career; from it Betty Comden and Adolph Green (who also played the Miller and Munshin roles) derived a 1944 Broadway hit with music by Leonard Bernstein, and, when MGM brought them to Hollywood, wrote the screenplay. Direction by Kelly and Stanley Donen had exhilarating zest; Arthur Freed's production sparkled; Roger Edens' and Lennie Hayton's scoring won an Academy Oscar. The six leads were supported by Alice Pearce, in her original stage role, and Florence Bates.

1949

The Yellow Cab Man *starred Red Skelton as a disaster-prone inventor, here with James Gleason, Gloria DeHaven and Charles Hughes. Edward Arnold, Walter Slezak, Jay C. Flippen, Paul Harvey, Polly Moran were in it. Writers Devery Freeman and Albert Beich, director Jack Donohue and producer Richard Goldstone kept the sight gags coming almost without respite.*

Once again the MGM air was heavy with imaginary anaesthetics as Pandro Berman's crew opened up the old hospital sets for **The Doctor and the Girl**, *dusted off the scalpels and pulled rubber gloves on a handsome new surgeon: Glenn Ford in his first of dozens of Metro roles. Patients with him here: Janet Leigh (walking) and Gloria DeHaven (emergency). Charles Coburn, Bruce Bennett, Warner Anderson, Nancy Davis, Arthur Franz and Basil Ruysdael were also cast under Curtis Bernhardt's direction. Theodore Reeves' script streamlined 'Bodies and Souls' by Maxence van der Meersch, a massive best-seller—but not as a film.*

Farley Granger and Cathy O'Donnell—golly, what those poor kids went through to get to this happy ending of **Side Street**. *Audiences had their nerves frazzled too, as the lovers got caught up in robbery and murder, tensely plotted by Sydney Boehm and directed at a fast clip by Anthony Mann. He shot exteriors in Manhattan, most effectively in the climactic chase through the streets. Sam Zimbalist produced, casting James Craig against type as a vicious gangster, and Jean Hagen, Paul Jergens, Edmon Ryan, Harry Bellaver, Whit Bissell, John Gallaudet.*

Marcia Davenport's **East Side, West Side** *brought the total of novels filmed by MGM in 1949 to ten. It wasn't exactly a best-seller at the ticket-windows, but worked out at a profit thanks to its cast's drawing power: Van Heflin, Barbara Stanwyck, James Mason (left to right); plus Ava Gardner, Cyd Charisse, Gale Sondergaard, Nancy Davis, William Conrad, Raymond Greenleaf, Beverly Michaels, William Frawley. Mervyn LeRoy directed Isobel Lennart's screenplay, produced by former story department head Voldemar Vetluguin.*

Top names were again sent to London for the new studio's second production, **Conspirator**, *with even more disappointing results than* Edward My Son, *and producer Arthur Hornblow Jr faced a 'what can we do with this?' dilemma back at Culver City, where it lay on the shelf for several months. Robert Taylor reprised his* Undercurrent *performance of charming husband/vicious villain, while Elizabeth Taylor as his wife made a premature start as an adult actress. Sally Benson's script, from a novel by Humphrey Slater, and Victor Saville's direction were equally uninspired. Others cast: Robert Flemying, Honor Blackman, Harold Warrender, Thora Hird, Wilfrid Hyde White, Marjorie Fielding, Marie Ney, Helen Haye, Karel Stepanek.*

Ann Sothern went dramatic in a minor domestic thriller, **Shadow on the Wall**. *Zachary Scott co-starred, supported by little Gigi Perreau and Nancy Davis, who was to become California's first lady as Mrs Ronald Reagan; also cast were Tom Helmore, John McIntire, Marcia Van Dyke, Barbara Billingsley. Robert Sisk produced and Pat Jackson was imported from Britain to direct the William Ludwig script, from a Hannah Lees–Lawrence Bachmann story.*

Any Number Can Play *was a lacklustre affair, only moderately popular, although the novel by Edward Harris Heth seemed ideal Clark Gable stuff: woman trouble and business trouble for the boss of a posh gambling hell. It got the best names money could buy: writer Richard Brooks; producer Arthur Freed (what, no music?); director Mervyn LeRoy; cast Barry Sullivan, Darryl Hickman, Alexis Smith and the King himself (left to right) and Wendell Corey, Audrey Totter, Frank Morgan, Mary Astor, Lewis Stone, Marjorie Rambeau, William Conrad, Leon Ames, Edgar Buchanan, Mickey Knox, Richard Rober, Dorothy Comingore (the 'Marion Davies' in* Citizen Kane*).*

Critics raved over **Intruder in the Dust**; *Clarence Brown's production and direction of William Faulkner's novel demonstrated just how well a novel can be filmed. A master at bringing out the best in decades of MGM actors, from Garbo to Claude Jarman Jr, he got memorable performances from young Claude, Elizabeth Patterson and David Brian (here) and Juano Hernandez as the Negro they saved from lynching. Ben Maddow's script made no detours into comic or romantic relief from its grim theme of racial bigotry, personified by Porter Hall, Will Geer and Charles Kemper.*

The well-cast and beautifully mounted Pandro Berman production of **Madame Bovary** *took ▷ the odd course of framing the story in a depiction of Flaubert's trial for corrupting morals by writing it. Thus Emma's drama was put at one remove from the audience, who could admire without becoming engrossed. Vincente Minnelli directed the Robert Ardrey screenplay, and Jennifer Jones played the title role, Louis Jourdan (with her here) her lover. Also cast were James Mason as the author, Van Heflin as Bovary, Christopher Kent (the young Swedish actor, Alf Kjellin, renamed), Gene Lockhart, Gladys Cooper, Frank Allenby, John Abbott, Henry Morgan, George Zucco, Ellen Corby, Eduard Franz, Paul Cavanagh. Two previous versions: Hollywood, 1932 (as* Unholy Love!*); Paris, 1934 by Jean Renoir.*

1949

The movie of the year for many: Spencer Tracy, Judy Holliday and Katharine Hepburn in **Adam's Rib**. Mr and Mrs Garson Kanin (Ruth Gordon) wrote the witty story of married lawyers at professional loggerheads especially for Tracy and Hepburn, who were at their best ever. Director George Cukor and producer Lawrence Weingarten zipped them through this moneyspinner in a record 'A' schedule of 37 days. Judy's film debut as the dimwit on trial for husband-shooting was wildly funny, while three other newcomers from Broadway, David Wayne (glimpsed behind Tracy here), Tom Ewell and Jean Hagen also scored. Hope Emerson, Clarence Kolb and Polly Moran, back after 13 years, played bright bits and

Cole Porter contributed a song, 'Farewell Amanda'.

Frank Morgan's last appearance was in **Key to the City**, an amiable, forgettable comedy teaming Clark Gable and Loretta Young (here). He died at 59 after 17 years of fine MGM work. Albert Beich's original about a convention of mayors was hoked up with gags and action by scripter Robert Crutcher and director George Sidney in Z. Wayne Griffin's production. Marilyn Maxwell, James Gleason, Raymond Burr, Lewis Stone, Raymond Walburn, Pamela Britton, Clinton Sundberg, Marion Martin, Bert Freed, Emory Parnell, Clara Blandick supported.

A new star of the first magnitude arrived in **That Midnight Kiss***: Mario Lanza, given the ▷ lead opposite Kathryn Grayson for a debut that excited the public, had the critics talking about a new Caruso, and revived MGM's reputation for talent-spotting. In the somewhat auto-biographical role of a singing truck-driver he disclosed a theatre-shaking voice and a person-ality to match. The Joe Pasternak musical, directed by Norman Taurog, actually gave him fourth billing below Grayson, Jose Iturbi and Ethel Barrymore, with Keenan Wynn, Jules Munshin, J. Carrol Naish, Thomas Gomez, Arthur Treacher, Marjorie Reynolds and Amparo Iturbi in support. Script: Bruce Manning, Tamara Hovey.*

Nancy Goes to Rio *was Ann Sothern's last at MGM, where she started as a chorus girl named Harriet Lake in 1929. She's shown (below) with Louis Calhern in this typically tuneful, fluffy, popular Joe Pasternak musical. Jane Powell co-starred with Ann in the Jane Hall–Frederick Kohner–Ralph Block yarn about mother and daughter chasing the same singing role and the same man (unbeknownst*

to each other, mind you), re-scripted by Sidney Sheldon from a Deanna Durbin movie Paster-nak made at Universal ten years before, It's a Date. *Robert Z. Leonard directed with Carmen Miranda, Barry Sullivan, Scotty Beckett, Fortunio Bonanova, Nella Walker, Hans Conreid in the cast.*

The studio's year ended with a Yippee! as Robert Taylor rode down the wicked Apaches who dared to capture a White Woman. **Am-bush** *was a superior Western, as might be expected from Sam Wood (who died at 66 soon after directing it), and it did strong business. Armand Deutsch produced Marguerite Robert's screenplay from Luke Short's story, with John Hodiak, Jean Hagen, Don Taylor, Bruce Cowling, Leon Ames, John McIntire and the beauteous Arlene Dahl (here with Taylor)*

231

RENAISSANCE
1950

The industry generally was in the dumps. US attendances dwindled to 60m weekly (lowest since 1933), the British average to 26m. But it was a nice little year for MGM–Loew's, the 1950 net rising a million from 1949, and a new studio vitality making itself felt with hits like *Annie Get Your Gun, Father of the Bride* and *The Asphalt Jungle.*

The weak and medium attractions were the ones chiefly affected by the fall-off in attendances; big was still big. In this category came two show business stories: Bette Davis in J. L. Mankiewicz's Academy-Awarded *All About Eve*, and William Holden in Billy Wilder's Hollywood drama *Sunset Boulevard* with its galaxy of old-timers: Gloria Swanson, Erich von Stroheim, Buster Keaton, Anna Q. Nilsson, H. B. Warner and Cecil B. DeMille. Cecil B. was up to his old epic tricks in *Samson and Delilah.* Britain's best was *The Third Man*, reuniting *Kane's* Joseph Cotten and Orson Welles.

James Stewart in *Harvey* and Gregory Peck in *12 O'Clock High* clicked. Marlon Brando made an exciting debut in *The Men. Born Yesterday* hilariously starred this year's Oscar winner, Judy Holliday, and 1949's, Broderick Crawford. Jose Ferrer also won the Academy accolade in *Cyrano de Bergerac* but it flopped, as did Harold Lloyd's last movie, *Mad Wednesday.*

With the dawn of the Fifties, Val Lewton, beloved of horror buffs for his Zombies and Cat People of the Forties, turned nice and produced **Please Believe Me**. *Maybe the ghouls resented it: it was his last picture. This romantic comedy cast (left to right) Robert Walker, Peter Lawford, Deborah Kerr and Mark Stevens; also James Whitmore, Spring Byington, J. Carrol Naish, George Cleveland. Norman Taurog directed the Nathaniel Curtis screenplay.*

Niceness also permeated **Stars In My Crown**, *a gentle drama of a country parson and his family – Joel McCrea, Ellen Drew, Dean Stockwell. Jacques Tourneur returned to direct Joe David Brown's adaptation of his own novel, scripted by Margaret Fitts, produced by William Wright. Also cast: Lewis Stone, James Mitchell, Alan Hale, Juano Hernandez, Amanda Blake, Connie Gilchrist, Arthur Hunnicutt.*

Red Skelton played three roles in **Watch the Birdie**: *a camera nut, his father and his grandfather. Three roles too many, quipped Buster Keaton buffs, faithful unto death to* The Cameraman. *Ann Miller and Arlene Dahl shared leading lady chores, supported by Leon Ames, Pamela Britton and Richard Rober. Jack Donohue directed; Harry Ruskin produced and collaborated on the script with Ivan Tors and Devery Freeman; original by Marshall Neilan Jr.*

Elizabeth Taylor, Rosemary DeCamp, Leon Ames and Van Johnson in **The Big Hangover**, *a silly failure featuring a talking dog. It did nothing for Liz, Johnson, or the auteur theory of film-making: Norman Krasna wrote, produced and directed it all by himself. Also cast: Percy Waram, Fay Holden, Edgar Buchanan, Selena Royle, Gene Lockhart, Philip Ahn, Matt Moore, Pierre Watkin, Russell Hicks...*

The Skipper Surprised His Wife *was not in the same class as* Father of the Bride, *but still a bright domestic comedy. Robert Walker starred with (left to right) Jan Sterling, Spring Byington, Joan Leslie and Edward Arnold. Dorothy Kingsley's story of an ex-captain running his home as he did his ship brought director Elliott Nugent back to MGM after 17 years. William H. Wright produced, with Leon Ames, Paul Harvey, Kathryn Card in the cast.*

The Magnificent Yankee *was Louis Calhern's great stage success: he played it for two years on Broadway and another on the road. Rewarding him for his many fine MGM supporting jobs, Schary scheduled a film version, although aware it was more of a prestige than a profit entry. Its author, Emmet Lavery, wrote the script, Armand Deutsch produced, John Sturges directed, and Ann Harding ably partnered Calhern's splendid portrayal of Oliver Wendell Holmes, the liberal US Supreme Court Justice. Eduard Franz, Philip Ober, Ian Wolfe, Richard Anderson and James Lydon were cast. Its British title,* The Man with Thirty Sons, *referred to the Harvard law graduates Holmes sponsored.*

Richard Brooks' script and direction made a real gripper of **Crisis**, *George Tabori's story of an ailing dictator and an American surgeon forced to operate on him. Brooks and Arthur Freed, producing one of his rare non-musicals, had the pleasant idea of casting erstwhile matinee idols in support of Cary Grant, Jose Ferrer and Signe Hasso: Antonio Moreno, with them here (right), was one of MGM's first stars; Ramon Novarro and Gilbert Roland were also featured with Paula Raymond, Leon Ames and Teresa Celli.*

ON WITH THE DANCE
1951

Although MGM-Loew's profits in 1951 ($7.6m from $178m gross) equalled those of 1950, other companies were skidding. The number of television sets in American homes doubled during the year to 15m. All companies refused to sell their huge backlogs of movies to this threatening ogre, but Columbia, Universal and Paramount announced plans to film TV material. Better news from abroad, where restrictions on Hollywood product were eased or removed by Britain, Australia, Italy, France, West Germany and Argentina.

Three films vied for any prizes *American in Paris* didn't win: Vivien Leigh (Academy Award) and Marlon Brando in *A Streetcar Named Desire*; Elizabeth Taylor and Montgomery Clift in *A Place in The Sun*, Humphrey Bogart (Academy Award) and Katharine Hepburn in *The African Queen*. Also highly regarded were Alfred Hitchcock's *Strangers on a Train*, William Wyler's *Detective Story* and Jean Renoir's *The River*. Biblical box-office: Gregory Peck and Susan Hayward as *David and Bathsheba*. Doris Day and the Dean Martin–Jerry Lewis team achieved Top Tendom, joining Wayne, Crosby, Hope, Cooper, Tracy, Betty Grable, Randolph Scott, Abbott and Costello.

Lone Star *was produced on a big scale by Z. Wayne Griffin, with proportionate box-office response. Starring Clark Gable and Ava Gardner, it was a good old slam-bang Western with Gable and Broderick Crawford slugging it out for the land and the gal. Vincent Sherman directed the stars and Lionel Barrymore and Beulah Bondi (repeating their* Gorgeous Hussy *roles), Ed Begley, James Burke, William Farnum (the Gable of 40 years earlier), Lowell Gilmore, Moroni Olsen, Russell Simpson, William Conrad. Story, Howard Estabrook; script, Borden Chase.*

Westward the Women *veered from the usual to trace the trek of a wagon train full of nubile ladies destined to help pioneering males populate the wilderness. Dore Schary personally produced the movie, an original by Frank Capra scripted by Charles Schnee and directed by William Wellman. John McIntire helped Robert Taylor quell marauding Injuns and squalling trekkers Denise Darcel, Hope Emerson, Lenore Lonergan and Julie Bishop.*

Crowds loved and critics hated **Soldiers Three** *with Cyril Cusack, Robert Newton, Stewart Granger and David Niven (from left to right). Producer Pandro Berman had won acclaim for* Gunga Din *at RKO a dozen years before, but his* Soldiers Three *was kippered Kipling, hardly worthy of the studio that had done so well by* Captains Courageous *and* Kim. *Indian location shots from the latter backgrounded the jolly horseplay directed for laughs and action, junior grade, by Tay Garnett. The Marguerite Roberts–Tom Reed–Malcolm Stuart Boylan screenplay also employed Walter Pidgeon, Greta Gynt, Frank Allenby, Robert Coote and Dan O'Herlihy.*

By Pierre of the Plains *out of* Rose Marie, *Frank Fenton's story of a trapper versus a Mountie,* **The Wild North**, *was MGM's third outdoor hit in a row. It was given a spacious production (in AnscoColor) by Stephen Ames and plenty of action by Andrew Marton. Stewart Granger and Cyd Charisse canoed and canoodled; Wendell Corey played the NWMP constable, supported by Morgan Farley, J. M. Kerrigan, Howard Petrie, and those never-out-of-work Indians.*

Home Town Story *was a cuckoo's egg in the MGM nest, laid by General Motors who had commissioned it from director-writer Arthur Pierson as a propaganda piece. It naïvely told how newsman Jeffrey Lynn learned the error of his pinko ways, realizing the goodness of Big Business when his kid sister, trapped by a cave-in, was rescued by the machinery of tycoon Donald Crisp. In this scene: Lynn, Nelson Leigh, moppet Melinda Plowman, Alan Hale Jr, Crisp and Marjorie Reynolds. Also cast: Barbara Brown, Marilyn Monroe, Glenn Tryon.*

The Red Badge of Courage *was one of the ▷ sparks that set off the final Mayer–Schary–Schenck explosion. Schary scheduled the Stephen Crane Civil War classic, Mayer vetoed it, Schary insisted, Mayer appealed to Schenck for support. He didn't get it, and this, together with other ego-bruising incidents, resulted in Mayer's exit in the summer of 1951. Meanwhile, John Huston's script and direction captured the mood of Crane's novel, although its tenuous story suffered when disastrous sneak previews cued severe cutting. Producer Gottfried Reinhardt desperately added narration (spoken by James Whitmore) to explain the action, but movie fans still couldn't get the hang of it and it failed to recover its $1.6m cost. Audie Murphy, the mild-mannered youth who won more World War II medals than any other soldier, ably led the cast: Bill Mauldin, Douglas Dick, John Dierkes, Royal Dano, Arthur Hunnicutt, Andy Devine.*

The **Belle of New York** had a famous title once listed for Judy Garland. She might have pepped up this perfunctory version of the old Hugh Morton play (script, Robert O'Brien, Irving Elinson) and new but hitless songs by Harry Warren and Johnny Mercer. More was expected from the talents of Fred Astaire and Vera-Ellen (here dancing in the clouds), and those of producer Arthur Freed, director Charles Walters, and Marjorie Main, Keenan Wynn, Alice Pearce, Clinton Sundberg, Gale Robbins.

An operatic musical, **The Great Caruso**, surprised many showmen by becoming an absolute smash hit, thanks chiefly to the rapidly developing Mario Lanza furore. The real Caruso's widow, Dorothy, wrote the biographical framework ornamented by the Sonya Levien–William Ludwig screenplay. It was the singingest movie ever made, featuring no fewer than 27 vocal items, most of them sung by Lanza with tremendous brio. In nine operatic scenes he was joined by Metropolitan stars Dorothy Kirsten, Blanche Thebom, Jarmila Novotna (with him here), Giuseppe Valdengo and others. The Pasternak production even yielded a pop hit, 'The Loveliest Night of the Year', sung by Ann Blyth as Caruso's wife. Richard Thorpe directed in showmanly style. In the cast: Carl Benton Reid, Eduard Franz, Ludwig Donath, Richard Hageman, Alan Napier. Douglas Shearer's sound department won an Oscar for its recording quality.

Larry Parks, a big name since portraying Al Jolson in two film biographies, starred for the last time in **Love is Better than Ever**/The Light Fantastic opposite Elizabeth Taylor. He was then engulfed in the miasma of the McCarthy anti-Red hearings. Not much more was heard of the movie, either; a frail comedy about a dancing school, written by Ruth Brooks Flippen, directed by Stanley Donen, produced by William Wright. Also cast: Josephine Hutchinson, Tom Tully, Ann Doran, Kathleen Freeman.

Universally acclaimed as the company's great artistic triumph of 1951, **An American in Paris** brought the musical movie to an imaginative peak, especially in the 18-minute ballet (its 'Toulouse-Lautrec' sequence is seen here) danced by Gene Kelly and Leslie Caron. Show Boat outgrossed it as the year's most popular musical, but it brought MGM back into the Academy Award class with a bang, winning eight Oscars: best film; best story and screenplay, Alan Jay Lerner; best scoring, Johnny Green, Saul Chaplin; best art direction, Cedric Gibbons, Preston Ames, Edwin B. Willis, Keogh Gleason; best cinematography, Alfred Gilles; best costume design, Orry-Kelly, Walter Plunkett, Irene Sharaff; Thalberg Memorial Award, producer Arthur Freed; special award for choreography, Gene Kelly. The last deserved another two for his performance and his discovery of Mlle Caron in the Ballets des Champs Elysées – a new star for Metro. Vincente Minnelli's cast had only three other principals: pianist-comedian Oscar Levant, French singer Georges Guetary and the superb Nina Foch. The score was a Gershwin feast, ranging from one of George and Ira's earliest songs, 'I'll Build a Stairway to Paradise' (1922) to their last, 'Love is Here to Stay' (1937) and including 20 other numbers sung or played, plus the Concerto in F (third movement) and the title suite, which was first staged in Ziegfeld's 'Show Girl' (1929).

A musical that always does business: **Show Boat**, this time starring (left to right) Kathryn Grayson, Joe E. Brown and Howard Keel, with Agnes Moorehead, Marge and Gower Champion glimpsed in the background. Ava Gardner co-starred in the 'Julie' role intended for Judy Garland, and Robert Sterling, Adele Jergens, Leif Erickson, William Warfield (singing 'Ol' Man River') and Regis Toomey supported. George Sidney directed and Arthur Freed produced this handsome and hugely profitable version of Edna Ferber's goldmine, originally a best-selling novel, then a 1927

Ziegfeld show on Broadway, then filmed twice by Universal in 1929 (mostly silent) and 1936, and revived repeatedly on New York and London stages. Jerome Kern's music, one of the best show scores ever, drew fine performances from Keel and Grayson on 'Make Believe', 'Why Do I Love You?' and 'You Are Love', while Gardner was voice-dubbed for 'Bill' and 'Can't Help Lovin' That Man'. New songs he composed for the 1936 film were omitted, but included was 'After the Ball', which strangely is always interpolated as one of the big climactic numbers in the otherwise all-Kern score. Script: John Lee Mahin.

Excuse My Dust, a nice little musical about a dizzy inventor of an 1895 horseless carriage, gave Red Skelton a less slapsticky role than usual, and a new girl in Sally Forrest. Script was by George Wells; director Roy Rowland; producer Jack Cummings. Macdonald Carey, Monica Lewis, Raymond Walburn, Jane Darwell, Lillian Bronson, Guy Anderson and Paul Harvey were cast. Arthur Schwartz and Dorothy Fields did the songs, Hermes Pan the dances, and exhibitors the no-business.

Crime drama stalwart of the year was Walter Pidgeon, who returned to Culver City after Bulldog Drummond for two more double-feature melos. **The Sellout** featured John Hodiak, Audrey Totter and Karl Malden (left to right) with Pidgeon as a corruption-fighting newspaper editor. Paula Raymond, Cameron Mitchell, Thomas Gomez and Everett Sloane were also in the Nicholas Nayfack–Matthew Rapf production, directed by Gerald Mayer, written by Charles Palmer from Rapf's original . . . **The Unknown Man** had Pidgeon as a murder trial lawyer, supported by Dawn Addams, Richard Anderson and Ann Harding (with him here) and Barry Sullivan, Keefe Brasselle, Lewis Stone, Eduard Franz, Philip Ober and Mari Blanchard. Veteran Richard Thorpe directed and newcomer Robert Thomsen produced the Ronald Millar–George Froeschel screenplay.

SINGIN' IN THE RAIN
1952

This is Cinerama, with its curved picture six times the normal size, opened to great acclaim. It was the television-nagged industry's first film since sound to revive public enthusiasm via innovation, although a limited one.

Conventional screens were faring best with the super-hokum of *The Greatest Show on Earth*, so ably made by Cecil B. DeMille that it won the best film Oscar. The critics, more aware of art than box office, preferred Fred Zinnemann's *High Noon*, which did get an Academy prize for Gary Cooper. Jennifer Jones and Laurence Olivier in *Carrie*, Fredric March in *Death of a Salesman*, Burt Lancaster and Shirley Booth (Academy Award) in *Come Back, Little Sheba* were worthy but lugubrious. Cheerfulness broke in with John Wayne in Ford's *The Quiet Man*, Alec Guinness in *The Lavender Hill Mob*, Michael Redgrave in *The Importance of Being Earnest*, and Chaplin's *Limelight*, his last Hollywood movie.

A lower ratio of MGM hits dropped Loew's profits $3m below 1951, the least since 1933.

No 1952 blues while Gene Kelly and Debbie Reynolds were **Singin' in the Rain**. *It made a star of Debbie and was the third of the really superlative musicals Kelly made for Arthur Freed; many rate it even higher than* On the Town *and* American in Paris. *It made more money, and it had more laughs, with its only slightly exaggerated picture of the studios' silents-into-talkies panic of the late Twenties, enhanced by nostalgic tunes from the Freed–Brown catalogue: the title song, 'You Were Meant for Me', 'All I Do is Dream of You', a 'Broadway Melody' ballet danced excitingly by Kelly and Cyd Charisse, plus some new ones. Like* On the Town, *it was written by Adolph Green and Betty Comden, directed by Kelly and Stanley Donen, photographed by Harold Rosson. It won applause for Donald O'Connor's clowning and dancing, and raves for Jean Hagen's wildly funny caricature of a dumb movie queen. Also cast: Millard Mitchell, Rita Moreno, Douglas Fowley, Madge Blake.*

Debbie Reynolds and Donald O'Connor (right) carried their Singin' in the Rain *ebullience into* **I Love Melvin**, *a smaller musical but large in entertainment value, and a tidy profit-maker. Don Weis directed them and Una Merkel, Allyn Joslyn, Noreen Corcoran, Richard Anderson, Jim Backus and Barbara Ruick in the George Wells production. Robert Taylor popped up in a dream sequence when Debbie sang the brilliant 'A Lady Loves' number staged, like the others, by Robert Alton. Wells scripted Laslo Vadnay's story.*

MGM filmed **The Merry Widow** *a third time, and starred Lana Turner and Fernando Lamas, directed by Curtis Bernhardt, produced by Joe Pasternak. It was once too often. No top notes at the paybox as Lehar's music played third fiddle to Technicolor glamour and the laborious sophistication of a new script by Sonya Levien and William Ludwig. Just as she had in 1934, Una Merkel led the supporting cast, now including Richard Haydn, Thomas Gomez, John Abbott, Marcel Dalio and Robert Coote.*

Skirts Ahoy!, *with Joan Evans, Vivian Blaine and Esther Williams (here) was a sex change on the customary three-sailors musical. Otherwise no surprises. But look, Gene—Esther could do her ballet under water! Isobel Lennart wrote, Sidney Lanfield directed, Joe Pasternak produced; with Barry Sullivan, Keefe Brasselle, Dean Miller, Margalo Gillmore, Jeff Donnell, Thurston Hall, and specialties by Billy Eckstine, the DeMarco Sisters, Debbie Reynolds, Bobby Van, Keenan Wynn.*

Lots of talent in **Lovely to Look At**: *Ann Miller, Zsa Zsa Gabor, Red Skelton (seated); Kurt Kasznar, Kathryn Grayson, Howard Keel, Marge and Gower Champion (standing). Two fine singers, three great dancers, a top comedian, a good character actor and an international blonde—what more could you want? Add Jerome Kern songs ('Smoke Gets in Your Eyes', 'I Won't Dance', 'Yesterdays', 'The Touch of Your Hand', 'You're Devastating', 'Lovely to Look At', etc), smooth Mervyn LeRoy direction, posh Jack Cummings production and you've got a hit. George Wells and Harry Ruby rewrote* Roberta *which was first filmed by RKO in 1934 from the Broadway show based on Alice Duer Miller's novel.*

Supporting spots in Show Boat *and* Lovely to Look At *won Marge and Gower Champion a musical of their own.* **Everything I Have is Yours**. *They practically played themselves, a brilliant, married dance team, and Dennis O'Keefe made a welcome return as their producer. Enjoyable entertainment for its none-too-crowded audiences. Robert Z. Leonard directed for writer-producer George Wells, with Monica Lewis, Dean Miller, Eduard Franz, John Gallaudet, Jonathan Cott cast.*

Jane Powell and a new talent, Bobby Van, scored in **Small Town Girl**, *a middling Pasternak musical much revised by Dorothy Cooper and Dorothy Kingsley from the 1936 Janet Gaynor movie. Farley Granger, Ann Miller, S. Z. Sakall, Robert Keith, Fay Wray, Billie Burke, Nat King Cole, Dean Miller and William Campbell took Leslie Kardos' direction, with numbers staged by Busby Berkeley.*

249

Plymouth Adventure *was supposed to be an epic of the 'Mayflower's' voyage to the New World, but the script sprang a leak. Helen Deutsch wrote it, from Ernest Gebler's novel. Spencer Tracy was only too convincing as the surly, contemptuous captain; audiences started wishing he'd fall overboard around Reel Three. But later it was Gene Tierney who did, leaving husband Leo Genn (right). They, Van Johnson, Dawn Addams, Lloyd Bridges, Barry Jones, John Dehner, Lowell Gilmore, Rhys Williams, Kathleen Lockhart, John Dierkes and Paul Cavanagh made quite a cast, and producer Dore Schary gave Clarence Brown quite a budget to work on. Pity.*

Surgeon and nurse were at it again in **Battle Circus.** *You had to read the credits twice to believe that this soggy romance in a Korean M.A.S.H. unit was scripted and directed by Richard Brooks and produced by the prestigious Pandro Berman. You knew it couldn't be a 'B' quickie, because up there on the screen were big stars, Humphrey Bogart and June Allyson, trying to breathe some life into it. Others cast: Keenan Wynn, Robert Keith, William Campbell, Patricia Tiernan, Jonathan Cott, Philip Ahn, Steve Forrest, Jeff Richards. Allen Rivkin and Laura Kerr wrote the 'original'.*

The last Tracy-Hepburn picture at MGM was one of their best. Written for them by Ruth Gordon and Garson Kanin, **Pat and Mike** *had Spencer as a shady sports promoter and Kate as his whiz-bang tennis and golf protégée, with Aldo Ray (right) as his bone-head boxer. Director George Cukor and producer Lawrence Weingarten gave it everything needed for a comedy winner, including a good cast: William Ching, Sammy White, Phyllis Povah, Loring Smith, George Mathews, Charles Buchinski (later Bronson), Jim Backus, Chuck Connors (debut) and sports stars Alice Marble, Donald Budge, Gussie Moran, Frank Parker, Babe Zaharias.*

Scaramouche *cut a fine dash, both in the person of Stewart Granger (in Ramon Novarro's 1923 role) and at the box-office. Janet Leigh (here sharing the happy-ending smiles) was one of his lady-loves, and Eleanor Parker the other; Mel Ferrer was his splendidly sword-swinging foe. They were supported by Henry Wilcoxon, Nina Foch, Richard Anderson, Lewis Stone (who was also in the original), Robert Coote, Elisabeth Risdon, Howard Freeman, John Dehner, John Litel. Carey Wilson supplied a Technicolorful production, briskly directed by George Sidney and much rewritten by Ronald Millar and George Froeschel from the old Rex Ingram version of Sabatini's story.*

Vittorio Gassman, a star MGM had just imported from Italy, with Nina Foch (left) and Yvonne de Carlo in **Sombrero.** *This complication of romantic dramas was directed by Norman Foster, written by him and Josefina Niggli from her novel, 'Mexican Village'. It was sleepy-time down south at the paybox, despite a strong cast that included Ricardo Montalban, Cyd Charisse, Walter Hampden, Kurt Kasznar, Rick Jason, Thomas Gomez and dancer Jose Greco. Produced in Technicolor by Jack Cummings.*

Kurt Kasznar and Leslie Caron (foreground), Ralph Meeker, Gilbert Roland, John McIntire, Dick Simmons and Louis Armstrong in **Glory Alley.** *This drama, set 'way down yonder in New Orleans and centred on a boxer (Meeker) and a honky-tonk dancer (Miss Caron), was director Raoul Walsh's first at MGM for 17 years. It didn't click. Written by Art Cohn, produced by Nicholas Nayfack.*

New Orleans also backgrounded the mingled dramas of four young people caught up by Mardi Gras fever in **Holiday for Sinners.** *Gig Young and Janice Rule (seen here), Richard Anderson and William Campbell did their best, aided by veterans Keenan Wynn, Edith Barrett, Michael Chekhov and Porter Hall and directed by Gerald Mayer, but it flopped harder than Glory Alley. 'Hush mah roar', said Leo, hurrying north. John Houseman produced the Hamilton Basso screenplay, from a story by A. I. Bezzerides.*

Director Mitchell Leisen and writer Arthur Sheekman moved over from Paramount to bring out Glenn Ford's unexpected skill as a light comedian in **Young Man With Ideas.** *Here shy businessman Ford's wife underestimates her alcoholic capacity in one of the many funny scenes in this Gottfried Reinhardt –William Wright programmer. Ruth Roman (the wife), Denise Darcel, Nina Foch, Donna Corcoran, Ray Collins, Mary Wickes, Sheldon Leonard supported.*

The acting phase of George Murphy's extraordinary career ended in 1952 after 15 MGM years. A Broadway hoofer in the Twenties, he became a politician in the sixties (after much experience of industry politics as Screen Actors Guild president, Academy vice-president and Metro's ambassador at large) and was elected as Senator from California–one up on Governor Ronald Reagan. The latter's wife, Nancy Davis, played Murphy's wife in **Talk About a Stranger** *with Billy Gray (here) as their son. This 'B'-minor drama about a family's mysterious neighbour was written by Margaret Fitts from Charlotte Armstrong's original, produced by Richard Goldstone, directed by David Bradley, and featured Kurt Kasznar and Lewis Stone.*

Coveting the fortune June Allyson inherited from her murdered uncle, wicked Angela Lansbury guides her to a 19th-floor balcony while she sleepwalks. Before long, **Remains To Be Seen** audiences were sleepsitting, despite bursts of music from June, Van Johnson and Dorothy Dandridge. Producer Arthur Hornblow, scribe Sidney Sheldon and director Don Weis made this quote comedy thriller unquote from a Howard Lindsay–Russell Crouse play. Also cast: Louis Calhern, John Beal, Barry Kelley, Sammy White, Kathryn Card, Helene Millard, Paul Harvey, Morgan Farley and Howard Freeman.

Morocco was the location site for Mel Ferrer and Cornel Wilde in **Saadia**, a strange mixture of desert love, bandit raids and witchcraft. Albert Lewin directed, scripted and produced in Technicolor, casting Rita Gam, Michel Simon, Cyril Cusack, Wanda Rotha, Richard Johnson. Not a box-office oasis in sight.

In **Torch Song** Joan Crawford was back at MGM after ten years and still a very big name. It wasn't a very big picture though, according to the rental returns. As a Broadway star, Joan sang and danced (once in blackface, yet) and loved blind pianist Michael Wilding, who got some terrible parts at Metro. Writers John Michael Hayes and Jan Lustig bubbled sparkling dialogue into I. A. R. Wylie's soap-opera original, directed by Charles Walters, produced in Technicolor by Henry Berman and Sidney Franklin Jr. Also cast: Gig Young, Marjorie Rambeau, Henry Morgan, Dorothy Patrick, Paul Guilfoyle, Benny Rubin.

Dangerous When Wet, a bright Esther Williams musical, had her swimming the English Channel and romancing Fernando Lamas, who later became her off-screen husband. Producer George Wells added good Arthur Schwartz–Johnny Mercer songs, a Tom and Jerry underwater cartoon sequence and an enthusiastic cast: Jack Carson, Charlotte Greenwood (still high-kicking 22 years after her last MGM musical), Denise Darcel, William Demarest, Donna Corcoran. Charles Walters directed Dorothy Kingsley's screenplay.

William Holden and Eleanor Parker succouring conked-out Richard Anderson in **Escape from Fort Bravo**, a rousing tale of North versus South and Indians versus everybody. Frank Fenton wrote Nicholas Nayfack's Ansco-Colored production, directed by John Sturges. Also cast: John Forsythe, Polly Bergen, William Demarest, John Lupton, William Campbell and Carl Benton Reid. Profitable bookings everywhere.

Not a whit deterred by the dull thud of The Merry Widow, *Joe Pasternak starred Lana Turner in another semi-musical swooner,* **Latin Lovers**, *as a rich girl living it up in Rio. Ricardo Montalban co-tangoed; with Louis Calhern, John Lund, Jean Hagen, Beulah Bondi, Eduard Franz, Robert Burton and Rita Moreno. Mervyn LeRoy, who brought Lana with him to MGM 15 years before, directed as if regretting it. Script: Isobel Lennart.*

Greer Garson and Walter Pidgeon reached their co-starring nadir with **Scandal at Scourie**, *a tedious period piece about small-town politics, Catholic-Protestant antagonism and an adopted child. The latter gave Donna Corcoran the best part in the picture, indicating the failure of Norman Corwin, Leonard Spigelgass and Karl Tunberg to turn Mary McSherry's story into a real Garson–Pidgeon vehicle. Jean Negulesco directed and Edwin Knopf produced, vainly throwing in Technicolor. Also cast: Margalo Gillmore, Rhys Williams and Philip Ober (with the stars here) and Agnes Moorehead, Arthur Shields, John Lupton, Ian Wolfe, Philip Tonge.*

Another great star of the Forties shone dimly in 1953: Mickey Rooney in **A Slight Case of Larceny** *with Marilyn Erskine and Eddie Bracken. Tapping an oil company's pipeline to feed their gas station was the idea of Jerry Davis' script, directed by Don Weis and produced by Henry Berman with medium results. Elaine Stewart, Douglas Fowley, Robert Burton, Charles Halton supported.*

Deborah Kerr, Movita, Betta St John, Cary Grant, Patricia Tiernan and Richard Anderson in **Dream Wife**, *a bit of fluff received by press and public well this side of ecstasy. Schary produced the Sidney Sheldon–Herbert Baker– Alfred Levitt comedy, directed by Sheldon. It co-starred Walter Pidgeon, with Eduard Franz, Buddy Baer, Bruce Bennett, Dan Tobin, Gloria Holden, June Clayworth, Dean Miller, Steve Forrest.*

The Great Diamond Robbery *was the last for Red Skelton after 13 MGM years. Robert Leonard directed and Edwin Knopf produced the lacklustre comedy by Laslo Vadnay, with (left to right) Harry Bellaver, Skelton, George Mathews, Dorothy Stickney, Cara Williams and Kurt Kasznar; also cast were James Whitmore, Reginald Owen, Connie Gilchrist.*

Two well-made 'B's in AnscoColor rounded out 1953. Earl Holliman, Dewey Martin and Keenan Wynn in a prizefight-plus-religion drama, if you can imagine it: **Tennessee Champ**, *written by Art Cohn, directed by Fred Wilcox, produced by Sol Fielding; Shelley Winters and Yvette Duguay were ringside girls . . . Frances Dee, Donna Corcoran and Ward Bond gave* **Gypsy Colt** *his oats; Martin Berkeley scripted Eric Knight's story for the William Grady Jr–Sidney Franklin Jr production, directed by Andrew Marton, with Lee Van Cleef, Larry Keating, Bobby Hyatt.*

THIS YEAR OF GRACE

1954

Warner Bros. studio and distribution were operating separately from their theatres, leaving only MGM–Loew's holding out against the US government's divorcement order. *The Caine Mutiny, The Glenn Miller Story, Rear Window, On the Waterfront, White Christmas, Three Coins in the Fountain, From Here to Eternity, Moulin Rouge, How to Marry a Millionaire, Genevieve* and *Shane* were main rivals to MGM's biggest. *Waterfront* succeeded *Eternity*, the previous winner, as the Academy's best film; Marlon Brando in the former followed William Holden in *Stalag 17* as best actor; Grace Kelly in *The Country Girl* took over from Audrey Hepburn in *Roman Holiday* as best actress. Biggest box-office star was John Wayne, in his sixth year among the Top Ten: after him came Dean Martin and Jerry Lewis, Gary Cooper, James Stewart, Marilyn Monroe, Alan Ladd, Holden, Bing Crosby, Jane Wyman and Brando.

Frances Goodrich–Dorothy Kingsley script from Stephen Vincent Benet's 'Sobbin' Women'. It was in AnscoColor and CinemaScope.

Variations on the war theme: the raw realism that keynoted **Prisoner of War** was too depressing for financial success. Steve Forrest, Dewey Martin and Ronald Reagan played Americans suffering tortures in a Korean camp, with Stephen Bekassy, Leonard Strong, Darryl Hickman, Jerry Paris and John Lupton among Andrew Marton's well-directed cast. Henry Berman produced the Allen Rivkin screenplay.

Better audience reaction greeted another Marton–Berman war movie, **Men of the**
▽ **Fighting Lady** scoring with its wild blue yonder heroics and a typically sincere performance by Van Johnson. Art Cohn's screenplay, filmed in AnscoColor, was strongly cast with Walter Pidgeon, Louis Calhern, Frank Lovejoy, Dewey Martin, Keenan Wynn, Robert Horton, Dick Simmons. Bert Freed.

Disappointingly delivering less warmth, erotic or otherwise, than its title promised, **Flame and the Flesh** dawdled through a triangle story of temptress Lana Turner and nightclub singer Carlos Thompson (here) and innocent bambina Pier Angeli. Filmed in Italy, England and Technicolor by Richard Brooks, the Auguste Bailly original was scripted by Helen Deutsch and produced by Joe Pasternak. Also cast: Bonar Colleano, Peter Illing, Charles Goldner.

John Justin and Gene Kelly in **Seagulls Over Sorrento**/Crest of the Wave, a workmanlike version of Hugh Hastings' stage success, about British and American sailors on a Scottish island. Shot in 1953 at MGM British by John and Roy Boulting, it emerged entertainingly but with little paybox impact a year later. Script: Frank Harvey and Roy Boulting. Also cast: Jeff Richards, Bernard Lee, Sidney James, Patrick Doonan, Ray Jackson, Patrick Barr.

Howard Keel could hardly believe it when Jane Powell tamed his backwoods brothers, Marc Platt, Matt Mattox, Jacques d'Amboise, Tommy Rall, Jeff Richards and Russ Tamblyn in
△ **Seven Brides for Seven Brothers**. Neither could the studio when the movie became the year's most sensational hit—and it was still getting bookings around the world 20 years later. Jack Cummings produced it on the back lot, so to speak, while more expensive musicals with stage-famous titles were being made front and centre. It did for the screen what 'Oklahoma' had done for the theatre: created a new style of musical, roaring with vitality, prancing with open-air freshness. Credit Stanley Donen's direction, Michael Kidd's choreography, the Gene de Paul–Johnny Mercer songs ('When You're in Love', 'Wonderful Day', 'Bless Yore Beautiful Hide', 'Spring', 'Lonesome Polecat', etc.) and the Albert Hackett–

Betrayed *ended the 24-year reign of MGM's king of stars, Clark Gable; the company found that he was no longer the surefire draw of yore, and he was eager for the lucrative freelancing which occupied his remaining six years. His last for Leo was an outdated drama of spies in German-occupied Europe, written by Ronald Millar and George Froeschel, directed by Gottfried Reinhardt at the British studio. Victor Mature (left) and Lana Turner co-starred, with Louis Calhern, Wilfrid Hyde White, O. E. Hasse, Ian Carmichael, Niall MacGinnis, Nora Swinburne, Roland Culver. Gable's subsequent percentage deals at other studios paid him better than his MGM annual salary of $500,000.*

Also out, as overhead cuts reached the star list, went Greer Garson after a mere 15 years. Her great prestige had dwindled in unworthy vehicles for several years, and **Her Twelve Men** *wasn't strong enough to halt the trend. She looked a treat in AnscoColor as a boys' schoolteacher in the pleasant William Roberts–Laura Z. Hobson screenplay, with Robert Ryan (right), Barry Sullivan, Richard Haydn, Barbara Lawrence, James Arness, Rex Thompson, Tim Considine, Ian Wolfe. Robert Z. Leonard directed John Houseman's production.*

Carlos Thompson, Robert Taylor and Eleanor Parker in **Valley of the Kings**, *or Clap Hands if You Believe in Pharaohs. Written (with Karl Tunberg) and directed by Robert Pirosh; featuring Kurt Kasznar and Victor Jory; produced in Eastman Color by one whose wish to remain anonymous we must respect.*

The studio set a speed record on **Rogue Cop**, *only four months elapsing between story buy and final preview. Director Roy Rowland and producer Nicholas Nayfack kept it fast on the screen too, and Robert Taylor thankfully climbed out of Valley of the Kings to higher paybox levels in the title role. Left to right: Alan Hale Jr, Taylor, Robert Simon, George Raft and Anne Francis as underworld czar Raft's floozie. Sidney Boehm's script from William McGivern's novel had parts for Steve Forrest, Vince Edwards and Robert Ellenstein.*

Esther Williams was dropped from the MGM contract list after **Jupiter's Darling**; *so were Marge and Gower Champion and director George Sidney (from left here with Miss Williams, George Sanders and producer George Wells). This CinemaScope musical co-starred Howard Keel and featured Richard Haydn, William Demarest, Norma Varden and Douglass Dumbrille. The product of their labours was an expensive flop, adapted by Dorothy Kingsley from Robert E. Sherwood's Broadway success of the Twenties, 'The Road to Rome'. Keel played Hannibal singing his way across the Alps; Esther swam in a mini-toga.*

Off-key results, too, from **The Glass Slipper**, *hopefully the successor to Lili by Leslie Caron, writer Helen Deutsch, director Charles Walters and producer Edwin Knopf. It was straight Cinderella, with Michael Wilding*

swanning around in tights as Prince Charming, and Caron apparently almost as ill at ease, except while dancing with Roland Petit's Ballet de Paris. Also cast: Keenan Wynn, Elsa Lanchester, Estelle Winwood, Barry Jones, Amanda Blake, Lurene Tuttle, Liliane Montevecchi.

Victor McLaglen fixes a shotgun wedding for daughter Eleanor Parker and trapper Robert Taylor in **Many Rivers to Cross**, *watched by Russ Tamblyn, Jeff Richards and Ralph Moody. About as subtle as a school performance of Taming of the Shrew, which the Guy Trosper–Harry Brown script often resembled, the backwoods comedy rattled along with uninhibited hokum and action. Nobody liked it but the public. Directed by Roy Rowland; produced by Jack Cummings in CinemaScope and Eastman Color; with James Arness, Rosemary DeCamp, Josephine Hutchinson, Sig Ruman, Alan Hale Jr, Rhys Williams.*

Van Johnson joined the exodus of MGM-made stars after **The Last Time I Saw Paris**—*but he would be back. Here he and Elizabeth Taylor are caught up in VE-Day celebrations in Paris during the unconvincing drama Richard Brooks and Julius and Philip Epstein based roughly on Scott Fitzgerald's story of expatriate Americans, 'Babylon Revisited'. Good acting in a handsome Technicolor production by Jack Cummings, directed by Brooks, but spotty box-office. Also cast: Walter Pidgeon, Donna Reed, Eva Gabor, Kurt Kasznar, George Dolenz, Roger Moore (debut), Celia Lovsky.*

Vittorio Gassman finished his Metro contract and John Ericson started his with **Rhapsody**, *a feverish romance about temperamental musicians. It had a splendid musical score (Rachmaninov, Tchaikowsky, etc.) with violinist Michael Rabin and pianist Claudio Arrau dubbing for Gassman and Ericson (with Elizabeth Taylor here). Louis Calhern, Michael Chekhov, Barbara Bates, Richard Hageman, Celia Lovsky, Richard Lupino and Stuart Whitman were in Charles Vidor's cast. Lawrence Weingarten produced the Fay and Michael Kanin screenplay from Henry Handel Richardson's 'Maurice Guest'.*

The dramatic intensity of **Trial** was such that even the stills were exciting, like this one of Dorothy McGuire, Katy Jurado, Rafael Campos, Glenn Ford and Arthur Kennedy. Don Mankiewicz brilliantly scripted his own novel and director Mark Robson got every atom of suspense and spectacle from the murder trial of Campos, and its communist-inspired sideshows. Stunning performances by the above and John Hodiak, Juano Hernandez (as the screen's first black judge), Robert Middleton, Elisha Cook Jr, John Hoyt, Paul Guilfoyle, Whit Bissell, Barry Kelley. Charles Schnee produced.

Hit the Deck, *the daddy of all sailors-on-leave musicals, was a Broadway smash in 1927 and filmed by RKO-Radio in 1930 and 1936 (the latter as* Follow the Fleet *with Fred Astaire, Ginger Rogers, and Irving Berlin songs). Left to right: Jane Powell, Tony Martin, Debbie Reynolds, Walter Pidgeon, Vic Damone, Gene Raymond, Ann Miller, Russ Tamblyn and Kay Armen, a rich cargo of talent. Joe Pasternak's production, directed by Roy Rowland, had a fine Vincent Youmans score, retaining 'Hallelujah', 'Sometimes I'm Happy' and 'Why Oh Why?' from the original show and 'Keeping Myself for You' from the first movie, while adding numbers from other Youmans shows. Richard Anderson, Jane Darwell and J. Carrol Naish were featured in the Sonya Levien–William Ludwig screenplay.*

Shouts of praise from the critics greeted **It's Always Fair Weather**, *starring (left to right) Gene Kelly, Cyd Charisse, Dan Dailey, Dolores Gray and Michael Kidd. But it somehow fell short of the public enthusiasm aroused by its Gene Kelly/Stanley Donen/Arthur Freed/Betty Comden–Adolph Green predecessors,* On The Town *and* Singin' *in the Rain. All the same elements were present: songs, dances, fun, wit, production style, story ideas, speed. So why didn't they add up?*

The enormously successful **Love Me or Leave Me** *brought to MGM two of the few big stars who had never worked at Culver City: Doris Day and James Cagney. Unusually for a musical about real people, the protagonists were not noble goodies: Daniel Fuchs' Oscar-winning story and his script with Isobel Lennart didn't shirk showing the ruthless ambition that took Ruth Etting from honky-tonks to Ziegfeld stardom, or the crude violence of her racketeer husband. Charles Vidor's deft direction helped Miss Day to her best performance, while Cagney fairly scorched the celluloid, again proving himself one of the most exciting actors the screen has displayed.*

Ten Ruth Etting hits of the Twenties became Doris Day hits of the Fifties in Joe Pasternak's cavalcade of Prohibition-era show business. Also cast: Cameron Mitchell, Harry Bellaver, Robert Keith, Tom Tully.

gave him a delicious heroine in Kay Kendall. Director Richard Thorpe and producer Pandro Berman again officiated, lavishly and colourfully transposing Sir Walter Scott's story to film via a George Froeschel–Robert Ardrey script. Also cast: Robert Morley, Wilfrid Hyde White, Duncan Lamont (right), Alec Clunes, George Cole, Marius Goring, Eric Pohlmann, Ernest Thesiger.

Guys and Dolls, 2½ *hours of Damon Runyon's oddball characters and Frank Loesser's clever songs, directed by Joseph L. Mankiewicz, was the only Samuel Goldwyn production distributed by MGM; the deal paid off handsomely. It had been a great show and was a good film. Left to right: Marlon Brando, Jean Simmons, Frank Sinatra and Vivian Blaine. Goldwyn wanted Gene Kelly for the lead and may have had an even better movie with him in it; Brando was no song-and-dance man. On the other hand, his scenes with Miss Simmons had unusual conviction for a musical. Loesser added another winner, 'A Woman in Love', to those like 'If I Were a Bell', 'Luck Be a Lady' and 'Take Back Your Mink' of the stage smash, from which Miss Blaine, Stubby Kaye and B. S. Pully were recruited, joining Robert Keith, Sheldon Leonard, George E. Stone, Regis Toomey, Veda Ann Borg in the cast. Mankiewicz adapted the Abe Burrows–Jo Swerling play; Michael Kidd choreographed.*

Meet Me in Las Vegas/Viva Las Vegas, *a successful collaboration of producer Joe Pasternak and director Roy Rowland, teamed Cyd Charisse with Dan Dailey in a gambling story by Isobel Lennart. Here are Liliane Montevecchi, John Brascia and Miss Charisse in the exciting 'Frankie and Johnny' ballet, with off-screen singing by Sammy Davis Jr. The movie was liberally bedizened with musical numbers by the stars plus Lena Horne, Frankie Laine, Jerry Colonna and Cara Williams. Also present: Agnes Moorehead, Jim Backus, Lily Darvas, Oscar Karlweis, Paul Henreid.*

'Love is the Tender Trap' warbled Frank Sinatra, thus simultaneously scaling the top of the music and movie hit parades in **The Tender Trap**. *Debbie Reynolds was his bubbling, bachelor-trapping foil in this lively comedy, adapted by Julius Epstein from the Max*

Shulman–Robert Paul Smith stage success. Celeste Holm and David Wayne increased the paybox bait, with Lola Albright, Carolyn Jones, Jarma Lewis, Tom Helmore, James Drury. Charles Walters directed Lawrence Weingarten's production.

Lucille Ball, James Mason and Desi Arnaz in **Forever Darling**, *a comedy in which Mason was an angel bringing Lucy heavenly guidance. None was forthcoming for writer Helen Deutsch, director Alexander Hall or producer Arnaz. Also cast: Louis Calhern, John Emery, Natalie Schafer, John Hoyt, Mabel Albertson.*

The visual charms of Paris were the chief asset of **Bedevilled**. *In it Anne Baxter and Steve Forrest (brother of Dana Andrews) coped gamely with highly theatrical dramatics scripted by Jo Eisinger, directed by Mitchell Leisen—the tireless Richard Thorpe completed it when Leisen fell ill—and produced by Henry Berman. Also cast: Victor Francen, Robert Christopher and Joseph Tomelty.*

Equally theatrical but with undeniable emotional power: **Interrupted Melody**, *which was the high point of Eleanor Parker's 20-year starring career. She won much praise for a heartrending performance and William Ludwig and Sonya Levien won the script Academy Award. It was based on the true story of Australian soprano Marjorie Lawrence, stricken with polio at the height of her operatic fame. Glenn Ford as her husband matched Eleanor's acting skill, and her miming matched the dubbed voice of Eileen Farrell in eight arias; magnificent soundtrack music. Jack Cummings produced, Curtis Bernhardt directed; with Roger Moore, Cecil Kellaway, Ann Codee, Doris Lloyd, Dick Simmons.*

Quentin Durward *took Robert Taylor to MGM's British studios for the fifth time. While not a success of* Ivanhoe *proportions, it brought his London score to four hits out of five, and*

Kismet *had always looked like the libretto for a musical and it became one at last when Charles Lederer and Luther Davis adapted the old Edward Knoblock play, and Robert Wright and George Forrest composed a glorious score, the tunes borrowed from Borodin. After running for years as a stage show (originally financed by Lederer's aunt, Marion Davies) it reached CinemaScope screens in a sumptuous Arthur Freed production. Howard Keel and Dolores Gray (here), who once were rival London sensations in* Oklahoma *and* Annie Get Your Gun *respectively, appeared together for the first time and made every note of their numbers count. So did Ann Blyth and Vic Damone. But, as in* Brigadoon, *the usual sparkle was missing from Vincente Minnelli's direction, and business fell short of hopes. Also cast: Monty Woolley, Sebastian Cabot, Jay C. Flippen, Ted de Corsia, Jack Elam, Mike Mazurki. Its best-selling songs included 'Stranger in Paradise', 'And This is My Beloved', 'Baubles, Bangles and Beads' and the sizzling 'Not Since Nineveh'.*

I'll Cry Tomorrow *was the strongest of MGM's three 1955 biographical movies – all hits – about female singing stars; its depiction of acute alcoholism had more shock value than the polio of* Interrupted Melody *or the conflict of* Love Me or Leave Me. *Susan Hayward as Lillian Roth (here scraping bottom on skid row) did a highly professional job of acting, both in these sordid sequences and in the sunny days of Miss Roth's Broadway and Hollywood fame. She won the Cannes Festival award for it, but the costumes by Helen Rose got its only Academy Oscar. A batch of old songs, actually sung, surprisingly well, by Miss Hayward; the source book by Miss Roth, Mike Connolly and Gerold Frank; and Alcoholics Anonymous all got powerful plugs from its success. Director, Daniel Mann; producer, Lawrence Weingarten; cast, Eddie Albert, Richard Conte, Don Taylor, Jo Van Fleet, Ray Danton, Margo, Don Barry; script, Helen Deutsch, Jay Richard Kennedy.*

Lana Turner's long MGM career ended with one of her better pictures, Edwin Knopf's handsome production of **Diane**, *directed by David Miller. In Christopher Isherwood's literate script from John Erskine's romance of 16th-century France, she was Diane de Poitiers, beloved of Henry II – played by Roger Moore (here stripped for wrestling with Sean Mc-Clory). Pedro Armendariz (right), Cedric Hardwicke, Marisa Pavan (Pier Angeli's sister), Taina Elg, Torin Thatcher, Henry Daniell, John Lupton, Geoffrey Toone, Paul Cavanagh, Melville Cooper, Ian Wolfe and Gene Reynolds also performed ably, which is more than can be said for the box-office. This was the best of the few parts MGM gave Roger Moore after bringing him from England under contract; it was left to television to make him a star.*

John Houseman must have been a case for the couch when his elegant all-star production of the highly regarded novel **The Cobweb** *suffered a box-office trauma. William Gibson's book about psychiatrists and patients in a plush nuthouse had no mass appeal as scripted by John Paxton and directed by Vincente Minnelli. But what a cast: from front, Richard Widmark, Lauren Bacall, Charles Boyer, Lillian Gish in her first MGM movie for 22 years, John Kerr (debut), Oscar Levant, Jarma Lewis, Susan Strasberg (another debut) and Paul Stewart; also cast were Gloria Grahame, Fay Wray and Adele Jergens.*

Editor at work: Ben Lewis, veteran MGM cutter, views a scene from **The Last Hunt** *through his movieola. Among the most important and least publicized of film-makers, the editor usually works closely with director and/or producer to give each movie its distinctive pace, shape and character, if any. This Schary production, starring Robert Taylor as heavy and Stewart Granger as hero, dealt with the slaughter of huge herds of buffalo in the West, a subject that repelled more customers than it attracted. With Lloyd Nolan, Debra Paget, Russ Tamblyn, Constance Ford and Joe de Santis in his cast, Richard Brooks directed and wrote it from Milton Lott's original.*

The King's Thief *was Robert Z. Leonard's last movie in a record-breaking 31 years exclusively with MGM. It starred Edmund Purdom, Ann Blyth, George Sanders and David Niven (here), supported by Roger*

Moore, Melville Cooper, Sean McClory, Isobel Elsom, Rhys Williams, Alan Mowbray, John Dehner, Paul Cavanagh; script, Christopher Knopf, from Robert Andrews' story; producer, Edwin Knopf . . . Another sword-swinger buckling its swashes rather late after Scaramouche's *success:* **The Scarlet Coat** *with Cornel Wilde, Anne Francis and Michael Wilding (here), also Robert Douglas, John McIntire, Bobby Driscoll and Sanders, Williams, Dehner and Cavanagh again; script, Karl Tunberg; director, John Sturges; producer, Nicholas Nayfack. Both films paid their way.*

1955's belle of the 'Bs' was Jarma Lewis, a fetching brunette who leading-ladied **The Marauders**, *a Civil War drama with a hook-handed Keenan Wynn and Dan Duryea; also Jeff Richards, Harry Shannon, Richard Lupino; script, Earl Fenton; director, Gerald Mayer; producer, Arthur Loew Jr . . . In* **It's a Dog's Life** *the terrier got the best lines and Jarma got Jeff Richards; script, John Michael Hayes from Richard Harding Davis' The Bar Sinister, filmed by Pathé in 1927 as* Almost Human; *director, Herman Hoffman; producer, Henry Berman; cast, Edmund Gwenn, Dean Jagger, Richard Anderson, Sally Fraser, J. M. Kerrigan.*

Last off the 1955 assembly line was the latest Ford model – the fourth in a year which took Glenn to the forefront of Hollywood's dramatic actors. **Ransom** *showed with agonizing suspense the conflict between a kidnapped child's parents, he refusing to submit to the criminals, she (Donna Reed) eager to pay any price. Customers' nerves and theatres' seat-edges took a beating from the Cyril Hume–Richard Maibaum screenplay, tautly directed by Alex Segal. Leslie Nielsen, Juano Hernandez, Juanita Moore, Robert Keith, Mabel Albertson, Richard Gaines, Robert Burton and Alexander Scourby were in Nicholas Nayfack's production.*

HIGH SOCIETY PAYS

1956

Warner Bros. and 20th-Century Fox sold their pre-1948 films to television, while MGM put a cautious toe into that whirlpool by leasing *The Wizard of Oz* for four telecasts, netting $900,000. Mary Pickford followed Chaplin in selling her share of United Artists, which they had created with Douglas Fairbanks and D. W. Griffith in 1919.

A world survey counted approximately 108,500 cinemas in operation: USA 18,500; Russia 15,500; Italy 9,500; France 5,500; West Germany 5,000; Spain 5,000; Britain 4,500; Japan 3,500; India 3,000; East Germany 3,000; Mexico 2,500; Sweden 2,500.

Practically the entire membership of the Screen Actors Guild were in Cecil B. DeMille's record-smashing remake of *The Ten Commandments* or Mike Todd's *Around The World in Eighty Days*, which won the Academy and practically every other award. (Sir Cedric Hardwicke and John Carradine managed to get into both.) King Vidor also colossaled with *War and Peace* in Italy. *Bus Stop, The King and I, Carousel, Picnic, The Man with the Golden Arm* and *Friendly Persuasion* clicked.

Frank Sinatra, Kim Novak, Marilyn Monroe, Glenn Ford and Burt Lancaster displaced Gable, Bogart, Brando, Martin and Lewis and June Allyson in the Top Ten.

The Swan, *Ferenc Molnar's romance of never-never-land royalty was released, by a triumph of timing, as Grace Kelly (with Louis Jourdan here) became Her Serene Highness Princess Grace of Monaco; an event celebrated by all news media for weeks on end (MGM even had a half-hour documentary,* The Wedding in Monaco*). She was every inch a star as well as a princess, gentle, graceful and subtly humorous, in this remake;* Lillian Gish played it in 1930 as *One Romantic Night. Charles Vidor directed elegantly. Schary coaxed Alec Guinness to Hollywood as its superb co-star, with Agnes Moorehead, Brian Aherne, Jessie Royce Landis, Estelle Winwood, Leo G. Carroll and Robert Coote featured. Script: John Dighton.*

Excessive heat in the Colorado locations and in his exchanges with director Robert Wise resulted in Spencer Tracy walking out of **Tribute to a Bad Man** *and his 21-year MGM contract. So James Cagney stepped into Tracy's shoes and set a high acting example for newcomers Don Dubbins and Irene Papas in the first movie to come out of the cutting rooms in 1956. Sam Zimbalist produced Michael Blankfort's screenplay of domestic conflict on a ranch: a fairly good ticket-seller, with Stephen McNally, Onslow Stevens, Vic Morrow, Jeanette Nolan, Lee Van Cleef, Royal Dano.*

Clashing charismas and high voltage acting shook the sprockets as Anthony Quinn and Kirk Douglas took on their roles as Paul Gauguin and Vincent van Gogh in **Lust for Life**. *Douglas gave his finest performance and Quinn won the best supporting actor Oscar. Vincente Minnelli directed. The Metrocolor (new trade name) cameras of F. A. Young and Russell Harlan, filming French and Dutch exteriors and MGM-British interiors, and Norman Corwin's script (from Irving Stone's book) brought further assets to John Houseman's production. So did the work of James Donald, Pamela Brown, Everett Sloane, Niall MacGinnis, Henry Daniell, Madge Kennedy, Noel Purcell, Jill Bennett, Lionel Jeffries, Laurence Naismith, Eric Pohlmann, Jeanette Sterke and Isobel Elsom.*

◁ **Les Girls** *marked Gene Kelly's last MGM appearance until* That's Entertainment, *and Cole Porter's last score written for a film. Its approving audiences included the Queen and Prince Philip at its London première. Under George Cukor's direction the story of Kelly and his three Europe-touring dancing girls (left to right: Taina Elg, Kay Kendall and Mitzi Gaynor) shimmered with elegant fun. All four principals drew praise, Miss Kendall being hailed as America's most effervescent English import since Schweppes; they were supported by Jacques Bergerac, Leslie Phillips, Henry Daniell and Patrick Macnee. Orry-Kelly won an Oscar for his costumes. But the script John Patrick wrote for producer Sol C. Siegel was a bit too sophisticated to put it in the big-money class.*

Ray Milland (here with Barbara Everest as his mother) directed **The Safecracker** *and played the criminal whom the army let out of prison to open a safe in Nazi-occupied Belgium. Milland did a good job on both counts. Scripted by Paul Monash. Produced independently by David E. Rose at MGM's British studio, with Barry Jones, Jeanette Sterke, Victor Maddern, Ernest Clark, Cyril Raymond, Melissa Stribling, Anthony Nicholls, John Welsh.*

More Garbo memories were evoked by **Silk** △ **Stockings**, *a musical* Ninotchka, *rescripted by Leonard Spigelgass. Cyd Charisse played it acceptably without coming near the original magic—except in one rapturous scene when, alone in her hotel suite, she discarded her Russian serge and donned Paris silks while dancing to Cole Porter's lovely title number. This was never sung, leaving 'All of You' as the one real hit in a below-par Porter score. Fred Astaire (here with Cyd, Joseph Buloff, Jules Munshin and Peter Lorre) was in peak form; this was his last MGM appearance until* That's Entertainment *17 years later. Janis Paige had a showy part. Directed by Rouben Mamoulian, produced by Arthur Freed, it duplicated its Broadway stage success.*

One of the year's biggest money-spinners and laugh-rousers, **Don't Go Near the Water** *told* ▽ *a daffy tale about US Navy press officers on a Pacific isle miles away from World War II guns. Glenn Ford winningly starred, with Anne Francis and Earl Holliman (here); also cast were Gia Scala, Keenan Wynn, Eva Gabor, Russ Tamblyn, Jeff Richards, Romney Brent. Fred Clark stole scenes wholesale as the pompous CO. The funniest gag in the Dorothy Kingsley–George Wells script (from William Brinkley's novel) had Mickey Shaughnessy, chosen for publicity as the ideal sailor, unable to speak without using that (then) unprintable word, continually bleeped out on the soundtrack. Directed by Charles Walters, produced by Lawrence Weingarten.*

Eleanor Parker, who had once had to stand up to comparisons with Bette Davis in one Maugham remake, Of Human Bondage, *now had the even tougher assignment of following Garbo when she starred in* **The Seventh Sin**, *a remake of his* The Painted Veil. *English director Ronald Neame took a crew to Hong Kong for exteriors, but needn't have bothered. The movie was a dead duck that not even the kiss of life from Miss Parker and Jean Pierre Aumont (here), George Sanders, Bill Travers and Francoise Rosay could revive. David Lewis produced Karl Tunberg's screenplay.*

1958

Company results varied widely. MGM recovered from its first losing year; 20th Century-Fox, getting royalties from oil wells on its studio property, reported a $7½m profit; Paramount zoomed to $12½m; Republic had the best of its 13 years with $1½m and Disney the best of its 18 with nearly $4m, the same as United Artists. On the other hand, Columbia dived into red ink, losing $5m; Universal lost $2m and Warner Bros. $1m.

Dramatized novels dominated the release schedules, all the way from *The Brothers Karamazov* to *Peyton Place*. Predictably, the latter was bigger box-office. Others: *The Old Man and The Sea* (Spencer Tracy), *Room at the Top* (Laurence Harvey), *Ten North Frederick* (Gary Cooper), *The Naked and The Dead* (Aldo Ray), *Lonelyhearts* (Montgomery Clift), *The Roots of Heaven* (Errol Flynn), *The Last Hurrah* (Tracy), *God's Little Acre* (Robert Ryan), *A Time to Live and a Time to Die* (John Gavin), *Marjorie Morningstar* (Natalie Wood), *The Young Lions* (Marlon Brando, Clift), *Never Love a Stranger* (Steve McQueen), *The Quiet American* (Audie Murphy), *A Farewell to Arms* (Rock Hudson, Jennifer Jones).

1958–actually one of the best years in all-round product quality during MGM's second 25–opened with a laugh or two, but not many more, from **Merry Andrew** *with Danny Kaye and Pier Angeli. The much admired comic played an English schoolmaster who became a circus clown in Paul Gallico's story, scripted by Isobel Lennart and I. A. L. Diamond. Choreographer Michael Kidd was upped to full directorship by producer Sol C. Siegel, but did a patchy job. Business varied too. Operatic basso buffo Baccaloni, Robert Coote, Noel Purcell, Rex Evans, Patricia Cutts, Tommy Rall, Walter Kingsford and six songs were in it.*

Gigi *was the biggest grosser of all Arthur Freed musicals (world rentals about $15m.), champion prizewinner of 1958, and, to many, one of the most delightful movies ever made. MGM at its best, it sparkled like the champagne here being extolled by Hermione Gingold, Louis Jourdan and Leslie Caron. The movie danced off with no fewer than ten Academy Awards: best film; best direction, Vincente Minnelli; photography, Joseph Ruttenberg; screenplay, Alan Jay Lerner; scoring, André Previn; song, 'Gigi', Lerner and Frederick Loewe; editing, Adrienne Fazan; costumes, Cecil Beaton; art direction, William Horning and Preston Ames; honorary award, Maurice Chevalier. The last-named, now a jaunty 71, had three matchless songs: 'I'm Glad I'm Not Young Any More', 'Thank Heaven for Little Girls' and, with Miss Gingold, 'I Remember It Well'. Miss Caron, either as an anxious school-girl begging her cat to 'Say a Prayer for Me Tonight' or as an assured charmer queening it at Maxim's, was exactly right; she had played Gigi in a non-musical stage version of Colette's story in London. Jourdan, with the film's biggest role, acted and sang it to perfection. Miss Gingold and Isabel Jeans were elegant old bags, wickedly funny; Eva Gabor, Jacques Bergerac and John Abbott supported handsomely.*

A box-office stir was caused by Tennessee Williams' **Cat on a Hot Tin Roof**. *Not only was it the top moneymaker of 1958, it was the tenth biggest in all the company's years. Richard Brooks' direction and (with James Poe) script preserved the play's highly-charged atmosphere of dramatic conflict and sexual tension. The story was motivated by a husband's refusal to bed his wife, with a clear implication of his homosexual tendency, and the Lawrence Weingarten production took a step forward (or backward, as you will) in movie permissiveness from* Tea and Sympathy's *pussyfooting around the subject two years before. Paul Newman's brooding force as the husband came as no surprise, but Elizabeth Taylor's wife was a revelation: beautiful kitten became fiery cat in a stunning performance. Burl Ives repeated his Broadway success as Big Daddy; Jack Carson, Judith Anderson, Madeleine Sherwood and Laddy Gates supported ably.*

Russ Tamblyn swung with acrobatic élan *into his first star role as* **Tom Thumb** *(always billed as 'tom thumb'). Its production brought the full resources of MGM's British studio into play, and the heavy budget paid dividends as it became a perennial holiday booking. The Grimms' fairytale was cleverly expanded by producer-director George Pal to include songs, dances, animated puppets, and a riotous pair of villains in Peter Sellers and Terry-Thomas. Jessie Matthews was featured (23 years after being signed by MGM to star with Clifton Webb in a musical that never started) along with Bernard Miles, Alan Young, June Thorburn and Ian Wallace. Script: Ladislas Fodor.*

Andy Hardy Comes Home, *a faint echo of the movies that had made Mickey Rooney a star, tried to turn him into a young Judge Hardy. If the late Lewis Stone had tried to play Andy it wouldn't have been much sillier. The Hardy family, 1958: Fay Holden, Teddy Rooney (aged eight), Gina Gillespie, Patricia Breslin, Rooney, backed up by Sara Haden, Johnny Weissmuller Jr, Cecilia Parker. Very little was added to the series' $25m. in rentals by this independent production by Red Doff, directed by Howard Koch. Script: Edward Hutshing, Robert Donley.*

Rod Steiger forces James Mason, Inger Stevens and their daughter Terry Ann Ross to join his plot to extort $500,000 from an airline via a planted bomb. This started a series of suspense-fraught situations in **Cry Terror**, *written and directed by master withers-wringer Andrew L. Stone in his most unnerving style. Great stuff. Stone co-produced with his film editor wife, Virginia. Also cast: Neville Brand, Angie Dickinson, Jack Klugman, Kenneth Tobey, Jack Kruschen, Carleton Young and Mason's real daughter, Portland . . .*

Up for a breather: Virginia Core, Ross Martin, Dan Dailey and Claire Kelly in one of the drier moments from **Underwater Warrior**, *Ivan Tors' independent production about frogmen in the Pacific. Andrew Marton directed Gene Levitt's actionful script; James Gregory and Raymond Bailey completed the cast . . .*

Andrew and Virginia Stone dipped their picture-making brushes into the grue again for **The Decks Ran Red**, *which had captain James Mason and Dorothy Dandridge besting villain Broderick Crawford after a mutiny that killed off a shipload of actors like Stuart Whitman. David Cross, Joel Fluellen, Jack Kruschen and John Gallaudet; actionful direction by Stone. It turned a nice profit.*

Some Came Running *would have been a mishmash with less assured performers than Frank Sinatra, Dean Martin and Shirley MacLaine. James Jones' sprawling novel about a homecoming GI, a gambler and a goodtime girl was worked over by John Patrick and Arthur Sheekman and directed by Vincente Minnelli to yield several good scenes (mostly Miss MacLaine's), but little dramatic unity. Others in Sol C. Siegel's production were Martha Hyer, Arthur Kennedy, Nancy Gates, Leora Dana, Betty Lou Keim, Larry Gates, Steven Peck, Connie Gilchrist. The stars meant money in the paybox.*

Fun on the farm with Debbie Reynolds and Tony Randall in **The Mating Game**, *which transferred H. E. Bates' rambunctious 'Darling Buds of May' family to Maryland via William Roberts' adaptation. George Marshall directed, with Paul Douglas and Una Merkel as Pa and Ma Larkin, Fred Clark, Philip Ober, Charles Lane, Philip Coolidge and Trevor Bardette. Philip Barry Jr's production prospered.*

An arresting new face arrived in **Nowhere to Go**: *Maggie Smith, signed to a joint Ealing–MGM contract, and cast opposite George Nader as a girl giving refuge to a criminal on the run. Nader was impressive in his first movie away from Hollywood, a strong chase drama written by Seth Holt and Kenneth Tynan from Donald Mackenzie's novel and directed by Holt in London locales. Michael Balcon's production cast Bernard Lee, Geoffrey Keen, Bessie Love (her first for MGM in 28 years), Andree Melly, Howard Marion-Crawford, Harry H. Corbett, Lionel Jeffries.*

BEN HUR LIVES!

1959

MGM–Loew's, last of the hold-outs against the government's anti-trust action, finally divided itself in March into two unconnected companies: Loew's Theatres and Metro-Goldwyn-Mayer. Six months later the latter announced its profit, $7,698,951, the highest since 1951's total for the old company.

Censorship was still alive and well. The Production Code Administration (heir of the old Hays Office) refused to approve United Artists' David Niven–Mitzi Gaynor comedy *Happy Anniversary* until this speech was added: 'I never should have taken Alice to that hotel room before we were married. What

Two of the greatest strokes of good fortune in MGM's history were called **Ben-Hur**. *In 1925 the success or failure of the new company depended on it. In 1958 the continuance of MGM's prestige and its financial stability were risked with a $15m. investment in a remake of the same subject. A flop would have been disastrous. But its triumph was even*

more overwhelming than the original one; it brought MGM over $80m. in world-wide rentals. Then, in 1971, it had the biggest audience for a single screening of any film when it was seen by 32,630,000 Americans on TV. Those who pigeonhole it as just an inflated supercolossal may be surprised to know that it was received by the critics, almost without exception, as a masterly piece of film-making; praise was showered on every aspect of its production, and this welcome was echoed in the Academy's prizegiving for 1959. A record 12 Oscars were voted to it as the year's best picture and for best direction (William Wyler); actor (Charlton Heston in a portrayal of great spiritual and physical strength); supporting actor (Hugh Griffith); cinematography (Robert Surtees); scoring (Miklos

Rozsa); editing (Ralph Winters, John Dunning); costumes (Elizabeth Haffenden); art direction (William Horning, Edward Carfagno); sound recording (Franklin Milton); visual effects (Arnold Gillespie, Robert MacDonald); and sound effects (Milo Lory). Those special effects were greatly responsible for the spectacular sea battle and the breathtaking chariot race sequences; they in turn were prime reasons for the phenomenal crowds it drew. It was produced in Rome by Sam Zimbalist, whose making of Quo Vadis *there was a picnic in comparison; the mounting pressure of producing this now-or-never winner hastened his death shortly before its completion. Karl Tunberg got solo credit for a script also worked on by Christopher Fry (who was on the set with Wyler throughout), Maxwell* could I have been thinking of?' What indeed! But details in two murder trial dramas, *Compulsion* and *Anatomy of a Murder*, were unusually frank.

I Want to Live and *Separate Tables,* which had won Oscars for Susan Hayward and David Niven respectively, were hits. So were *Auntie Mame* (Rosalind Russell), *The Defiant Ones* (Tony Curtis, Sidney Poitier), *Some Like It Hot* (Marilyn Monroe, Jack Lemmon, Curtis), *The Nun's Story* (Audrey Hepburn, Peter Finch), *Pillow Talk* (Doris Day, Rock Hudson), *Rio Bravo* (John Wayne, Dean Martin).

Anderson, S. N. Behrman and Gore Vidal. Six 65-millimetre cameras were focused on its (give or take a thousand) 3,000 sets and 50,000 people, who included Stephen Boyd (at left, clashing with Heston in the chariot race) and Jack Hawkins, Haya Harareet, Martha Scott, Cathy O'Donnell, Sam Jaffe, Finlay Currie, Frank Thring, Terence Longdon, André Morell, Marina Berti, George Relph, Lawrence Payne and Duncan Lamont. Important contributions were made by second unit directors Andrew Marton, Yakima Canutt and Mario Soldati.

Shirley MacLaine and David Niven, making a comedy team as refreshing as Loy and Powell, or Hepburn and Tracy, blended their dry wit and offhand charm in **Ask Any Girl**, a box-

office winner for director Charles Walters and producer Joe Pasternak. George Wells' script, from a novel by Winifred Wolfe, took wicked swipes at business and merchandising morals while telling the story of how a girl who didn't smoke, drink, or anything, coped with three men about New York town. Also cast: Gig Young, Rod Taylor, Claire Kelly, Jim Backus and Elisabeth Fraser.

North by Northwest *was Alfred Hitchcock's first at MGM and, say many aficionados, his best ever. The studio replaced CinemaScope with Paramount's big-screen process, Vista-Vision, just this once; the whole production was going to be made for Paramount at one time. The movie had Cary Grant and Eva Marie Saint whirling in the vortex of Ernest Lehman's devilishly clever script to its climax among the great stone faces of Mount Rushmore. Thrilling Hitchcock touches abounded, and so did hefty grosses in all cinemas. Also cast: James Mason, Jessie Royce Landis, Leo G. Carroll, Philip Ober, Josephine Hutchinson, Martin Landau, Edward Platt, Adam Williams, Robert Ellenstein, Philip Coolidge.*

It Started with a Kiss *which Debbie Reynolds sold to Glenn Ford for charity, then Charles Lederer's script continued at this skirt-tearing level of humour. Profitable, though. Eva Gabor, Gustavo Rojo, Fred Clark, Edgar Buchanan, Henry Morgan and Robert Warwick were in George Marshall's cast; Aaron Rosenberg produced.*

Glenn Ford and Debbie Reynolds, working in perfect rapport with George Marshall, who had been directing either or both of them in five successive movies, hit the laugh jackpot with **The Gazebo**, *a neat moneyspinner. Alex Coppel's black comedy featured a pet pigeon, a body that wouldn't stay buried, Carl Reiner, John McGiver, Doro Merande, Mabel Albertson and ZaSu Pitts. Screenplay, George Wells; production, Lawrence Weingarten.*

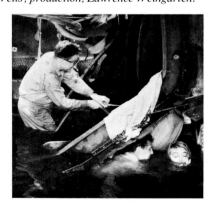

'I get 'em into trouble in the first reel and keep 'em in trouble till the end' said Andrew Stone explaining his cliffhanger technique. He wrote, directed and, with editor Virginia Stone, produced **The Last Voyage** *– and, boy, did he get Robert Stack and Dorothy Malone into trouble! The ship was on fire, captain George Sanders was having a crise de nerfs, Dorothy was trapped under wreckage and the water was rising steadily... Also cast: Edmond O'Brien (left), Woody Strode, Jack Kruschen and moppet Tammy Marihugh. As usual eschewing studio sets, Stone bought the famed liner 'Ile de France' which was headed for the scrapyard, filmed in and on her, and sank her as cameras turned. Short of drowning the extras, realism could go no further.*

Never So Few, *an uneasy mixture of comedy* ▷ *and action drama, sold well on the strength of its cast: Frank Sinatra and Gina Lollobrigida (here) and Steve McQueen, Peter Lawford, Brian Donlevy, Paul Henreid, Richard Johnson, Dean Jones, Charles Bronson, Philip Ahn, John Hoyt, Whit Bissell, Richard Lupino. It was whipped up by Millard Kaufman from Tom Chameles' best-seller. John Sturges directed the Edmund Grainger production.*

Maurice Chevalier and Deborah Kerr in **Count Your Blessings** *were sparkling players in need of something sparkling to play. The public, warned by most critics, gave a cold shoulder to this tedious filming (in Paris) of Nancy Mitford's novel 'The Blessing', whose brittle fun crumbled under the heavy hands of director Jean Negulesco, producer-scripter Karl Tunberg and actor Rossano Brazzi as Deborah's French husband. Martin Stephens as their son had a key part, with Tom Helmore, Ronald Squire, Patricia Medina, Mona Washbourne, Steve Geray and Lumsden Hare.*

Also made at the London studios with profitable results, **Libel** hinged on a look-alike coincidence as phoney as The Scapegoat's. It starred Dirk Bogarde as a Sir who might really have been somebody else, Olivia de Havilland (his wife) and Robert Morley (his barrister). Paul Massie, Wilfrid Hyde White, Anthony Dawson, Richard Wattis, Martin Miller, Richard Dimbleby, Millicent Martin, Robert Shaw, Joyce Carey, Kenneth Griffith and Richard Pearson were also in Anthony Asquith's cast. A lot of talent for producer Anatole de Grunwald to lavish on a creaky melodrama, adapted by him and Karl Tunberg from Edward Wooll's 1934 play.

The first 'Tarzan' made at the MGM studios since 1942, **Tarzan the Ape Man** introduced a new, collegiate-type vine-swinger in 6' 4" Denny Miller. Both he and Joanna Barnes as Jane were less nude than their predecessors, which possibly explains why it was the company's least popular 'Tarzan'. It went back to the first (1932) MGM entry's story, re-scripted by Robert Hill, directed by Joseph Newman, produced by Al Zimbalist, with Cesare Danova and Robert Douglas featured.

Green Mansions like 'Alice in Wonderland', should not be filmed. The magic melts under the arc lights. Vincente Minnelli had briefly attempted a 1954 version with Pier Angeli and Edmund Purdom. Writer Dorothy Kingsley, director Mel Ferrer and producer Edmund Grainger now made a brave try at the W. H. Hudson classic and got generally poor reviews and receipts for their trouble. Anthony Perkins and Audrey Hepburn (then Mrs Ferrer) brought an appropriately fey quality to their jungle dalliance, and were supported by Lee J. Cobb, silent star Sessue Hayakawa, Henry Silva, Nehemiah Persoff and Michael Pate.

Dowager countess Bette Davis is confronted by bogus son Alec Guinness in the most over-dressed set of the year, and one of her too few scenes in **The Scapegoat**. Once they'd swallowed the incredible premise of Daphne du Maurier's novel (an English tourist looking and sounding so much like a French count that the latter's family couldn't tell the difference) audiences relished a tasty dish of drama confected by writers Gore Vidal and Robert Hamer, directed by Hamer for producer Michael Balcon. Also cast: Nicole Maurey, Irene Worth, Pamela Brown, Geoffrey Keen, Peter Bull and Noel Howlett.

Alfred Hitchcock had been going to direct **The Wreck of the Mary Deare** but did North by Northwest instead. He might have tightened up the suspense in Eric Ambler's script from the Hammond Innes novel; but Michael Anderson found enough dramatic conflict and action in it to make a superior thriller. Gary Cooper as captain of a deserted ship and Charlton Heston as a salvage claimer tackled their he-man roles with spirit, supported by Michael Redgrave,

1959

Output slackened in 1959, and to keep the company's overseas exchanges busy the studio packaged three features from an MGM television series, seen only in America, based on 'Northwest Passage'. Actionful programmers, they were produced by Adrian Samish and written by Gerald Drayson Adams. Shown here are Keith Larsen, Buddy Ebsen and Don
△ Burnett (who were in them all) in **Fury River**, directed by Jacques Tourneur, Alan Crosland Jr, George Waggner and Otto Lang . . . the
▽ three men and Lisa Gaye in **Frontier Rangers**, directed by Tourneur, with Philip Tonge and Angie Dickinson . . . Larsen and Taina Elg in **Mission of Danger**, directed by Tourneur and Waggner, with Tonge, Alan Hale Jr and Patrick Macnee.

The Big Operator marked a departure for ▷ Mickey Rooney, cast as a sadistic gang-leader in the movie he co-sponsored with Albert Zugsmith. A remake of Paul Gallico's Joe Smith, American, directed by Charles Haas, produced by Red Doff, scripted by Robert Smith and Allen Rivkin, it featured Steve Cochran (here getting the 'we have ways of making you talk' treatment), in Robert Young's 1941 part. Also cast: Mamie Van Doren, good as a housewife, Mel Torme, Ray Danton, Jim Backus, Ray Anthony, Jackie Coogan, Charles Chaplin Jr. Billy Daniels, Jay North, Grabowski (left), Leo Gordon (right).

Watusi was a road company King Solomon's Mines. Said caption on this scene: 'George Montgomery and Taina Elg suddenly realize that their hatred has given way to love.' Those hot African nights do it every time. The movie was scripted by James Clavell from Rider Haggard's sequel, directed by Kurt Neumann and produced by Al Zimbalist, using much stock footage from the Mines location trip. Also cast: David Farrar, Rex Ingram, Dan Seymour.

Mamie Van Doren almost gave her all for cinema art at frequent intervals, as Albert Zugsmith productions kept zugging. In **The Beat Generation** she generated a beat in Ray Danton. Steve Cochran, Fay Spain, Louis Armstrong, Margaret Hayes, Jackie Coogan, Jim Mitchum, Charles Chaplin Jr, Ray Anthony, Cathy Crosby, Billy Daniels, Dick Contino, Maxie Rosenbloom and one Grabowski were in the Richard Matheson–Lewis Meltzer screenplay . . . In **Girls' Town** she turned Contino on in the woods, while Mel Torme, Paul Anka, Gigi Perreau, Elinor Donahue, Sheilah Graham, Gloria Talbott and Harold Lloyd Jr joined other Zugsmith regulars Anthony, Mitchum, Chaplin, Grabowski, the Misses Hayes and Crosby to interpret Robert Smith's script. Charles Haas directed both and they made money.

294

A unique spectacle was presented by a normal sized, black-and-white film, **The World, the Flesh and the Devil**, sponsored by Harry Belafonte and Sol C. Siegel. It showed the vast canyons of Manhattan emptied by some super-weapon, and only Belafonte left alive. These sequences, brilliantly photographed by Harold Marzorati in early mornings before New York crowds and traffic got too thick to keep out of camera range, gave way to a bizarre triangle story when Inger Stevens and Mel Ferrer brought the city's population to three. Scripted and directed by Ranald MacDougall, from Ferdinand Reyher's adaptation of an M. P. Shiel tale; produced by George Englund.

For the First Time was Mario Lanza's ironically titled swansong. While it was drawing crowds on his name, he was dying after years of massively excessive eating and drinking; a sad waste of an extraordinary vocal gift. But he looked and sounded good in this movie featuring Zsa Zsa Gabor (here), Johanna von Koszian and Kurt Kasznar. Independently produced in Italy by Alexander Gruter, in Techni-rama, the Andrew Solt screenplay was directed by Rudy Mate.

Robert Mitchum, Kieron Moore (centre) and Gia Scala in **The Angry Hills** which also starred Elisabeth Mueller and Stanley Baker, with Theodore Bikel, Sebastian Cabot, Peter Illing, Marius Goring, Leslie Phillips and Donald Wolfit. Robert Aldrich directed the thriller for producer Raymond Stross, using A. I. Bezzerides' script from the Leon Uris novel about resistance fighters in German-occupied Greece. Fair results.

Robert Taylor and Linda Christian in **The House of the Seven Hawks**, a fair-to-middling adventure yarn produced in England and Holland by David E. Rose with Richard Thorpe directing. Nicole Maurey, Donald Wolfit, Eric Pohlmann and David Kossoff had parts in Jo Eisinger's script from a novel by Victor Canning.

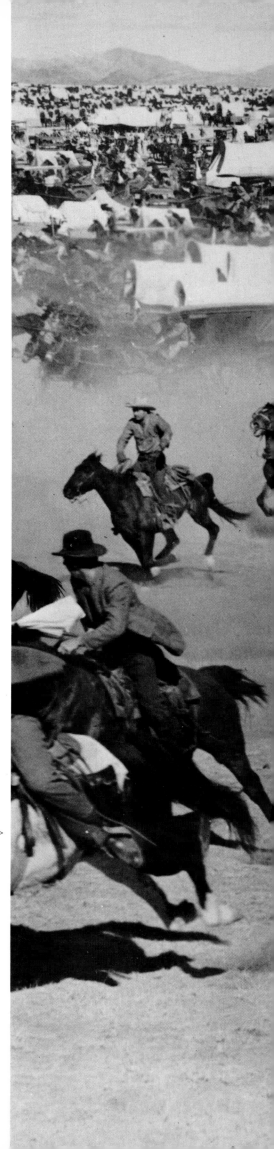

WELL IN THE BLACK
1960

The first full year of divorcement revealed the proportionate importance of Loew's Theatres ($2½m profit) and MGM ($9½m). No other company came near the MGM figure. But MGM production continued at a low ebb in 1960, only 12 features emerging from Culver City. Even including outside contributions, just 19 were finished for MGM release.

Britain had a rash of *Carry On* comedies, Oscar Wilde biographies (Peter Finch out-Oscaring Robert Morley), a labour union comedy, *I'm All Right, Jack*, and a ditto drama, *The Angry Silence*, both with Richard Attenborough.

Anthony Perkins starred with Gregory Peck, Ava Gardner and Fred Astaire in *On the Beach*, and with Janet Leigh in Hitchcock's most profitable shocker, *Psycho*. *South Pacific*, released in 1958, was threatening *GWTW's* long-run records.

After the *Ben-Hur* monopoly of 1959, the Academy spread its awards around a bit. Best picture, *The Apartment*; actor, Burt Lancaster in *Elmer Gantry*; actress, Elizabeth Taylor in *Butterfield 8*; director, Billy Wilder, *The Apartment*.

Winning prizes elsewhere was D. H. Lawrence's *Sons and Lovers*, directed in England by Jack Cardiff, making amends for his previous movie, *Scent of Mystery*, the first (and last?) in Smell-o-Vision.

Judy Holliday was one of the screen's true jewels, and **Bells Are Ringing**, *the last movie she made before her death in 1965, was a bright setting for her. This Betty Comden–Adolph Green musical had been a Broadway hit for Judy. Arthur Freed's production and Vincente Minnelli's direction shone, but its paybox performance disappointed: musicals were unfashionable. Dean Martin shared the excellent Comden–Green–Jule Styne score containing 'The Party's Over', 'Long Before I Knew You', 'Just in Time', 'Drop That Name' and the poignant 'I'm Going Back to The Bonjour Tristesse Brassiere Company!' Also cast: Fred Clark, Eddie Foy Jr, Jean Stapleton, Ruth Storey, Frank Gorshin, Steven Peck, Gerry Mulligan, Nancy Walters.*

To celebrate the 75th anniversary of Mark Twain's book, and perhaps earn an honest penny, Samuel Goldwyn Jr produced **The Adventures of Huckleberry Finn** *with Eddie Hodges a sprightly Huck and world light-heavyweight champ Archie Moore surprisingly*

good as Jim. It had been filmed by MGM before (and better), and twice by Paramount. This version was written by James Lee and directed by Michael Curtiz, with Tony Randall, Patty McCormack, Neville Brand, Judy Canova, Mickey Shaughnessy, Andy Devine, Buster Keaton, Finlay Currie, Josephine Hutchinson, John Carradine, Royal Dano, Sterling Holloway. Alan Jay Lerner and Burton Lane wrote four songs for it.

Edna Ferber's **Cimarron**, *once a massive hit for* ▷ *RKO-Radio, was a major box-office disappointment for MGM 30 years later. The great Oklahoma land rush of settlers staking their claims in 1889 made a thrilling sequence in CinemaScope, but the romance and marriage of adventurer Glenn Ford and city girl Maria Schell seemed to have faded since Richard Dix and Irene Dunne played them. Edmund Grainger's production went on – and on – for 140 minutes. It was directed by Anthony Mann, scripted by Arnold Schulman, with Anne Baxter, Russ Tamblyn, Mercedes McCambridge, Vic Morrow, Aline MacMahon, Arthur O'Connell, Edgar Buchanan, Robert Keith, Henry Morgan, Charles McGraw, David Opatoshu, Royal Dano, Vladimir Sokoloff.*

1961

After 23 years in movies Bob Hope finally did one for MGM, **Bachelor in Paradise**, and Lana Turner returned to her old studio for the occasion. They were the only two singles in a California housing estate; their progress to togetherness mildly amused crowds of fairly profitable proportions. Script, Hal Kantor and Valentine Davies; original, Vera Caspary; director, Jack Arnold; producer, Ted Richmond; cast, Janis Paige, Jim Hutton, Paula Prentiss, Don Porter, Virginia Grey, Agnes Moorehead, Clinton Sundberg, John McGiver.

Susan Hayward, director Daniel Mann and producer Lawrence Weingarten came together again for more I'll Cry Tomorrow acclaim, but didn't get it with **Ada**, a turgid drama of power politics with weak husband and strong wife in conflict. Arthur Sheekman and William Driskill based their script on Wirt Williams' novel 'Ada Dallas'. Left to right: Dean Martin, Martin Balsam, Hayward, Ralph Meeker, Wilfrid Hyde White; also cast were Larry Gates, Robert Simon.

Ingrid Thulin and Paul Henreid (here) were two of the important talents trapped in the disastrous remake of **The Four Horsemen of the Apocalypse**. Glenn Ford, Charles Boyer, Paul Lukas, Yvette Mimieux, Karl Boehm and Lee J. Cobb also starred under Vincente Minnelli's direction. All were either miscast (Thulin even had to be voice-dubbed, by Angela Lansbury) or off-form or both, and Minnelli's sensitivity was out to lunch. The dialogue in the Robert Ardrey–John Gay script was so banal, and the depiction of wartime Paris in Julian Blaustein's production so faulty, that giggles punctuated its press screenings. None was heard at MGM: a $6m. flop was no laughing matter.

The Green Helmet had enough human interest to satisfy average audiences; but it missed the full charge of excitement its subject–racing drivers–could have sparked off. Directed by Michael Forlong and produced by Charles F. Vetter at MGM British, the Jon Cleary screenplay was based on his own novel. Left to right: Nancy Walters, Bill Travers, Ed Begley, Peter Collingwood; also cast were Sidney James, Megs Jenkins, Ursula Jeans, Sean Kelly, Tutte Lemkow, Ferdy Mayne and driving champ Jack Brabham.

Another respectable if unsensational programmer from the British studio, **The Secret Partner** starred Stewart Granger as a fugitive trying to prove his innocence before the law caught up with him. Director Basil Dearden and producer Michael Relph brought their experienced teamwork to bear on the David Pursall–Jack Seddon screenplay. Also cast: Haya Harareet, the Ben Hur heroine, Bernard Lee, Hugh Burden, Lee Montague, Melissa Stribling, Conrad Phillips, John Lee, Peter Illing and Norman Bird.

Long famed for her inimitable supporting performances, Margaret Rutherford became a movie star at 70 when **Murder She Said** supplied her best part since the dotty medium in Blithe Spirit. As Agatha Christie's Miss Marple, she detected a cunning killing and gave MGM British a tidy moneymaker, economically produced by George Brown and slickly directed by George Pollock. Also cast: Conrad Phillips and Thorley Walters (here) and Arthur Kennedy, Muriel Pavlow, James Robertson Justice, Charles Tingwell, Joan Hickson, Ronald Howard. The David Pursall–Jack Seddon script was based on Miss Christie's '4.50 from Paddington'.

At MGM British the sumptuous feasts of yesteryear had been replaced by double-feature fare; a smorgasbord of slapstick was served up in **Invasion Quartet**. Spike Milligan, Gregoire Aslan, John Le Mesurier and Bill Travers were the comics in the Nazi-occupied France imagined by writers Jack Trevor Story and John Briley (using a Norman Collins original), and director Jay Lewis. Ronald Kinnoch produced, casting Thorley Walters, Maurice Denham, Thelma Ruby, Millicent Martin, Cyril Luckham and (briefly) Eric Sykes.

Spike Milligan had British radio and TV fans slapping their knees for years, but the guffaws were too widely spaced in his first solo-starring movie, **Postman's Knock**. It was one of MGM's few London-made pictures not released in the US. Barbara Shelley played the nutty postman's loved one, supported by John Wood, Miles Malleson, Wilfred Lawson, Ronald Adam, Mario Fabrizi, Bob Todd, Warren Mitchell, Lance Percival. Written by Jack Trevor Story and John Briley, directed by Robert Lynn, produced by Ronald Kinnoch.

As a comedy **A Matter of WHO** was about as funny as a smallpox epidemic–and that's what it was about. Somewhere along the line the Patricia Lee–Paul Dickson story, scripted by Milton Holmes, had become a Terry-Thomas fun film when it should have been a drama about WHO (World Health Organization). Alex Nicol and Sonja Ziemann, here with the star; Richard Briers, Honor Blackman, Carol White, Guy Deghy, Geoffrey Keen, Clive Morton, Vincent Ball, Andrew Faulds and Bruce Beeby were in it. Don Chaffey directed; Walter Shenson and Holmes produced at MGM British. Spotty business.

Arthur Freed's **Light in the Piazza** shone fitfully. No rush to the box-office was occasioned by its stars (left to right) Olivia de Havilland, Rossano Brazzi, Yvette Mimieux, George Hamilton—good as they were, and magnificent as the views of Florence looked in Cinema-Scope and Metrocolor. Elizabeth Spencer's novel on which Julius Epstein based his script had a depressing element in that the Yvette Mimieux character was mentally handicapped. Guy Green directed; Barry Sullivan and Isabel Dean were featured.

Having done everything else for suspense but tie a heroine to a railroad track, Andrew Stone tried a forest blaze in **Ring of Fire**, trapping everybody including vamp Joyce Taylor, cop David Janssen and gangster Frank Gorshin. Writer-producer-director Stone and co-producer Virginia scored another hit with the nail-biting masses.

George Hamilton and Richard Boone as 1870 US Cavalry officers who fought Apache raids when not snarling at each other in **A Thunder of Drums**. The well-worn territory covered by James Warner Bellah's script was observed in a harsher light than usual by director Joseph Newman in Robert J. Enders' production. Also cast: Luana Patten, Charles Bronson, Arthur O'Connell, Richard Chamberlain (debut), Duane Eddy, James Douglas and Tammy Marihugh.

Donald O'Connor's ebullience lightened the rather heavy-handed fantasy of **The Wonders of Aladdin**, a lavish Italian production directed by Henry Levin for Lux Films. Noelle Adam (here) and Vittorio de Sica, Aldo Fabrizi and Michele Mercier had other leads in Luther Davis' screenplay. The kiddies enjoyed it.

Arthur Loew filled out his overseas release lists with three features MGM TV made for △ American home consumption. Loaded with bullets, corpses, cops and robbers, they were: . . . **The Crimebusters** with Mark Richman, Martin Gabel, Carol Rossen, Philip Ober; producer, Charles Russell; director, Boris Sagal; script, Paul Monash, Wallace Ware . . . **The Lawbreakers** with Jack Warden, Vera Miles, Robert Douglas, Arch Johnson; producer, Jaime Del Valle; director, Joseph Newman; script, Paul Monash, W. R. Burnett **The Murder Men** with Dorothy Dandridge, Mark Richman, James Coburn, Shelley Manne; producer, Paul Monash; director, John Peyser; script, Mel Goldberg.

Out of the ordinary but out of the money was **Two Loves**/Spinster, with Shirley MacLaine as an inhibited schoolteacher who backed away whenever her temperamental boyfriend (Laurence Harvey) tried to consummate their love. The audience was as frustrated as the characters by the time Julian Blaustein's production ended with Shirley still more or less pure. Director Charles Walters got some value from the unfamiliar New Zealand setting and Maori characters in Ben Maddow's adaptation of Sylvia Ashton Warner's book. The miscast stars were supported by Jack Hawkins, Nobu McCarthy, Juano Hernandez, Ronald Long and Norah Howard.

Two more beefcake epics (both remakes of Douglas Fairbanks movies) starring Steve ▽ Reeves were picked up by MGM after the success of Giant of Marathon. **The Thief of Baghdad** was directed by Arthur Lubin and produced by Bruno Vailati, with Georgia Moll, Arturo Dominici, Edy Vessel and George Chamarat. **Morgan the Pirate** was made by another Hollywood director, André de Toth, with Valerie Lagrange, Armand Mestral and Chelo Alonso. Breakneck action and spectacular production effects brought profitable bookings.

1961 was the first year in MGM's history that didn't yield one major success. **The Honeymoon Machine**, which wound it up, at least meant to be funny, and was; Lawrence Weingarten's production turned a nice profit in 1962. Based on a play by Lorenzo Semple about an officer who used his ship's computer to break the bank at a Venice casino, George Wells' screenplay got a fast pace from Richard Thorpe's direction and sprightly performances from Brigid Bazlen, Paula Prentiss, Steve McQueen and Jim Hutton (left to right) and Jack Weston, Dean Jagger, Jack Mullaney.

1962

The twin emergence of *Cleopatra*, the most expensive movie ever made, and the 20th Century-Fox annual report of a $39,796,094 loss (the all-industry all-time record) demonstrated what one supercolossal dud can do to a company's balance-sheet. It was a pretty dismal year altogether. MGM sank $10m to a profit of $2½m.

Charlton Heston in *El Cid*, Gregory Peck in *Guns of Navarone*, Kirk Douglas in *Spartacus* and Paul Newman in *Exodus* were among the best draws after over a year in release. Best of the new ones were Britain's *A Taste of Honey* and the flamboyant display of vintage star quality by Bette Davis and Joan Crawford in *Whatever Happened to Baby Jane?*, until *Lawrence of Arabia* arrived just in time to win the Academy Award and an Oscar for director David Lean. Best performance prizes went to Peck for *To Kill a Mockingbird* and Anne Bancroft for *The Miracle Worker*. Doris Day recaptured the No. 1 spot in the *Motion Picture Herald's* Top Ten which she had held in 1960; Frank Sinatra and Burt Lancaster nudged out William Holden and Tony Curtis.

All Fall Down *came out of the cutting room to give 1962 a good start, doubly welcome after the mediocrity of 1961 product. With Warren Beatty as the dissolute wanderer and Brandon de Wilde as his idolizing young brother, plus Angela Lansbury and Karl Malden as their parents and Eva Marie Saint as their fateful visitor, John Houseman gave his production the perfect players to bring James Leo Herlihy's novel to screen life. John Frankenheimer as director and playwright William Inge as scripter were ideal casting too. Their one mistake was allowing the constant reiteration of the Beatty character's silly name, Berry-Berry, to irritate the movie's admiring (but none too numerous) spectators.*

Tarzan Goes to India *was the 36th feature filmed from Edgar Rice Burroughs' brainchild, and surefire box-office. In it a new Tarzan entrepreneur, Sy Weintraub, introduced a more mature title-roler than usual: Jock Mahoney, a top Hollywood stunt man for years. This scene shows him with elephant boy Jai and Gajendra, king (said his billing) of the elephants. John Guillermin directed the movie which was shot in India and given the full CinemaScope-Technicolor treatment. Mark Dana and Leo Gordon had parts in the Guillermin–Robert Hardy Andrews script.*

Cairo *borrowed its title from an old Jeanette MacDonald movie and its plot from* The Asphalt Jungle. *The latter, closely followed in Joanne Court's script, looked almost as good as new in its Egyptian setting, and Ronald Kinnoch's production made a useful double-biller. Directed by Wolfe Rilla, with George Sanders and Richard Johnson (here), Faten Hamama, John Meillon, Eric Pohlmann, Walter Rilla.*

Spaghetti spectaculars relished by 1962 action fans: **Damon and Pythias**/The Tyrant of Syracuse *had Guy Williams and Don Burnett as the BC pals, supported by Illaria Occhini, Liana Orfei, Arnoldo Foa and Marina Berti under Curtis Bernhardt's direction; script by Bridget Boland and Barry Oringer; produced by Sam Jaffe and Samuel Marx . . . In* **The Son of Spartacus** *vamp Gianna Maria Canale batted false eyelashes in appeal for mercy from Steve Reeves' henchmen; Jacques Sernas, Ivo Garrani and Enzo Fiermonte were featured in*

the Titanus production directed by Sergio Corbucci.

Period of Adjustment, *a bubbly comedy, came from a Tennessee Williams play. It drew smaller crowds than his breast-heavers did, but a good time was had by all while Anthony Franciosa, Jane Fonda and Jim Hutton (left to right) sorted out their matrimonial affairs with Lois Nettleton, John McGiver, Mabel Albertson and Jack Albertson. George Roy Hill directed the Isobel Lennart screenplay, Lawrence Weingarten produced.*

Cinerama joined forces with MGM to tell a story: **How the West was Won**. *After ten years* ▷ *of cashing in on sheer size, it needed a shot in the arm. This widest of wide-screen processes (using three linked cameras in production and three synchronized projectors in specially adapted theatres to achieve a panorama filling the whole field of vision) had exhausted its travelogue possibilities. Completed in 1962, the massive production by Bernard Smith covered the adventures of a pioneering family with enough plot twists and spectacular climaxes to equip a dozen movies. It was a prodigious money's worth—and worth approximately $50m. in world-wide rentals. Much of this came from non-Cinerama theatres, which were provided with conventional reels for one projector. Unfortunately they still showed the joins necessitated by Cinerama's triple width; incredibly, no single-camera version had been shot. Spencer Tracy's voice linked the episodes directed by Henry Hathaway, John Ford and George Marshall and enacted by Karl Malden, Carroll Baker, Debbie Reynolds and Agnes Moorehead (left to right below), also Henry Fonda, James Stewart, Gregory Peck, (with Debbie at right), John Wayne, George Peppard, Richard Widmark, Robert Preston, Carolyn Jones, Lee J. Cobb, Eli Wallach, Raymond Massey, Thelma Ritter, Walter Brennan, Brigid Bazlen, David Brian, Andy Devine, Russ Tamblyn, Henry Morgan and Mickey Shaughnessy. Writer James R. Webb, film editor Harold Kress and the MGM sound department won Academy Awards.*

'How Could They Make a Movie of **Lolita?**' demanded the ads. They didn't, quite. Stanley Kubrick's handling of the Vladimir Nabokov novel, scripted by the author, threw a discreet sheet over its bedroom details (this was back in 1962) and reduced the age disparity between Humbert and Lolita by casting James Mason and Sue Lyon (here with Shelley Winters as her mother). But it remained a fascinating depiction of the games some people play, and kept its big audiences alertly amused for over 2½ hours. Peter Sellers dazzled as Quilty. Others in James B. Harris' production for Seven Arts/MGM, made in England; Marianne Stone, Diana Decker, Jerry Stovin, Gary Cockrell.

Boris Karloff played a humanitarian surgeon in **Corridors of Blood**, although its advertising strove to indicate that he was up to his monstrous old tricks. The Jean Scott Rogers script, directed by Robert Day and produced by John Croydon for Producers Associates/MGM in England, dealt with his efforts to perfect an anesthetic in the bad old days when hospitals were like torture chambers. Betta St John, Christopher Lee, Francis Matthews, Adrienne Corri, Finlay Currie, Marian Spencer, Francis de Wolff and Frank Pettingell were featured.

With **Village of Daughters**, a forced farce not released in America, Eric Sykes followed his fellow television writer-comedian Spike Milligan into MGM British stardom. He played a travelling salesman vied for by well-upholstered maidens like Scilla Gabel. Script, David Pursall and Jack Seddon; director, George

Pollock; producer, George Brown. They were all below their Murder She Said standard. Also cast: Gregoire Aslan, Yvonne Romain, John Le Mesurier, Warren Mitchell, Eric Pohlmann, Carol White, Peter Illing.

For **The Password is Courage** Andrew and Virginia Stone dropped cliffhanger fiction and moved to England to film the true story of the war hero, inappropriately named Charlie Coward, who was captured by the Germans in 1940, escaped and was recaptured seven times. Dirk Bogarde (here with Lewis Fiander and John Gardiner) was excellent as Coward; others cast were Maria Perschy, Alfred Lynch, Nigel Stock, Reginald Beckwith, Bernard Archard, Ferdy Mayne, George Pravda and Colin Blakely. Stone's script and direction gripped throughout.

The Dock Brief/Trial and Error–John Mortimer's novel comedy about a wife murderer and his useless barrister–provided Peter Sellers with a rich part as the latter. He appeared in three guises while Richard Attenborough (here with Beryl Reid and David Lodge) had six, as an imaginary trial preceded the real one. This element of fantasy frightened mass audiences away from Dimitri de Grunwald's production, directed at the British studio by James Hill. Script: Pierre Rouve.

Kill or Cure took some hearty slaps at the public funnybone by teaming Eric Sykes and Terry-Thomas in a zany script, by David Pursall and Jack Seddon, about murders in a nature cure hotel. Dennis Price, Lionel Jeffries, Moira Redmond, Katya Douglas, David Lodge, Ronnie Barker, Hazel Terry and Derrin Nesbitt joined the fun in this popular MGM-British entry from director George Pollock and producer George Brown.

Valentina Cortese and Broderick Crawford in Leonardo Bercovici's **Square of Violence**. Grim and powerful, it arrived too late in the long succession of dramas about underground resistance to Nazi brutality. Bibi Andersson was featured in the screenplay by Eric and Leonardo Bercovici . . .

Bigger crowds bought tickets for another stimulating drama, **Sweet Bird of Youth**, starring Paul Newman and Geraldine Page. They repeated their Broadway success in Tennessee Williams' play as the passée movie star and the stud selling himself for a chance at Hollywood. As in Cat on a Hot Tin Roof the distinctive Williams blend of raw emotionalism and poetic imagery found a vivid film translator in writer-director Richard Brooks, who had to deodorize some of the play's gamier details. Rip Torn and Madeleine Sherwood also played their stage roles, with Ed Begley (best supporting actor Academy Award), Shirley Knight, Mildred Dunnock, Philip Abbott, Corey Allen and James Douglas in the Pandro Berman production.

Boys' Night Out was more suspect morally than Lolita. It offered for laughs a story of four men, three of them married, who rented a flat and equipped it with a blonde for their use on different nights. She kept them drooling at arm's length until the wives arrived to turn the movie from unappetizing comedy into wild farce. Tony Randall was the mainstay of a cast that included Kim Novak and Janet Blair (with him here) and James Garner, Howard Duff, Patti Page, Howard Morris, Jessie Royce Landis, Oscar Homolka, Anne Jeffreys, Zsa Zsa Gabor, William Bendix, Fred Clark, Jim Backus and Larry Keating. Producer, Martin Ransohoff; director, Michael Gordon; script, Ira Wallach, Marion Hargrove, from a Marvin Worth–Arne Sultan story. Business was brisk.

Two Weeks in Another Town scored a near-miss when Kirk Douglas, Vincente Minnelli, John Houseman and Charles Schnee tried to repeat the success of their Bad and The Beautiful with another drama about temperamental movie-makers. Schnee's script seemed confused and Minnelli's direction overheated; perhaps through too much cutting, the characters of Irwin Shaw's novel lost motivation. They were played at top pitch by Douglas and Cyd Charisse (here on a wild ride in Rome) and Edward G. Robinson, George Hamilton, Claire Trevor, Daliah Lavi, Rosanna Schiaffino and James Gregory.

Scissors had apparently been used freely, too, on another movie-star story, **A Very Private Affair**, with Brigitte Bardot and Marcello Mastroianni. The bumpy continuity of Louis Malle's film gave fitful glimpses into Bardot's real life while telling the tale of a press-hounded sex symbol's loves and sorrows. MGM picked up fairly profitable bookings with a dubbed English version of the French production, written by Malle, Jean Paul Rappeneau, Jean Ferry; producer, Christine Gouze Renal.

Escape from East Berlin/Tunnel 28 was based on an actual escape of 28 East Berliners by digging under the Wall. Gabrielle Upton, Peter Berneis and Millard Lampell scripted the film which Don Murray sustained with one of his deeply felt performances, aided by Christine Kaufmann (here), Werner Klemperer and Karl Schell in an accomplished German cast directed by Robert Siodmak. Walter Wood's independent production, shot entirely in West Berlin, kept tension high; but grosses moderate.

Ride the High Country/Guns in the Afternoon has a special place in the history of Westerns. After joining forces for it. Randolph Scott and Joel McCrea, two of the genre's most durable stars, went into wealthy retirement (Scott was reputed to be Hollywood's richest actor). And it was the first cinema success for director Sam Peckinpah, long a maker of television Westerns. Unexpectedly a winner of critics' raves and international awards, it had wry humour in its N. B. Stone Jr script about two tired lawmen going into action again and finding many excitements in their last adventure. Richard Lyons produced, with Mariette Hartley, Ronald Starr, Edgar Buchanan, R. G. Armstrong, John Anderson, L. Q. Jones, Warren Oates, James Drury and John Davis Chandler in the cast.

▽ **Jumbo**, a big-budget circus musical that stubbornly refused to come to life either on the screen or at the paybox, failed to revive the glory that was MGM musicals; they became very few and far between. Left to right: Stephen Boyd, Doris Day, Martha Raye, Jimmy Durante. The credits bulged with important names: director Charles Walters, producers Joe Pasternak and Martin Melcher, associate Roger Edens, songs by Rodgers and Hart, script by Sidney Sheldon, original by Ben Hecht and Charles MacArthur, photography by William Daniels, and (in 36th place) second unit director Busby Berkeley. Dean Jagger and 15 circus acts supported the stars, whose best number was 'The Most Beautiful Girl in the World'. Hardly anybody used the movie's contractual title, Billy Rose's Jumbo, an acknowledgment of the stage show's producer.

The fans liked Jim Hutton and Paula Prentiss in The Honeymoon Machine so MGM top-starred them in **The Horizontal Lieutenant**. It was made by the team that paired them first in Where the Boys Are; producer Joe Pasternak, director Richard Thorpe and writer George Wells. This time the latter's script, based on a novel by Gordon Cotler about a 1944 clean-up operation on a Pacific island, verged on the inane and business was blah. Also cast: Charles McGraw (right), Jack Carter, Jim Backus.

In **I Thank a Fool** doctor Susan Hayward was convicted of mercy killing, went to jail, came out jobless, answered an ad for a nurse and discovered the advertiser was her trial prosecutor (it's a small world in movies) whose wife, Diane Cilento was having mad fits. Now read on . . . Karl Tunberg's script from Audrey Erskine Lindop's novel was directed by Robert Stevens, produced by Anatole de Grunwald and neglected by the public. Peter Finch, Kieron Moore, Cyril Cusack and Athene Seyler were in the MGM British production.

Pat Boone was a noted advocate of purity in life and entertainment, and fan club members' eyebrows rose in unison as their idol shared scenes of illicit passion with Mai Zetterling in **The Main Attraction**. Non-members were indifferent, judging by the receipts. Daniel Petrie directed the circus melodrama, written and produced by John Patrick in England for Seven Arts/MGM. Also cast: Nancy Kwan, Kieron Moore, Yvonne Mitchell, John Le Mesurier, Warren Mitchell and Lionel Blair.

◁ The remake of **Mutiny on the Bounty** ran for 179 minutes and cost $19m. (ten times the 1935 original's budget), most of which MGM eventually got back through strong selling. Carol Reed started directing the movie in 1961, but he found the South Seas location no paradise. After many troubles—especially with Marlon Brando—he gave up and was replaced by Lewis Milestone, whose assignment recalled his exchange of cables with Harry Cohn when directing a boatload of bibulous actors in another sea epic, for Columbia in 1934. 'Hurry up, the cost is staggering', wired Cohn. 'So is the cast', replied Milestone. No such levity was suitable on the Bounty film, whose cost escalated from the staggering to the catastrophic as Brando supervised direction and script, delays multiplied and tempers frayed. It had a mixed reception and was best enjoyed by those who hadn't seen the old version. The spectacle was magnificent but the drama lost tension after the mutiny and ended dismally with the Bounty burning and Brando indulging in a long death scene. Otherwise his Fletcher Christian was more original and detailed than Clark Gable's. Trevor Howard (with him here) also impressed as Captain Bligh but—like John Gielgud in the Barretts remake—lacked the alarming flicker of madness that Charles Laughton could give his tyrants. Others in the Aaron Rosenberg production: Richard Harris, Hugh Griffith, Richard Haydn, Tim Seely, Percy Herbert, Gordon Jackson, Noel Purcell, Duncan Lamont, Chips Rafferty, Torin Thatcher, Frank Silvera, and Tarita, who became Brando's permanent offscreen partner (coincidentally, Movita, who played a major role in 1935, was once his wife; he is the father of sons by leading ladies of both Bountys). Script credit went to Charles Lederer; camera, Robert Surtees.

Polishing off his fencing foes in bunches, Stewart Granger was a 16th-century mercenary in **Swordsman of Siena**. That city's Palio horserace made the climax for Jacques Bar's Italo-French production, Étienne Perier directing the Michael and Fay Kanin–Alec Coppel script. It sold a lot of tickets. Also cast: Sylva Koscina, Christine Kaufmann, Tullio Carminati, Marina Berti, Ricardo Garrone.

Nothing if not international in 1962, MGM went south of the border down Mexico way (actually Spain) with **The Savage Guns**, a bandits versus ranchers actioner, written by Edmund Morris, directed by Michael Carreras, produced by Jimmy Sangster and Jose Maesso for Carreras' Capricorn Productions. Alex Nicol (left), Don Taylor (right) and Richard Basehart led an otherwise Spanish cast.

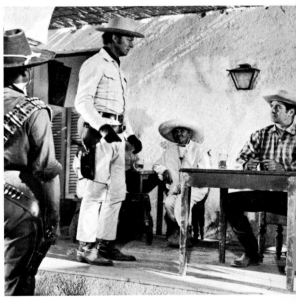

High-tension finish for the 1962 studio schedule: **The Hook** with (left to right) Nick Adams, Kirk Douglas, Robert Walker (son of the late star) and Enrique Magalona. To kill or not to kill their prisoner-of-war was the question turning Henry Denker's characters (from a novel by Vahe Katcha) against each other. Power in the acting and George Seaton's directing got William Perlberg's production nowhere at the box office.

309

INTO THE RED
1963

Chapter Two of the Wages of Extravagant Film-making came from MGM, whose release of *Mutiny on The Bounty* was followed by an appalling annual statement: $17½m below zero. (P.S.: Marlon Brando did not appear for MGM again until 1980.) United Artists also dipped into the red, but only $831,000 worth, a situation corrected by its release of Steve McQueen and James Garner in *The Great Escape*, Jack Lemmon and Shirley MacLaine in *Irma La Douce*, Frank Sinatra and Laurence Harvey in *The Manchurian Candidate*, Sean Connery in the first James Bond hit, *Dr No*, and Albert Finney in *Tom Jones*. The last won the best film and best director (Tony Richardson) Oscars. Patricia Neal in *Hud* and Sidney Poitier in *Lilies of The Field* were voted the best performances.

Fellini's *8½*, Zanuck's *The Longest Day*, Rosalind Russell and Natalie Wood in *Gypsy*, and Lemmon and Lee Remick in *Days of Wine and Roses* were also impressive. Lemmon and Paul Newman joined the Top Ten list, displacing Sinatra and Burt Lancaster.

1963 opened with **The Courtship of Eddie's Father.** *Dire prospects had been indicated by the star-director-writer team who helped unsaddle* The Four Horsemen of the Apocalypse, *and one of those find-Dad-a-wife stories. So the warmth of this one surprised critics and delighted audiences. In this scene Ronny Howard, splendid as Eddie, signals to father Glenn Ford his disapproval of Dina Merrill because she has 'skinny eyes'. Shirley Jones, Stella Stevens, Roberta Sherwood and Jerry Van Dyke completed Vincente Minnelli's principals in the Joe Pasternak production, written by John Gay from a novel by Mark Toby. It later sparked off an MGM TV series.*

Julie Andrews startled her fans in **The Americanization of Emily**. *They had never expected to see their Mary Poppins popping into bed with James Garner, who also nonplussed his public by playing a shameless coward. William Bradford Huie's novel and Paddy Chayefsky's script, set in wartime London, sparkled with surprises, expertly sprung by director Arthur Hiller. Melvyn Douglas, James Coburn, Joyce Grenfell, Keenan Wynn, Liz Fraser, William Windom, Edward Binns, Gary Cockrell and Edmon Ryan were in Martin Ransohoff's production. It pulled the crowds but they weren't as big as it deserved.*

Advance to the Rear/Company of Cowards *was a rowdy Civil War comedy that pleased the masses. Melvyn Douglas and Glenn Ford (left and right) as officers in a troop of misfits, were easily distracted from battle plans by the town's strumpets. Stella Stevens and Joan Blondell (here leading the daughters of joy) had featured roles with Jim Backus, Alan Hale Jr, Whit Bissell and Michael Pate in the Ted Richmond production directed by George Marshall. Written by Samuel Peeples and William Bowers from originals by Jack Schaefer and William Chamberlain.*

The heroine of **The Unsinkable Molly Brown** *really existed, and her life supplied so much 'book' for the original stage show (by Richard Morris) and script for the movie (by Helen Deutsch) there was hardly room for Meredith Willson's songs, making it something of a musical manqué. Debbie Reynolds was the life and soul of the film, despite miscasting as a Colorado mining camp hellion who became a social climbing millionairess and a heroine of the 'Titanic' disaster. She and Harve Presnell, who repeated his Broadway role of Molly's husband, punched across what numbers there were. Produced on the stage by none other than Dore Schary, it was filmed by Lawrence Weingarten on a lavish budget, amply returned from American box-offices but less so from overseas. Charles Walters directed, with Roger Edens as associate producer. Left to right: Hayden Rorke, Audrey Christie, Debbie, Hermione Baddeley and Vassili Lambrinos; also cast were Ed Begley, Jack Kruschen, Martita Hunt, Kathryn Card.*

Margaret Rutherford as Miss Marple made it three hits in a row for Lawrence Bachmann's MGM British series of Agatha Christie whodunits. **Murder Most Foul** *again had Charles Tingwell as the Scotland Yard man astounded by her percipience (and fabulous face) as she investigated murders in a theatrical troupe. Also cast: Ron Moody, Andrew Cruickshank, Megs Jenkins, Ralph Michael, James Bolam, Francesca Annis, Stringer Davis, Pauline Jameson, Dennis Price, Terry Scott. David Pursall and Jack Seddon adapted the Christie novel 'Mrs McGinty's Dead'; George Pollock directed; Ben Arbeid produced.*

Murder Ahoy, *made by the same MGM British people who had scored with* Murder Most Foul, *was Miss Marple's last fling. Business for this series was dropping. Lionel Jeffries was the captain hopelessly outgunned by Margaret Rutherford when she snooped after a killer aboard his ship. Others concerned: Charles Tingwell, William Mervyn, Joan Benham, Stringer Davis, Nicholas Parsons, Miles Malleson, Henry Oscar, Derek Nimmo, Francis Matthews, Terence Edmond.*

Honeymoon Hotel *offered a farrago of roguish misunderstandings and wink-and-nudge dialogue such as hadn't been displayed since* Getting Gertie's Garter *sent Grandpa rolling in the aisle. Inexplicably produced by Pandro Berman as a non-musical comedy, it starred two of the most talented performers of Broadway musicals, Robert Goulet and Robert Morse (here with Elsa Lanchester). The R. S. Allen–Harvey Bullock screenplay also employed Nancy Kwan, Jill St John and Keenan Wynn, desperately directed by Henry Levin for laughs, which were in short supply.*

The Rounders *with Henry Fonda, Sue Ane Langdon, Hope Holiday and Glenn Ford was all fun, no guns—a most unusual Western: Chill Wills, Edgar Buchanan, Kathleen Freeman and Barton MacLane supported. The Richard Lyons production was written from Max Evans' novel and directed by Burt Kennedy.*

The stomping rhythms of Sam Katzman's 'B' musicals were blended with a dramatic story in **Your Cheatin' Heart** *and his praiseworthy production scored at the paybox in many areas. The forbidding title hid an only slightly-sugared biography of Hank Williams, who drank himself to death after writing over 500 country & western songs and singing most of*

them: his discs continued to sell in the millions even after he died. George Hamilton and Susan Oliver made a convincing Mr and Mrs Williams; Hank Jr dubbed the songs for Hamilton. Gene Nelson directed Stanford Whitmore's screenplay, with Red Buttons and Arthur O'Connell featured.

Jeffrey Hunter, 37 and still looking like the most popular undergrad on campus, took the road to Rome for a less exacting role than Jesus Christ. He co-starred with Massimo Girotti and Mylene Demongeot (with him here) and Ron Randell in **Gold for the Caesars**. *Slave revolts and Celt-Roman battles broke out all over Arnold Perl's script, from a novel by Florence Seward, directed by Andre de Toth and profitably produced by Joseph Fryd.*

Hollywood's golden boy, Tab Hunter, went to Egypt to star in **The Golden Arrow** *with Rossana Podesta and (with him here) Dominique Boschero. He rode horses and magic carpets through a fast succession of Arabian Nights adventures in the Titanus production directed by Antonio Margheriti. Clever special effects in Technirama popped the eyes of its mostly juvenile audiences.*

Two minor musicals for the bubble-gum trade. Connie Francis, Jim Hutton, Susan Oliver and Joby Baker in **Looking for Love**, *produced by Joe Pasternak, directed by Don Weis, written by Ruth Brooks Flippen; with Barbara Nichols, Jay C. Flippen, Jesse White and, in cameo spots, George Hamilton, Yvette Mimieux, Paula Prentiss, Danny Thomas, Johnny Carson …Chad Everett, Frank's girl Nancy Sinatra and Mary Ann Mobley in* **Get Yourself a College Girl**/The Swingin' Set, *produced by Sam Katzman, directed by Sidney Miller, written by Robert E. Kent; with the Dave Clark Five, the Animals, Stan Getz and Astrud Gilberto.*

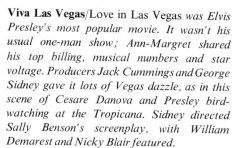

One Elvis Presley wasn't enough for **Kissin' Cousins**, *a mad hill-billy romp with Pamela Austin and Yvonne Craig, here flanking a blond Elvis and a brunet Elvis. Fans didn't know which way to look. Former dancing star Gene Nelson directed and, with Gerald Drayson Adams, wrote the profitable Sam Katzman production, featuring Glenda Farrell, Arthur O'Connell, Jack Albertson and Donald Woods. Elvis shared ten songs between him.*

Viva Las Vegas/Love in Las Vegas *was Elvis Presley's most popular movie. It wasn't his usual one-man show; Ann-Margret shared his top billing, musical numbers and star voltage. Producers Jack Cummings and George Sidney gave it lots of Vegas dazzle, as in this scene of Cesare Danova and Presley bird-watching at the Tropicana. Sidney directed Sally Benson's screenplay, with William Demarest and Nicky Blair featured.*

Joanne Woodward sharing a panic with Stuart Whitman in double-biller **Signpost to Murder**, *a stagey but effective thriller about an escaped prisoner from a mental hospital who forced a housewife to give him refuge. Monte Doyle's play was scripted by Sally Benson, directed by George Englund, produced by Lawrence Weingarten, with Edward Mulhare, Alan Napier cast.*

Catherine Deneuve was snatched from the altar by the Gestapo and whisked to what **Vice and Virtue**'s *publicity called a 'lust-crazed Nazi general's pleasure house'. Despite several orgies, more implied than shown, 'she retained her integrity'. Which was more than could be said for Roger Vadim's movie, co-produced by Gaumont and MGM in France, with Annie Girardot, Robert Hossein and O. E. Hasse taking care of the vice department. Script by Vadim and Roger Vailland.*

An intriguing plot set **36 Hours** *apart from other war movies (although it ended with the conventional chase) and made it a hit: a Nazi hoax convinced James Garner, US bearer of D-Day secrets, that he had been unconscious for six years and the war was long over. In it were Eva Marie Saint, Werner Peters and Garner (here) and Rod Taylor, Alan Napier, John Banner, Russell Thorson, Sig Ruman, Celia Lovsky, Martin Kosleck. George Seaton directed, and based his script on stories by Roald Dahl, Carl Hittleman and Luis Vance. Production by William Perlberg and Seaton.*

Flipper was the most lovable non-human star since Lassie, and **Flipper's New Adventure/** Flipper and the Pirates *was one sequel that didn't disappoint. The dolphin was again Luke Halpin's pet in producer Ivan Tors' story, scripted by Art Arthur, of how they helped a stranded British yachting family: Pamela Franklin (here), Francesca Annis, Helen Cherry and Tom Helmore. Leon Benson directed it in Florida and the Bahamas. A lengthy television series ensued.*

Ivan Tors veered from dolphin epics long enough to make **Rhino!** *a lively movie about wild beasts. Robert Culp and Harry Guardino, having felled a lion with a harmless tranquillizing dart instead of a bullet, hunted a pair of rare white rhino in order to save them from extinction. Shirley Eaton was there to show that no such danger threatened blondes. The Arthur Weiss–Art Arthur script was produced in South Africa by Ben Chapman for Tors, who directed.*

1964 ended impressively with the turbulent drama of **Young Cassidy**. *Rod Taylor vigorously played Sean O'Casey's autobiographical title role in the Robert Graff–Robert Emmett Ginna production. John Ford fell ill during its shooting in Ireland and Jack Cardiff took over direction of the John Whiting screenplay. A splendid cast included Maggie Smith and Michael Redgrave as W. B. Yeats (here with Taylor) and Flora Robson, Edith Evans, Jack MacGowran, Sean Phillips, T. P. McKenna, Pauline Delany, Philip O'Flynn, and Julie Christie in a star-making performance.*

Hollywood's second generation took charge of **The Young Lovers**/Chance Meeting. *It was produced and directed by Samuel Goldwyn Jr and starred Henry's son Peter Fonda (here with Sharon Hugueny). They and featured players Nick Adams and Deborah Walley did well, but the Julian Halevy story and George Garrett script about university students lagged.*

DR. ZHIVAGO
1965

Nervously cheerful described the MGM outlook at the start of 1965; profits stayed even with 1964, but expenditure on *Doctor Zhivago* made the accountants shudder. Meanwhile 20th Century-Fox unveiled one of the biggest money-makers in the industry's history: *The Sound of Music*, which won the Academy Award, another Oscar for Robert Wise, and almost as many customers as *GWTW*.

The acting prizes went to Lee Marvin in *Cat Ballou* and Julie Christie in *Darling*. The latter's director, John Schlesinger, won many international citations, as did Frederico Fellini for *Juliet of the Spirits*. The annual James Bond blockbuster was *Goldfinger*; *Those Magnificent Men in Their Flying Machines* drew big crowds; Rock Hudson and Doris Day had a comedy hit in *Send Me No Flowers*; Stanley Kramer, with *It's a Mad, Mad, Mad, Mad World* in its second year of success, brought Vivien Leigh back in *Ship of Fools*, which won raves for Oskar Werner. Sean 'Bond' Connery hit the top of the star list, leading John Wayne, Doris Day, Julie Andrews, Jack Lemmon, Elvis Presley, Cary Grant, James Stewart, Elizabeth Taylor and Richard Burton.

The first feature out of the factory in 1965 was **Quick, Before it Melts**. *George Maharis, Janine Gray, Anjanette Comer and Robert Morse (left to right) topped a cast that included James Gregory, Yvonne Craig, Norman Fell and Milton Fox, the last being a penguin. It was that kind of a picture. Delbert Mann directed and co-produced with Douglas Laurence; script by Dale Wasserman from Philip Benjamin's novel.*

Still cheerful but even sillier, **Girl Happy** *had Elvis Presley chasing Shelley Fabares around Fort Lauderdale, Florida. Producer Joe Pasternak had had better luck with this locale in* Where the Boys Are. *Director Boris Sagal seemed flummoxed by the limp Harvey Bullock–R. S. Allen script, but the Presley fans came anyway. Also cast: Harold J. Stone, Gary Crosby, Joby Baker, Nita Talbot, Mary Ann Mobley, Chris Noel, Jackie Coogan.*

To Trap a Spy–*a spin-off from television's* The Man from U.N.C.L.E.–*was no great shakes on its first playdates, but the rumblings of a minor box-office earthquake could be heard in the distance. Robert Vaughn as Napoleon Solo dominated a fast-moving screenplay pieced together by Sam Rolfe, with parts for Luciana Paluzzi, Patricia Crowley, Fritz Weaver, William Marshall, Will Kuluva, David McCallum and Victoria Shaw. Don Medford directed, Norman Felton produced.*

The immortal clowning of Stan and Ollie in their early two-reelers was preserved in **Laurel and Hardy's Laughing 20's**, *compiled by Robert Youngson, whose similar* MGM's Big Parade of Comedy *had demonstrated how to make money without actually filming anything. The 91-minute feature was released in the same year as Laurel's death at 75; Hardy had departed eight years earlier.*

Vat 69 got a free (?) plug but the belly-dancer got nowhere in this scene of **Where The Spies Are**: *English secret agents David Niven and Nigel Davenport were too true-blue to be distracted from duty. James Leasor's 'Passport to Oblivion' was scripted (with Wolf Mankowitz), produced (with Steven Pallos) and directed by Val Guest at MGM/British, with Francoise Dorleac, John Le Mesurier, Basil Dignam, Eric Pohlmann, George Pravda, Ronald Radd and Noel Harrison. A neat thriller that got good business.*

Joy in the Morning, *Betty Smith's story of young newly-weds, lacked the poignancy of her famous* Tree Grows in Brooklyn *but it had charm, emphasized in Alex Segal's direction and the playing of Richard Chamberlain (here with Arthur Kennedy as his father) and Yvette Mimieux. Oscar Homolka, Donald Davis, Joan Tetzel, Sidney Blackmer, Virginia Gregg, Chris Noel and Harvey Stephens had parts in the Sally Benson–Alfred Hayes–Norman Lessing screenplay, produced by Henry Weinstein. Not much joy for exhibitors, though.*

Operation Crossbow, *produced in a big way ▷ by Carlo Ponti at MGM British, was almost but not quite a box-office blockbuster. The Richard Imrie–Derry Quinn–Ray Rigby script about destroying the German V-Bomb bases was impressively authentic and excitingly theatrical by turns; Erwin Hillier's photography and Tom Howard's special effects, starring supercolossal climactic explosions, were outstanding. Sophia Loren, in briefly for name value, and George Peppard, prominent throughout, are seen here. Michael Anderson directed with a sure touch, employing Trevor Howard, John Mills, Richard Johnson, Tom Courtenay, Jeremy Kemp, Anthony Quayle, Helmut Dantine, Richard Todd, Lilli Palmer, Paul Henreid, Sylvia Syms, John Fraser, Barbara Rueting, Patrick Wymark (as Churchill), Moray Watson, Richard Wattis and a thousand or so others.*

Jean Paul Belmondo interrupted his race across the Sahara with Andrea Parisy and a truckload worth $100,000 to take potshots at his pursuers. The breakneck pace, culminating in a ferocious brawl, made strange seat-fellows of action fans and French film buffs for Henri Verneuil's picture, written by Michel Audiard and produced by Alain Poire for Gaumont/MGM. Also cast: Lino Ventura, Reginald Kernan, Gert Frobe, Bernard Blier . . . Made by

While making a successful television series of Flipper, *Ivan Tors varied the formula a bit for a feature,* **Zebra in the Kitchen,** *which brought Jay North and his pet puma into an action spree during which the boy set free a whole zoo. The Art Arthur screenplay (original, Elgin Ciampi) was directed by Tors; also featured were Martin Milner, Andy Devine, Jim Davis, Joyce Meadows, Robert Lowery.*

Hysteria, *a teasing puzzle from Britain's horror wholesalers, Hammer Films, was a useful MGM release. In this scene Robert Webber, Jennifer Jayne, Lelia Goldoni, Maurice Denham and Anthony Newlands find a corpse in the shower-stall. Jimmy Sangster produced his own screenplay, leaning heavily on that old story standby, amnesia: Freddie Francis directed.*

Italians, but a long way from home, was a wilder version of the 'Flipper' stories, **Tiko and the Shark.** *Produced by Goffredo Lombardo for Titanus/MGM and directed by Folco Quilici, Italo Calvino's story concerned a Polynesian boy keeping to the primitive life with his girl and his pet shark when civilization invaded their island. Beautifully filmed in the South Seas with a native cast.*

Clarence, the Cross-eyed Lion *was a feature-length try for theatre bookings in advance of another popular MGM television series,* Daktari. *Enjoyable, but it didn't repeat the 'U.N.C.L.E.' success. Written by star Marshall Thompson (left), Art Arthur, Alan Caillou, directed by Andrew Marton, produced by Leonard Kaufman; with Richard Haydn (right), Betsy Drake, Cheryl Miller.*

Two musicals in a minor key: **Harem Scarum/** Harem Holiday *had few rivals as the year's worst movie; in it Elvis Presley (here with Carolyn Carter) essayed a sort of singing Valentino role mixed with Fairbanks acrobatics. The comic-strip script by Gerald Drayson Adams was more or less directed by Gene Nelson, and produced by mistake and Sam Katzman. Also cast: Mary Ann Mobley, Fran Jeffries, Michael Ansara, Jay Novello, Philip Reed . . . .Katzman recovered from* Harem Scarum *in time to produce a cheap and cheerful remake of* Girl Crazy, *with Connie Francis and Harve Presnell assigned the hopeless task of replacing Judy Garland and Mickey Rooney.* **When the Boys Meet the Girls** *gave them fine Gershwin songs and support from Herman's Hermits, Louis Armstrong, Liberace, Sue Ane Langdon, Fred Clark, Frank Faylen, Joby Baker in a Robert E. Kent script directed by Alvin Ganzer.*

Three from abroad: Connoisseurs of the loin-cloth school of acting (there were plenty of them) applauded Richard Lloyd and Kirk Morris in **Hercules, Samson and Ulysses.** *These contenders for the Steve Reeves Scholarship left little footage for Enzo Cerusico as Ulysses, and Liana Orfei as Delilah never had time to reach for the scissors. Joseph Fryd's spaghetti spectacular was written and directed by Pietro Francisci . . . In* **Greed in the Sun**

Andrew and Virginia Stone came a cropper with fantastic comedy in **The Secret of my Success,** *a three-episode story by Andrew about a dimwitted policeman (James Booth). The funniest segment concerned a dizzy husband-killer (Stella Stevens), followed by a piece featuring Honor Blackman and giant spiders, and a messy conclusion with Shirley Jones and a South American revolution. Lionel Jeffries kept turning up; ticket-buyers didn't. Left to right: Booth, Jeffries, Miss Stevens.*

Ann-Margret, made in Sweden, in **Made in Paris,** *a wafer-thin comedy about the fashion industry. She kept the eye happily occupied while the brain dozed over Stanley Roberts' script, directed by Boris Sagal, produced by Joe Pasternak and enacted by Louis Jourdan, Richard Crenna, Chad Everett, Edie Adams, John McGiver and Marcel Dalio. Count Basie, Trini Lopez and the seductive A-M herself provided musical interludes.*

1965

The 'Man from U.N.C.L.E.' craze really lifted off with the release of **The Spy with My Face**; the television spin-off for cinemas became especially big in Britain, where MGM's distribution boss Michael Havas masterminded a sustained publicity campaign that turned these movies from bill-fillers into major money-makers. David McCallum as Illya Kuryakin, subordinated to Robert Vaughn's Napoleon Solo in the first feature, suddenly was equally idolized by the fans; Leo G. Carroll started his permanent job as the secret agents' chief; Senta Berger co-starred as their alluring enemy. It was written by Clyde Ware and Joseph Calvelli, directed by John Newland and produced by Sam Rolfe under the supervision of MGM's television executive Norman Felton.

MGM's last releases in CinemaScope, once the wonder of the movie world (and a future headache for TV companies) were a pair of Westerns produced in Spain by Lester Welch. **Gunfighters of Casa Grande** featured (left to right) Dick Bentley, Phil Posner, Jorge Mistral and Alex Nicol; also Steve Rowland, Mercedes Alonso, Maria Granada; director,

Roy Rowland; writers, Patricia and Borden Chase, Clarke Reynolds . . . In **Son of a Gunfighter** Russ Tamblyn (here flanked by Ralph Browne and Kieron Moore) was an improbable triggerman; James Philbrook, Fernando Rey and Miss Granada were also in Reynolds' screenplay. Paul Landres directed.

Louis B. Mayer's ghost must have been smiling down on **The Singing Nun**. It was just the family-type heart-wallop he loved; its stars—Debbie Reynolds and Ricardo Montalban (left and right)—were MGM discoveries in the good old days, and who should be playing the Mother Superior but our own Greer Garson! Commercially, Mayer would have been right, as usual: it contributed to the company's handsome 1966 profit. Based on a real character, the Belgian nun who recorded best-sellers as Soeur Sourire (it had 12 songs) the Sally Benson–John Furia Jr screenplay was directed by Henry Koster, produced by John Beck and Hayes Goetz. Also cast: Chad Everett and little Ricky Cordell (here) and Katharine Ross, Michael Pate, Agnes Moorehead, Juanita Moore, Tom Drake, Ed Sullivan, Marina Koshetz, Nancy Walters.

Hold On! was also an offspring of the disc business. It starred the British sub-Beatle group, Herman's Hermits, in particular its likeable lead singer, Peter Noone (here with Shelley Fabares). The title came from one of their hit songs, but takings indicated it could have come from another of them: 'A Must to Avoid'. Karl Green, Keith Hopwood, Derek Leckenby and Barry Whitwam of the group, Sue Ane Langdon, Herbert Anderson and Bernard Fox were in the Sam Katzman production which was written by James Gordon, directed by Arthur Lubin.

Tony Randall, Anita Ekberg and Robert Morley in **The Alphabet Murders**, a soft-boiled thriller from Lawrence Bachmann's British unit, directed by Frank Tashlin. Randall amusingly played Agatha Christie's sleuth Hercule Poirot in the David Pursall–Jack Seddon screenplay. Also cast: Maurice Denham, Guy Rolfe, Sheila Allen, Julian Glover, Clive Morton; Cyril Luckham, James Villiers, Richard Wattis, Austin Trevor.

Around the World Under the Sea was a well-made and well-received special effects thriller. In this scene Shirley Eaton, Brian Kelly, Marshall Thompson and Lloyd Bridges emerge

unscathed from a submarine volcano. David McCallum, Keenan Wynn and Gary Merrill also starred. The Art Arthur–Arthur Weiss screenplay was directed and produced for Ivan Tors by Andrew Marton.

Carlo Ponti's production **The 25th Hour** was overlong and often confusing in mood and incident, but it had the merit of being different from other war movies—maybe too much so: it drew meagre business. In it Anthony Quinn (left) playing a sort of Rumanian Don Quixote fighting the windmills of war, was taken prisoner successively by Germans, Russians and Americans. Henri Verneuil directed it in Budapest, Belgrade, Munich and Paris, casting Virna Lisi, Gregoire Aslan, Michael Redgrave, Serge Reggiani, Marcel Dalio, Alexander Knox, Marius Goring, John Le Mesurier. Script by Francoise Boyer, Wolf Mankowitz and Verneuil from C. V. Gheorghiu's novel.

Hotel Paradiso, Georges Feydeau's glorious Olympics of bed-jumping, corridor-running, door-slamming and wife-swapping, fell flat on the screen. It was produced and directed in Paris by Peter Glenville, who had successfully staged it in London (with Alec Guinness) and New York. Glenville collaborated with Jean-Claude Carriere on the script and played Feydeau in an introductory bit. Left to right: Gina Lollobrigida, Robert Morley, Peggy Mount, Leonard Rossiter and Guinness. Also cast: Akim Tamiroff, Marie Bell, Douglas Byng, Robertson Hare, Derek Fowldes, Ann Beach.

More dollars than sense: **The Glass-Bottom Boat** drew nearly $5m. from American theatres alone, thanks to dotty characters, crazy situations and Frank Tashlin's high-speed direction. And, of course, the durable popularity of Doris Day (here gagging it up with Dom de Luise). Other able farceurs who punched over Everett Freeman's script: Rod Taylor, John McGiver, Paul Lynde, Edward Andrews, Dick Martin, Eric Fleming, Elisa-

beth Fraser, Alice Pearce, George Tobias, Ellen Corby, Arthur Godfrey. Martin Melcher and Freeman produced.

The central figures of **Maya** were an elephant and her calf, in whose defence she was killed by tigers. Many customers found this hard to take: thou shalt not be cruel to elephants is a box-office commandment. Clint Walker and Jay North played an American hunter and his son in India, and John Berry directed the King Brothers production there; script by John Fante based on Gilbert Wright's adaptation of a Jalal Din–Lois Roth story.

James Garner and Jean Simmons starred in **Mr Buddwing**/Woman Without a Face, filmed from Evan Hunter's novel with considerably less success than his Blackboard Jungle. The identity problem of an amnesiac held interest, but too many romantic encounters clogged the narrative, scripted by Dale Wasserman, directed by Daniel Mann. Suzanne Pleshette, Angela Lansbury, Katharine Ross, Jack Gilford, Raymond St Jacques, Joe Mantell and ex-'Dead End Kid' Billy Halop were in the Mann–Douglas Laurence production.

The Dangerous Days of Kiowa Jones had an unusual title and a heroine who didn't look as if she'd just stepped out of a beauty shop; conviction in performance and direction set it above the average Western. Robert Horton, who'd been riding the television ranges for years, starred with Diane Baker and Sal Mineo (left and right), aided by Gary Merrill, Nehemiah Persoff and Royal Dano in the Max Youngstein–David Karr production, written by Frank Fenton and Robert Thompson, directed by Alex March.

1966

Big one of the year was **Grand Prix**, pro- ▷
duced by Edward Lewis for Cinerama screens;
it was a potent attraction in regular cinemas
too. In contrast to his All Fall Down, John
Frankenheimer's direction scored best in spectacular action; the intimate scenes of racing
drivers and their women (written by Robert
Alan Aurthur) were on the stodgy side. The
race sequences, filmed on real championship
circuits, had stunning impact, with remarkable
camerawork by Lionel Lindon and his crew,
and sound effects that won Academy Awards
for Gordon Daniels and the MGM sound
department. Editors Fredric Steinkamp, Henry
Berman, Stewart Linder and Frank Santillo
also won Oscars. Eva Marie Saint and Yves
Montand (here after a crash) were cast with
James Garner, Toshiro Mifune, Brian Bedford,
Jessica Walter, Antonio Sabata, Françoise
Hardy, Claude Dauphin, Geneviève Page,
Jack Watson, Rachel Kempson, Ralph Michael
and several driving champions.

Spinout/California Holiday combined all the
Elvis Presley movie clichés. He played a pop
singer and a racing-driver and a magnet for
every girl in sight and was referred to as The
Perfect American Male. What more could
the Legion of El Loyalists desire? 'Critics
don't buy tickets' was the motto of producer
Joe Pasternak, director Norman Taurog,
writers Theodore Flicker and George Kirgo.
Old-timers saw that Una Merkel, Cecil Kellaway and Frederick Worlock were alive and
well in a young cast: Shelley Fabares, Diane
McBain, Deborah Walley, Jack Mullaney,
Warren Berlinger, Dodie Marshall.

Robert Taylor, still stalwart in middle age,
and young Chad Everett shared star billing
and shoot-outs in **Return of the Gunfighter**, a
conventional Western with such familiar bad-
men as Butch Cassidy (John Crawford) and
the Sundance Kid (John Davis Chandler).
Frank and Maurice King produced and James
Neilson directed the Robert Buckner–Burt
Kennedy story, featuring Ana Martin, Lyle
Bettger and Michael Pate. This completed a
rather undistinguished production year, its
prosperity sparked by Zhivago income.

NEW DIRECTIONS
1967

Money poured into MGM's coffers: a record gross income of $227m yielding a profit of $14m. United Artists, the latest of the old-line companies to be absorbed, became a segment of Transamerica Corp.

Biggest surprise hit of the year: *Bonnie and Clyde* with Warren Beatty and Faye Dunaway made a fortune for producer Beatty and Warners. Biggest non-surprise hit: *You Only Live Twice*, yet another Bond mint for UA's new owners, who also got the Oscar winner, *In the Heat of the Night*. Rod Steiger won for his performance in this, while the best actress, said the Academy, was in Spencer Tracy's last film, *Guess Who's Coming to Dinner*: the astonishing Katharine Hepburn, whose previous Oscar was 35 years old.

The Sand Pebbles, Thoroughly Modern Millie, Barefoot in the Park and *Valley of the Dolls* were popular. France scored with *Un Homme et Une Femme* and *La Guerre est Finie*.

Blow-Up *had the cognoscenti discussing, dissecting and analyzing it during the late 1960's; a whole book of speculations about it was published. Non-cog crowds quickly gave up guessing what Michelangelo Antonioni was getting at and just enjoyed the 'swinging London' chic, the pervading air of mystery, the sometimes topless Vanessa Redgrave and David Hemmings (here topped), Sarah Miles 'in flagrante', and Hemmings tumbling with nude girls in his photographic studio. All of which made it a powerful ticket-seller. Antonioni brilliantly directed his baffling script, written with Tonino Guerra; Carlo Ponti produced.* ▷

Double Trouble *was one of the more idiotic Elvis Presley movies. His songs came as a relief from Jo Heims' script (original, Marc Brandel) about smuggling between England and Belgium—or something. Norman Taurog directed the Judd Bernard–Irwin Winkler production, with Annette Day (here) and John Williams, Yvonne Romain, Chips Rafferty and the Wiere Brothers.*

The Comedians, *scripted by Graham Greene from his novel about a group of Europeans and Americans in voodoo-ridden Haiti, was filmed in West Africa and France: Haitian dictator Papa Doc was unwelcoming. Performances by Richard Burton and Alec Guinness (here) and Elizabeth Taylor, Peter Ustinov, Lillian Gish and Paul Ford were the movie's best assets, artistically and financially, but results were patchy. Producer and director: Peter Glenville.*

△ **Dark of the Sun**/The Mercenaries *was too violent for some censor boards, but not for the public.* Jim Brown *and* Rod Taylor *led the roughneck action, which director* Jack Cardiff *kept moving at a terrific pace. Taylor had the year's most energetic role as he rescued a trainload of Congo villagers and a hoard of diamonds from attacking rebels.* Yvette Mimieux *as a refugee and* Kenneth More *as an alcoholic doctor co-starred in a cast that included* Paul Garsten, Andre Morell, Olivier *Despax, Guy Deghy, Calvin Lockhart and Alan Gifford. Quentin Werty and Adrian Spies scripted the George Englund production.*

Arthur Kennedy *and* Glenn Ford *in* **Day of the Evil Gun** ▷ *were rivals who joined forces when the woman they both loved was kidnapped by Apaches. Jerry Thorpe produced and directed the stark, depressing Charles Marquis Warren–Eric Bercovici horse opera, with* Dean Jagger, John Anderson, Paul Fix, Royal Dano.

341

1968 **2001: A Space Odyssey**, *science fiction without* ▷
death-rays or monsters, is one of the great
imaginative achievements of the movies. It was
produced in Cinerama – and deep secrecy – at
the MGM British studio. After an expendable
prologue resembling a preview of Planet of the
Apes, *Stanley Kubrick's film took an increas-*
ingly strong grip on its audiences as it went
to the moon and beyond, until its hero (Keir
Dullea, here) was hurtled into the unknown
regions of outer space. The final scenes were so
stunningly bizarre that almost every viewer had
a different explanation for them, with reactions
ranging from exaltation to baffled anger. The
talk it created had a cumulative effect on the
box-office: initial doubts that its cost would be
recouped changed to estimates of $50m. in
rentals, and by 1978 it was still drawing big
cinema crowds. Kubrick's direction and special
effects (which won an Academy Award) and,
with Arthur C. Clarke, script were enhanced
by a soundtrack which surprisingly featured
'The Blue Danube' and a bit of Richard Strauss'
'Thus Spake Zarathustra'; the latter became a
kind of theme tune for real space flights. Also
cast: Gary Lockwood as co-hero, a super-
computer named Hal as villain (with Douglas
Rain's voice), William Sylvester, Daniel Rich-
ter, Leonard Rossiter, Margaret Tyzack,
Robert Beatty, Sean Sullivan.

The other extreme of science fiction was **Battle**
Beneath the Earth/Battle Beneath the Sea, *a*
British flick about Chinese hordes tunnelling
below the Pacific with laser beams to plant
atom bombs under American cities. Wild, man.
Montgomery Tully directed, Charles Reynolds
and Charles Vetter Jr produced, L. Z. Har-
greaves wrote. The cast: Robert Ayres, Sarah
Brackett and Kerwin Mathews (here) and
Viviane Ventura, Peter Arne, Martin Benson,
Earl Cameron, Michael McStay, Carl Jaffe.

How to Steal the World *marked the end of*
'U.N.C.L.E.', with Eleanor Parker as the last
wicked victim of Robert Vaughn's and David
McCallum's THRUSH-crushing exploits;
Barry Sullivan, Leslie Nielsen, Tony Bill, Mark
Richman, Daniel O'Herlihy, Hugh Marlowe,
Ruth Warrick and Leo G. Carroll filled other
leads in Anthony Spinner's production, written
by Norman Hudis and directed by Sutton
Roley.

1970

Once again MGM got a hit-maker one movie removed from his hit: **Alex in Wonderland** was directed by Paul Mazursky, who'd had a winner in Bob & Carol & Ted & Alice. The new one was a disjointed study of a Hollywood director at loose ends, its brilliant moments insufficient to attract ticket-buying crowds. Donald Sutherland (here with Jeanne Moreau in one of two sequences shot on Hollywood Boulevard) made a long, difficult role look easy; Mazursky himself scintillated in a satirical sketch of a producer; Ellen Burstyn was fine as the director's wife. Larry Tucker produced and collaborated on the script with Mazursky.

Dirty Dingus Magee was one of Burt Kennedy's jolly Westerns and rowdier than most. Frank Sinatra (here with Michele Carey) had a high old time as a carefree outlaw in the Tom and Frank Waldman–Joseph Heller comedy from David Markson's novel, and its exhibitors enjoyed good response. Also cast: George Kennedy, Anne Jackson, Lois Nettleton, Jack Elam, John Dehner, Harry Carey Jr, Paul Fix.

Charming love scenes (including one in the obligatory Seventies' nude) between Sarah Miles and Christopher Jones relieved the otherwise sombre drama of **Ryan's Daughter**, David ▷ Lean's first film since Doctor Zhivago. With his usual background of war (the 1916 Irish revolt this time) it was essentially a simple triangle story of these two and Robert Mitchum as the village schoolmaster. Hence the public's expectation of another Lean super-epic—furthered by MGM's having to treat it as such in order to get back its incredible $12m. cost—was disappointed. Nevertheless, it was a splendidly acted, beautifully made picture, that won Oscars for John Mills' supporting performance as a hideous half-wit and Freddie Young's gorgeous photography. Trevor Howard, Leo McKern and Barry Foster had other leads in Robert Bolt's screenplay, produced by Anthony Havelock-Allan. MGM distribution could take bows during 1970–73 for reaping approximately double the cost of its prolonged 1969–70 production.

Kelly's Heroes was a hit in the USA and an ▷ outright smash in the UK and some other countries. The movie followed the wild adventures of Donald Sutherland, Clint Eastwood and Telly Savalas (left to right) along with Don Rickles, Carroll O'Connor, Hal Buckley, Stuart Margolin, Dick Davalos and other GIs robbing a bank behind the German lines. This was war? Troy Kennedy Martin wrote the Gabriel Katzka–Sidney Beckerman production, directed by Brian Hutton for slambang action.

Author Hugh Leonard's funny idea of a penis transplant was tediously developed in **Percy**, delivering little of what its subject matter promised to spice-seekers. 'Percy', the hero's coy name for his new organ, was never seen—mercifully or disappointingly, according to taste—but its box-office potency was decidedly

The year's most mixed-up family figured in **My Lover, My Son**, with Romy Schneider as mother giving son Dennis Waterman an incestuous come-on because she got him confused in her mind with her dead lover; sonny almost co-operated but instead went for a nude scene with Patricia Brake in a Thames houseboat; meanwhile father Donald Houston was bedding secretary Alexandra Bastedo, but came home in time for the big climax in which he got killed by Romy, who let Dennis think he'd done it, and do you remember the Hardy Family? Directed by John Newland, produced by Wilbur Stark, scripted by William Marchant and Jenni Hall from a story by Stark and a novel by Edward Grierson.

evident. Hywel Bennett was the recipient of the transplant, George Best (right) a footballer in a game Bennett imagined while searching for the identity of his member's original owner. Ralph Thomas' cast in the Betty Box EMI production also featured Elke Sommer, Britt Ekland, Denholm Elliott, Cyd Hayman, Janet Key, Patrick Mower, Pauline Delany, Adrienne Posta, Julia Foster.

British releases on both sides of the Atlantic increased; an average example in quality and drawing power was **The Walking Stick**—good, but not very good. David Hemmings and Samantha Eggar deftly played characters who were more interesting in themselves than in what they did: an introverted girl and a seductive thief. The robbery climax of George Bluestone's script, from Winston Graham's novel, missed much of its potential suspense. Emlyn Williams, Phyllis Calvert, Ferdy Mayne, Francesca Annis, Bridget Turner and Dudley Sutton were in the Elliot Kastner–Alan Ladd Jr production, directed by Eric Till.

After Easy Rider came out, American highways were crammed with leather-jacketed, black-glassed motorcycled wanderers aged 17, going on 30, who were either living life like it really is, man, or making more movies like Easy Rider. One of the latter. **Then Came Bronson**, was a television pilot released overseas with minimal box-office repercussions. Michael Parks played the drop-out and Bonnie Bedelia the pick-up, supported by Akim Tamiroff, Gary Merrill, Sheree North, Martin Sheen and Bert Freed. Written by Denne Bart Petticlerc, directed by William Graham, produced by Robert Justman.

Dark Shadows/House of Dark Shadows was brought up to date only by extra violence; otherwise all the old vampire clichés were on view in this hearse-opera based on a popular television series. Here Kathryn Leigh Scott, Joan Bennett and Louis Edmonds discover one of the movie's many corpses. Dan Curtis produced and directed the Sam Hall–Gordon Russell screenplay. Also cast: Grayson Hall, Jonathan Frid and Roger Davis.

Get Carter *went about as far as an 'X' would stretch. It lifted the lid on Newcastle, of all places, as a steaming sewer of violence and vice, with Michael Caine as a London racketeer seeking his brother's killer up north and (here) enjoying the co-operation of Geraldine Moffatt. A box office hit for writer-director Mike Hodges, produced by Michael Klinger, it featured John Osborne, Ian Hendry, Bryan Mosley, Britt Ekland, Glynn Edwards, Rosemarie Dunham, Terence Rigby and Bernard Hepton.*

The vogue for violence: 'First time I've had to fry a lady', said hot-seat operator Stacy Keach to murderess Mariana Hill in **The Traveling Executioner**, *which went into loving detail over the use of a 1918 electric chair that didn't always work. After a good deal of whoring and unofficial killing, he ended up in the chair himself, with his teen-age assistant Bud Cort throwing the switch. This fragrant nosegay was gathered by producer-director Jack Smight from author Garry Bateson and tossed to a wincing public, who ducked . . .*

Ex-star Cornel Wilde produced and directed **No Blade of Grass**, *a British contribution to MGM's share of the violence that filled the screens, but not always the cinemas, in 1970. The Sean Forestal–Jefferson Pascal screenplay was from John Christopher's novel. Wilde intended the tale of a future famine to be anti-pollution propaganda wrapped in exciting fiction, but it came out as conventional action melodrama. In this scene, Nigel Davenport, John Hamill and Anthony May arrive too late to save Jean Wallace and Lynne Frederick from some raping marauders.*

In **The Moonshine War** *the bullets flew as thick as when Warner Bros. had a franchise on the Prohibition era, but the public didn't seem to care any more. The movie starred Patrick McGoohan as a revenue agent and Richard Widmark as a bootlegger fighting over a booze-making still in Kentucky. Alan Alda, Lee Hazlewood, Will Geer, Melodie Johnson and Harry Carey Jr were in the Martin Ransohoff production, written by Elmore Leonard, directed by Richard Quine.*

DRUGS AND DREAMS
1971

MGM announced a healthy turnaround from 1970's operating loss; the 1971 operating profit was $7,835,000, which with further asset disposals of $8,523,000 brought the net income to $16,358,000 – the highest for 25 years.

Other companies prospered with the drug thriller *The French Connection*, the James Bond *Diamonds Are Forever*, the near-pornographic *Carnal Knowledge* and the nostalgic *Summer of '42*.

British payboxes were filled by spin-offs from television: *Dad's Army, On the Buses, Up Pompeii*, although cinemas had dwindled there to 1,529 (a third of their peak number) and attendances to 193m. *The French Connection*, its star Gene Hackman and director William Friedkin, and Jane Fonda in *Klute* took the Academy Awards. Walter Matthau, George C. Scott, Ali MacGraw and Sean Connery replaced Jack Lemmon, Barbra Streisand, Sidney Poitier and Katharine Hepburn in the Top Ten.

Production delays while producers Lester Perskey and Lewis Allen backed and filled about how close to the wind director Harvey Hart should sail with **Fortune and Men's Eyes** *resulted in this study of male homosexuality arriving well after the more entertaining* Boys in the Band *had pre-empted the subject's novelty value. The heartless story of a normal youth (Wendell Burton) debauched by a prison population incredibly devoted to sexual activities was filmed in a Quebec jail with, also incredibly, Canadian government assistance. Here aggressive hunter Zooey Hall and flam-* *boyant queen Michael Greer appraise the new fish in their tank. Greer, who played the same role on the stage, and Danny Freedman, as a pathetic cellmate, were outstanding. Script was by John Herbert from his Broadway play.*

The Boy Friend, *Sandy Wilson's little satire of Twenties musical comedies, with pretty tunes and ingenuous story, was staged in London originally in 1953 and became an international smash. MGM bought screen rights in 1956, but producers were afraid of its sheer simplicity; such a famous property had to be a BIG movie – but how? Lap-dissolve to 1971, London again; enter writer-director-producer Ken Russell, afraid of nothing. He gave the original show a backstage story outside the story, superimposed on the Twenties stage spoof a satire of Thirties movie musicals in the Busby Berkeley style, and added some Freed–Brown hits from the MGM music library. It was all brilliantly done and overdone. Here ex-model phenomenon Twiggy (disarmingly amateur) and ex-ballet star Christopher Gable are singing 'I Could Be Happy with You'. In an exuberant supporting cast Tommy Tune did a sensational Charleston and Glenda Jackson an unbilled bit; also Max Adrian, Brian Pringle, Murray Melvin, Moyra Fraser, Georgina Hale, Barbara Windsor. Box-office was patchy.*

Soylent Green *was Edward G. Robinson's last* ▽ *movie; he died in 1973, 50 years after his film debut and 80 after his birth. This original thriller pictured the horrendous future of a New York in which pollution and over-population had made everything scarce except people. Harry Harrison's story, scripted by Stanley Greenberg, hinged on the discovery by hero Charlton Heston (here cornering Chuck Connors) that the staple food for the masses, processed by a monopoly, was made from human corpses. Strong action and mob scenes; lively box-office response. Also cast: Leigh Taylor-Young, Joseph Cotten, Brock Peters, Paula Kelly, Mike Henry, Roy Jenson, Whit Bissell, Celia Lovsky. Director, Richard Fleischer; production, Walter Seltzer, Russell Thacher.*

The Man Who Loved Cat Dancing *had lots going for it: it was a love story combined with Western action, from a current best-seller (by Marilyn Durham), and starred Burt Reynolds and Sarah Miles, who received acres of news space when location filming was*

Trader Horn *was a remake of the 1930 epic in name and locale only. Every possible (and impossible) African jungle cliché was crammed into the tale as Rod Taylor quelled villainous natives, various beasts and detachments of the British and German armies in the unintentionally funny William Norton–Edward Harper screenplay. It was directed by Reza Badiyi after a fashion, produced by Lewis Rachmil. Also cast: Anne Heywood, Jean Sorel, Don Knight.*

*Black power was declining at the box-office, even for the third Shaft punch-up, **Shaft in Africa**, and the series continued on television. Richard Roundtree (here with most of the well-developed Neda Arneric) was cast with Frank Finlay, Vonetta McGee and Marne Maitland; directed by John Guillermin; produced by Roger Lewis; written by Stirling Silliphant . . . Also aboard ship in momentary non-violence were Jim Brown and Judy Pace in **The Slams** (meaning prison; also the reviews it got) a jail-break caper directed by Jonathan Kaplan; produced by Gene Corman; written by Richard Adams. Also cast: Roland Harris, Paul E. Harris and Frank de Kova.*

interrupted by the strange death of her male secretary. But the MGM paybox jinx was still on. Richard Sarafin directed and Martin Poll produced with Eleanor Perry, who wrote the script. Left to right: Miss Miles, Bo Hopkins, Reynolds; also cast were George Hamilton, Jack Warden, Lee J. Cobb, Robert Donner, Larry Littlebird, Jay Silverheels.

*Robert Ryan co-starred in **The Outfit**, his 80th and next-to-last movie: he died in 1973, aged 64. Here Robert Duvall forces information from Felice Orlandi, watched by Karen Black in this tough thriller about one man's war on a crime organization to avenge his brother's murder. Also in Carter DeHaven's production, written (from Richard Stark's novel) and directed by John Flynn: Joe Don Baker, Sheree North, Timothy Carey, Richard Jaeckel, Jane Greer, Marie Windsor, Elisha Cook Jr, Roy Roberts, Emile Meyer, Roy Jenson, singer Anita O'Day, boxer Archie Moore, tennist Tony Trabert.*

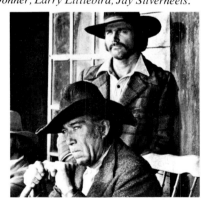

*The exploits of the gun-totin' pair featured in **Deaf Smith and Johnny Ears** were less out of the ordinary than their movie's title. The one novelty in its Texas turmoil, Italian style, was a deaf-mute hero (Anthony Quinn) whose affliction didn't prevent him and his younger pal (Franco Nero) from wiping out an entire garrison of baddies. Oscar Saul and Harry Essex, heading a posse of Italian writers, provided a script in which action fortunately precluded much dubbed dialogue. Director, Paolo Cavara; producers, Joseph Janni and Luciano Perugia; heroine, Pamela Tiffin.*

GOLDEN ENTERTAINMENT
1974

On January 4 the MGM Grand Hotel, Las Vegas, completed its first month of operation and reported capacity bookings. The world's largest resort hotel, with 2,084 rooms, it cost $120m. (estimated cost when construction started in April 1972 was $90m.) and had advance reservations into 1982.

Universal won its first best picture Academy Award since 1930's *All Quiet On The Western Front* with *The Sting*, which took seven Oscars altogether, including one to director George Roy Hill. Jack Lemmon in *Save the Tiger* was elected best actor and Glenda Jackson in *A Touch of Class* best actress. MGM won nothing, had few films on current release via its new distributors, and fewer imminent. But the 50th anniversary of the studio's opening on April 26th, 1924, was celebrated in the light of new President Frank E. Rosenfelt's statement: 'One of our principal objectives will be to provide a climate at MGM which will attract creative film-makers . . . Contrary to recent public speculation, the roar of Leo the Lion will not be reduced to a weak meow.'

The Super Cops *looked like the wildest fiction; actually it told the true story of two New York crime-crushers who racked up a record total of arrests and convictions in the tough, drug-ridden ghetto of Bedford-Stuyvesant. Nick-named 'Batman and Robin' by the press, they are Dave Greenberg and Bob Hantz, seen here in the background in minor roles, with David Selby as Hantz and Ron Leibman as Greenberg in the foreground. The script by Lorenzo Semple Jr (from L. H. Whittemore's book) and direction by Gordon Parks gave the William Belasco production cartoon-like speed and violence. Sheila Frazier, Pat Hingle, Dan Frazer and Joseph Sirola were featured.*

During 1974 Michelangelo Antonioni made his third film for MGM, produced by Carlo Ponti for 1975 release. **The Passenger** *had his usual fascinating ambiguities draped around a sturdy framework constructed by 25-year-old English writer Mark Peploe. Jack Nicholson, at the top of his profession after a succession of hits from* Easy Rider *to* Chinatown, *starred as a disenchanted television journalist taking*

on the identity of a look-alike dead man –and his surprising past. Here he encounters Maria Schneider (the Last Tango in Paris *girl), playing a nameless hippie who stayed to share his new life. Ian Hendry and Jennie Runacre had other leads in the drama, filmed in Spain, Algeria, Germany and England.*

Kazablan *was made in Tel Aviv with Israeli star Yehoram Gaon (centre) leading an all-singing, all-dancing. all-chutzpah street gang. High spirits, low grosses. Menahem Golan produced, directed and (with Haim Hefer) scripted the jolly Jewish musical.*

A contract for Dean Martin to headline at the MGM Grand Hotel included a movie commitment, so he made **Mr Ricco**. *They loved him in Las Vegas, but not in this minor murder melo, directed by Paul Bogart, scripted by Robert Hoban, produced by former MGM vice-president Douglas Netter. Thalmus Rasulala shared this brawl with him and featured billing with Cindy Williams, Geraldine Brooks, Eugene Roche, Philip Thomas, Denise Nicholas.*

That's Entertainment *was a rousing tribute to the first 50 MGM years and a heartening pace-setter for the second. It was completed in time for a May 1974 première and the most enthusiastic reception for any of the company's movies in years. Musical highlights from MGM's vast archives were dovetailed into a 132-minute feature written, directed and produced by Jack Haley Jr under the aegis of the studio's production chief, Daniel Melnick. Linked by newly filmed introductions and voice-over comments by Fred Astaire (seen in his astonishing walls-and-ceiling dance in* Royal Wedding*), Bing Crosby, Gene Kelly, Peter Lawford, Liza Minnelli, Donald O'Connor, Debbie Reynolds, Mickey Rooney, Frank Sinatra, James Stewart and Elizabeth Taylor, the excerpts made a dazzling show. Above, Jean Harlow in* Reckless. *Below, Deanna Durbin and Judy Garland in their film debut, the short* Every Sunday. *'While many may ponder the future of Metro-Goldwyn-Mayer', said* Variety *in its rave review, 'nobody can deny that it has one hell of a past!'*

RECORDS GO BOOM
1975

Inflation? Unemployment? International crises? 'Forget 'em and go to the movies' was one public reaction, especially in the USA and Canada, where cinema income reached $2 billion, the all-time high. More encouraging yet, the number of tickets sold was the highest for 12 years. Universal's *Jaws* chewed a big chunk of that total, becoming the greatest money-maker ever released (of course, thanks partly to ever-rising seat prices), with *The Towering Inferno, Earthquake, Young Frankenstein, The Godfather Part 2, Shampoo,* the British *Murder on the Orient Express* and *Tommy* among the runners-up in 1975 prosperity.

MGM joined the record-breaking spree: net profits ($31,862,000) were the best in the company's history. Over a third of the operating income came from feature films, despite the scarcity of new product–striking proof that the scrapping of distribution had worked. The remainder came from the MGM Grand, Las Vegas, now believed to be the most profitable hotel in the world.

Moviegoers often shun movies about movies. So **Hearts of the West**/Hollywood Cowboy, *with Jeff Bridges (Academy-nominated for his work in* The Last Picture Show*) as a B-picture cowboy softening crusty production manager Blythe Danner, was praised for its evocation of 1930s Hollywood but met box-office apathy. Andy Griffith, Donald Pleasence and Alan Arkin were others in Rob Thompson's warm comedy, directed by Howard Zieff and produced by Tony Bill, the young actor who made it big as a producer with* The Sting.

Completed as the year ended, **That's Entertainment, Part 2** *was planned by studio topper Daniel Melnick as a sequel in spirit to the previous year's winner, and more than that in substance. Along with musicals from MGM's bulging storehouse of golden oldies, some of its most renowned 'straight' successes were also represented (that still of Garbo and Taylor in* Camille *at the top of this set is indicative), and a good deal of new material was filmed under the direction of Gene Kelly, here reunited with Fred Astaire. In short–nostalgia, plus. Saul Chaplin, long a contributor to Leo's musicals (he won Oscars for* An American in Paris *and* 7 Brides for 7 Brothers*) co-produced with Melnick.*

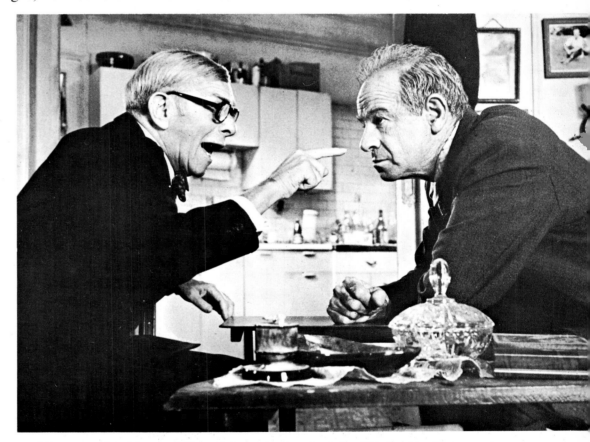

Sean Connery in **The Wind and the Lion** *had one of his best parts since turning in his 007 badge. As the last of the Barbary Pirates, he played a 1904 forerunner of today's terrorists kidnapping an American woman (Candice Bergen) in Morocco and making huge ransom demands on President Theodore Roosevelt (Brian Keith). John Milius directed his screenplay in Spain, with emphasis on spectacular action; Herb Jaffe produced; John Huston co-starred. MGM and Columbia collaborated in its making (a new Hollywood idea that once*

would have given L.B. Mayer and Harry Cohn coronaries) and shared its income. This split-the-risk procedure on an expensive project was also followed on the 20th Century-Fox/Warner Bros. Towering Inferno.

△ *A geriatric joy,* **The Sunshine Boys** *scored a resounding hit for the company and for Walter Matthau (right) and George Burns (returning to the screen at, incredibly, 79). Their character studies of ex-vaudeville partners who loved to hate each other were comedy acting of the richest quality, relished by critics and crowds alike. Director Herbert Ross smartly paced the laugh-peppered dialogue of Neil Simon, who scripted from his Broadway success, and producer Ray Stark gave it show-biz authenticity via New York location filming.*

GETTING GRANDER
1976

'New all-time highs for both income and gross revenues' was the 1976 report from MGM President Rosenfelt, forgivably bragging about a profit of $35,557,000. Biggest money-spinner in Leo's corporate empire was again the Grand Hotel, Las Vegas; so much so, that construction was begun on another giant hotel/casino, the MGM Grand, Reno, aimed for completion in 1978. And the studio announced a future remake of the 1932 all-starrer *Grand Hotel*, to be filmed at the Vegas palace. Also scheduled: what happened next to Scarlett and Rhett in a sequel to *Gone With The Wind*. The latter, still producing world-wide cinema income in 1976, broke all film-on-TV records with a USA viewership of 110m. in November. George Burns in *The Sunshine Boys* won one of the few Oscars not collected by *One Flew Over the Cuckoo's Nest* the year's top hits, along with *The Omen*, *All the President's Men*, *Silent Movie* and *Taxi Driver*.

No shock value left in 4-letter words, so **Norman . . . is that You?** *turned to 13-letter ones like miscegenation and homosexuality as subjects for rowdy comedy. Redd Foxx and Pearl Bailey starred as the perplexed parents of a fine brown son whose bedmate was not only white but male. The latter was played by Dennis Dugan, seen here with Tamara Dobson as a lady of the evening Dad hopefully presented to Norman (Michael Warren). Ron Clark and Sam Bobrick, authors of the Broadway flop it came from, collaborated on the script with producer-director George Schlatter, who filmed it on teletape to unlovely effect. Critics frowned and Metro accountants beamed: it took $4m. in its first month on release.*

Fang and claw in the TV jungle: Robert Duvall, Faye Dunaway and William Holden as three of the power-driven executives in the brilliant Paddy Chayevsky script for **Network***, MGM's most acclaimed 1976 creation (co-produced with United Artists). Hectic to the point of hysteria, it seemed about to fly off into noisy chaos at times, but director Sidney Lumet never lost sight of the sharp and bitter points it had to make. A fourth fine starring performance came from Peter Finch (his last); Wesley Addy, Ned Beatty, Beatrice Straight, Marlene Warfield and ex-child actor Darryl Hickman supported in Howard Gottfried's handsome production.*

Stockard Channing, whose off-beat heroines enlivened The Fortune *and* The Big Bus *and made her the comedienne discovery of 1976, became an arresting dramatic performer too in* **Sweet Revenge***. With Franklyn Ajaye as her black friend and fellow felon, she played a car-stealing hippie. Sam Waterston co-starred as her lawyer in the B. J. Perla story scripted with Marilyn Goldin. Jerry Schatzberg produced and directed, eschewing the over-exposed roads of Los Angeles and San Francisco to show Seattle traffic in this one, which got no green light from its Cannes Festival preview audience; a detour back to the studio for revisions ensued.*

Richard Jordan, the hunter, and Jenny Agutter and Michael York, the hunted, in **Logan's Run***,* △ *a science-fiction spectacular that had to go some to get back its cost. One of its huge 23rd century sets filled the largest sound stage in the world, MGM's No. 15; another needed two stages tunneled together; stunning special effects abounded; the credits bristled with items like Laser Consultant, Kenworthy Snorkel Camera Systems, Todd-AO, Holograms by Multiplex. But David Z. Goodman's script from a William Nolan–George Johnson novel soon ran out of bright ideas and settled for a prolonged chase ending in the ruins of the U.S. Senate, inhabited by dozens of cats and Peter Ustinov, sole survivors (unexplained) from our civilization. Michael Anderson directed the Saul David production, with Roscoe Lee Browne, Farrah Fawcett-Majors and Michael Anderson Jr. in his cast.*

Another sci-fi dazzler set in a nearer future, **Demon Seed** *had Julie Christie coping with emotional scenes that might have made Bernhardt quail, since they had to be acted against assorted electronic hardware. Such as an all-seeing TV eye – here displaying Gerrit Graham – and a berserk computer which, rashly over-equipped by her inventor husband (Fritz Weaver), sort of raped her. And that's how variations of the Frankenstein legend are born. Berry Kroeger, John O'Leary and Larry Blake were also in the excellent Herb Jaffe production, adapted by son Robert Jaffe from Dean Koontz's novel, directed by Donald Cammell and designed by MGM's thrice-Oscared veteran, Edward Carfagno.*

GOODBYE RECORDS
1977

Jubilee time! Britain celebrated the Queen's 25th anniversary; Hollywood the 50th of talking pictures, and it was golden indeed. Film business broke all records, thanks partly to the astounding draw of *Star Wars*. Among this unprecedented hit's nearest rivals (but well behind) were *A Star is Born*, *The Spy Who Loved Me*, *King Kong* and *The Deep*, all more commercially than artistically notable, and two which were both: *Rocky* and *Network*. They shared the major Academy Awards, *Network* bringing four to MGM, for players Peter Finch (posthumously), Faye Dunaway and Beatrice Straight and writer Paddy Chayefsky. With all its divisions increasing profits, MGM had another record year. And Leo's ego received a further fillip from the American Film Institute, whose 35,000 members voted *Gone With The Wind* 'the greatest American film of all time', and *The Wizard of Oz*, *Singin' in the Rain* and *2001: A Space Odyssey* also in the first ten.

By the end of its first year of distribution by co-sponsor Warner Bros. **The Goodbye Girl** *had become MGM's third highest-ever money maker in America, topped only by* Gone With the Wind *and* Zhivago. *Quite a feat for a small-scale comedy. But it had the Midas touch, also the gift of combining warmth with wit, of author Neil Simon, who throws out stage and screen hits like confetti. Marsha Mason (his wife) and Richard Dreyfuss (Academy Award, best actor) were superb as unwilling flat-mates; so was Quinn Cummings as her alarmingly perceptive daughter, the only other big part. Like Simon's* The Sunshine Boys, *it was directed by Herbert Ross and produced by Ray Stark.*

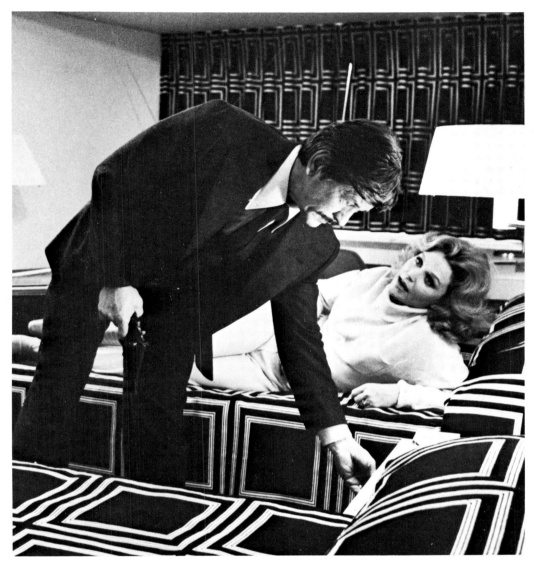

Telefon *pulled the neat trick of making an American spy story's hero (Charles Bronson) as Russian as its villain (Donald Pleasence), thus maintaining detente. It didn't maintain box-office profits too well, however, despite the added attraction of Lee Remick, here with Bronson. Don Siegel directed the Peter Hyams-Stirling Silliphant suspenser, from Walter Wager's novel. James B. Harris produced. Tyne Daly, Patrick Magee, Sheree North acted.*

Mark Hamill, star of Star Wars, *had only a jazzed-up sports car instead of galactic gadgets in* **Corvette Summer**/The Hot One. *Plus a fetching new girl, Annie Potts. But this youthful comedy, shot in Los Angeles and Las Vegas in*

1977, scored surprisingly strongly in 1978. Matthew Robbins directed and Hal Barwood produced their own breezy screenplay.

Those corpses dangling from the ceiling weren't the only people kept in suspense by **Coma**. *Its audiences had a fine nail-gnawing time watching Genevieve Bujold flee for dear life through a hospital where the anesthetics were terminal. A brilliantly clever thriller, and a big hit. Michael Douglas, Elizabeth Ashley, Richard Widmark and Rip Torn had other leads in Martin Erlichman's production, written and directed by Michael Crichton, from Robin Cook's novel.*

AGAIN THE CHAMP
1978

Once more, glad tidings from the MGM accountants: the year's profits totalled $49,341,000 easily the company's highest ever. Up went the film rentals, the laboratory income (7 million feet of film processed weekly), the television revenue, and – oh, yes, the hotel/casino gross, a cool $219m. A chunk of that hotel fortune came from the new MGM Grand, Reno, which opened on May 3rd. It has only 1,015 rooms, against twice as many in the MGM Grand, Las Vegas, but it does have the world's largest casino, gigantic stage shows in the Ziegfeld Room, a 2,000-seat tennis pavilion, a 50-lane bowling alley, 7 restaurants, 40 shops, 145 acres of ground . . . and a cinema.

Woody Allen's *Annie Hall* won Oscars. An old Hollywood legend revived when an unknown actor skyrocketed to superstardom: John Travolta in *Saturday Night Fever* and *Grease*. Also big were *Heaven Can Wait*, *Close Encounters of the Third Kind* and *Jaws 2*.

Was General 'Blood and Guts' Patton's death in 1945 really an accident? No – a plot! said **Brass Target**, *and the Arthur Lewis–Berle Adams production proceeded to get enmeshed in so much plot that excitement waned after a rousing robbery sequence early on. John Cassavetes, Sophia Loren, Max von Sydow, George Kennedy (as Patton), Patrick McGoohan, Robert Vaughn, Bruce Davison, Edward Herrman were directed by John Hough in the Alvin Boretz drama developed from Frederick Nolan's book,* The Algonquin Project.

Few exhibitors were living on velvet when they played Bryan Forbes' sequel to National Velvet, *which had made Elizabeth Taylor a star in 1944.* **International Velvet**, *the first MGM British film in six years, was painstakingly directed and beautifully produced by Forbes, but his script lost impetus on its way to an equestrian Olympics climax. Warm performances by Christopher Plummer and Tatum O'Neal (here), Anthony Hopkins, Nanette Newman (Mrs. Forbes, splendid as the original Taylor character grown up), Peter Barkworth, Dinsdale Landen, Jeffrey Byron. Seemed that people demanding wholesome movies were too busy writing to newspapers.*

For the first time, James Caan took on the double load of director and star in **Hide in Plain Sight**. *Here he is shown directing. This brisk little drama, based on fact by Leslie Waller and scripted by Spencer Eastman, concerned a man's search for his children, hidden by the US Government along with their mother and her new husband because the latter was an informer against crime czars. Aside from Caan, the Bob Christiansen–Rick Rosenberg production had a new-faces cast, headed by Jill Eikenberry, Robert Viharo, Barbra Rae.*

In the 47 years since **The Champ** *became a record-breaker and an Oscar-winner for author Frances Marion and star Wallace Beery, MGM used various versions of its basic story. But the first full remake was a major 1978 effort giving production chief Richard Shepherd and everyone else at the studio high hopes for history repeating in 1979. Franco Zeffirelli made his Hollywood directorial debut with the updated Spencer Eastman–Walter Newman script. Dyson Lovell, long an associate of Zeffirelli, produced. Jon Voight starred as the boxer making a comeback for his son (Ricky Schroder, the most appealing child actor to turn up in many a year) with Faye Dunaway as his wife; plus Jack Warden, Arthur Hill, Joan Blondell, Sam Levene, Elisha Cook Jr.*

The first movie made entirely in New Jersey since the silent days, **Voices** *was shot on a small budget in Newark – hardly the most romantic of cities. But it might have been Verona for the aspiring young singer and the deaf girl whose love story was played by newcomers Michael Outkean and Amy Irving. Alex Rocco, Barry Miller, Herbert Berghof and Viveca Lindfors supported them in Joseph Wizan's production, written by John Herzfeld, directed by Robert Markowitz.*

TWO FOR ONE
1979-1980

Production activity was at the lowest ebb in MGM's history during much of this period, but there was a flood tide coming. At the beginning of 1980 plans were laid for establishing an annual release total of 12 to 15 feature films, and David Begelman, former Columbia topper, was signed to supervise them. At the same time $20,000,000 was earmarked for studio additions and improvements during 1980–1. And in May 1980 the company was split into two separate corporations: Metro-Goldwyn-Mayer Film Co. (with Begelman as President, Frank Rosenfelt moving up to Chairman of the Board) and MGM Grand Hotels Inc. The former retained, of course, its name of 56 years' fame, MGM.

The Empire Strikes Back, sequel to the all-time record holder *Star Wars*, was the industry's biggest money-maker of 1979–80, with *Superman* not far behind. But the most highly praised were unspectacular family dramas: *Kramer vs. Kramer*, which won 5 major Oscars for '79, and *Ordinary People*, which took 4 for '80, including Robert Redford's first try at directing.

A down-to-earth Superman with no superhuman powers, **Hero At Large** *was a lovable character. TV star John Ritter (son of the famous singing cowboy Tex Ritter), played a struggling young actor hired to publicize a movie hero, Captain Avenger, which inspired him with an urge to rush to the aid of anyone in danger. The A. J. Carothers original, directed by Martin Davidson and produced by Stephen Friedman, was enhanced by New York location shooting and the performance of Anne Archer (here with Ritter), another second-generation talent: her parents, John Archer and Marjorie Lord, played many leads in the 40s and 50s. Kevin McCarthy, Bert Convy and Harry Bellaver also scored.*

Greeted by rude remarks from the critics and a salvo of silence from the box-office, **The Formula** *nevertheless boasted an intriguing story premise – the alleged conspiracy to suppress a method of mass manufacture of a fuel oil substitute – plus a fine cast and grade A production at Berlin and Culver City studios. Steve Shagan's novel, scripted and produced for the screen by himself, dealt with a synthetic oil formula which kept Germany fuelled through World War II and which then disappeared. Was the complex narrative's transfer from book to film an unwieldy task, or did something go wrong with the final cut? Anyway, audiences were too often left won-*

dering what the devil was going on. George C. Scott, here with Marthe Keller, co-starred with Marlon Brando (his first at MGM since the 1962 Mutiny on the Bounty*), supported by John Gielgud, G. D. Spradlin, Beatrice Straight, Richard Lynch, John van Dreelen, Robin Clarke. John G. Avildsen directed.*

Crazed killer Tom Rolfing clutches Caitlin O'Heaney by the throat as she reaches for a dissecting knife in **He Knows You're Alone***, a shrieker that kept knuckle-biting fans in transports of vicarious terror. Scott Parker's script had the fiend pursuing our heroine through a hospital morgue, a church, an amusement park and an art-deco movie palace, while beheading and slicing other innocent citizens en route. Director Armand Mastroianni, a young American cousin of Marcello making his feature debut, shot it in New York's Staten Island. Don Scardino and Elizabeth Kemp had leads in the new-faces cast; George Manasse produced. Well done, in an overdone genre.*

Many notable names bedecked the credit titles of **Sunday Lovers***, an MGM pick-up from Paris-based Leo L. Fuchs's Viaduc Productions. It consisted of separate tales about frustrated Lotharios in four countries: England, with LynnRedgrave, Roger Moore, Priscilla Barnes (here, r. to l.) and Denholm Elliott, directed by Bryan Forbes in a Leslie Bricusse script; France, with Lino Ventura, Robert Webber, Catherine Salviat, directed by Edouard Molinaro; Italy, with Ugo Tognazzi, Rosanna Podesta, Catherine Spaak, Sylva Koscina, directed by Dino Risi; and USA, with Gene Wilder, Kathleen Quinlan, Dianne Crittenden, directed by Wilder from his script. The credits were the best part.*

Two young performers with a talent for characterization in depth demonstrated it in **Why Would I Lie?***, but the question got a dusty answer from the ticket-buying public. Treat Williams starred as a compulsive fantasy-spinner whose job of social worker involved him in a tricky search for the mother of an adopted 7-year-old boy. Lisa Eichhorn played a withdrawn girl who blossomed into love for both man and boy. Treat (a hit in* Hair *and* 1941*), Lisa (memorable in* Yanks *and* The Europeans*) and young Gabriel Swann (with them here) deserved more than the mild response the new movie drew, as did Larry Peerce's direction of the Pancho Kohner production, a Peter Stone screenplay from Hollis Hodges's novel 'The Fabricator'.*

Wow! or words to that effect were elicited from practically everybody when Gene Anthony Ray and Carol Massenburg went into their dance in **Fame**. They, and what looked like hundreds of other young dancers, singers, musicians and – not least – actors, performed with an elan unsurpassed even in the Rooney–Garland heyday. They played pupils at New York's real High School of the Performing Arts, director Alan Parker focusing on eight of them (Ray, Maureen Teefy, Paul McCrane, Irene Cara, Barry Miller, Lee Curreri, Laura Dean, Antonia Franceschi) for interwoven stories of success, failure and love. A small miracle was the capture of Manhattan's atmosphere, in all its tawdry confusion and exhilarating glamour, by a largely British team: Parker, producer Alan Marshall, photography director Michael Seresin, designer Geoffrey Kirkland, editor Gerry Hambling and cameraman John Stanier. Writer Christopher Gore and co-producer David De Silva headed their brilliant collaborators; composer Michael Gore won two Oscars, for best original score and best song, 'Fame' with lyrics by Dean Pitchford. A Fame series for TV ensued.

LIVING DANGEROUSLY
1983

Profits for the joint company climbed to a peak of $42 million. Plainly the merger had saved both UA and MGM for extinction. UA, the slightly more productive partner, released nine movies to MGM's five; these included *War Games* and the 13th helping of agent 007 in *Octopussy*, served up to the insatiable Bond-hungry public. MGM's risk in financing the Australian movie, *The Year Of Living Dangerously*, paid off, but $20 million was squandered on *Brainstorm*, Natalie Wood's last picture, completed after her death.

This was also the year of two big sequels, *Return of the Jedi* (Lucasfilm/Fox), the completion of the *Star Wars* trilogy, and *Indiana Jones And The Temple Of Doom* (Lucasfilm/Fox), two of the six George Lucas and Steven Spielberg movies in the top ten grossers of all time. Two other films followed in their wake, *Star Trek III–The Search For Spock* (Paramount) and *Romancing The Stone* (20th Century-Fox).

Little Linda Hunt carried off the Best Supporting Actress Oscar for *The Year Of Living Dangerously* in the midst of the five that went to *Terms of Endearment* (Paramount).

At the centre of **Brainstorm** is a machine that records emotions and physical sensations so that others can relive them through playback. The inventors are research scientists Christopher Walken and Louise Fletcher, who want to use it in the exact understanding of how other people feel, but a group of heavies in the Pentagon want it for psychological warfare. Producer-director Douglas Trumbull, the man who created the impressive effects for Close Encounters of the Third Kind and Blade Runner, this time buried himself in technology to the detriment of the plot and the characters. On the Super Panavision screen, audiences were supposed to experience sex, romantic love and even dying. The film was dedicated to Natalie Wood, whose untimely death by drowning occurred before shooting was complete. It is sad that her last role, as Walkden's wife, should have given her so little to do except observe the events and look beautiful. Also cast in this botched sci-fi picture, written by Robert Stitzel and Philip Frank Messina, were Cliff Robertson, Jordan Christopher, Donald Hotton, Alan Fudge, Joe Dorsey and Bill Morey.

Sultry Brazilian sexpot Sonia Braga was **Gabriela**, the main attraction in the cacao-rich town of Ilheus in 1925, as well as being the centre of this Ibrahim Moussa and Harold Nebenzal production. In the mid-'70s, a serialized soap opera version of Jorge Amado's novel Gabriela, Clove and Cinnamon, starring the sensual Braga, broke all TV-rating records in Brazil. MGM bought the screen rights and got Leopoldo Serran and Bruno Baretto to adapt it to feature-film proportions, with Barreto directing. Marcello Mastroianni was cast as the middle-aged bar-owner who marries Gabriela with the mistaken idea that she would remain faithful. Lacking the satiric edge of the book, it was nevertheless an amiable enough raunchy romantic comedy with easy-on-the-eye Brazilian scenery, thanks to Carlo di Palma's photography, easy-on-the-ear samba music by Antonio Carlos Jobin and Gal Costa, and pleasant performances from the two leads, supported by Antonio Cantafora, Ricardo Petraglia, Paulo Goulart and Antonio Pedro.

Small town Indiana in the 1940s was the setting for **A Christmas Story**, based by screenwriters Jean Shepherd, Leigh Brown and Bob Clark on radio humorist Shepherd's novel, In God We Trust, All Others Pay Cash. *It tells of a nine-year-old boy's overwhelming desire to own a Genuine Red Ryder Carbine Action Air Rifle, and the ruses he devises to persuade his parents (Melinda Dillon and Darren McGavin) to give it to him as a present. Peter Billingsley winningly portrayed the bespectacled kid, with good support coming from Ian Peterella, Scott Schwartz, R. D. Robb, Tedde Moore, Yano Anaya, Zack Ward, Jeff Gillen and Colin Fox. Difficult to believe that the Bob Clark who directed this warm-hearted picture, had given the world the crass* Porky's *the previous year. Clark also produced with Rene DuPont.*

1983

The pop group Bauhaus sang 'Bela Lugosi is Dead' at a nightclub in **The Hunger**, a vampire movie which must have had the old Hollywood Dracula turning in his grave. A chic mixture of rock video, softcore porn, and blood-letting, written by Ivan Davis and Michael Thomas (from the novel by Whitley Streiber), it paired, in a slightly unlikely partnership, the immaculate Catherine Deneuve with rock star David Bowie. The two stars, acting as immortal lovers, live off the blood of innocents whom they attract to their New York apartment. After Bowie, in a hideous transformation, ages 200 years in 20 minutes while being kept in Dr Susan Sarandon's waiting room (we know how he feels!), Deneuve, after centuries of heterosexuality, turns her desires towards the more appealing prospect of the lady doctor. TV commercial maker Tony Scott, younger brother of Ridley 'Alien' Scott, directed this turkey for producer Richard A. Shepherd. Cliff De Young, Beth Ehlers, Dan Hedaya, Rufus Collins, Suzanne Bertish, James Aubrey, Ann Magnuson, John Stephen Hill, Shane Rimmer, Bessie Love, and Willem Dafoe (in one of his first roles) were other members of the cast.

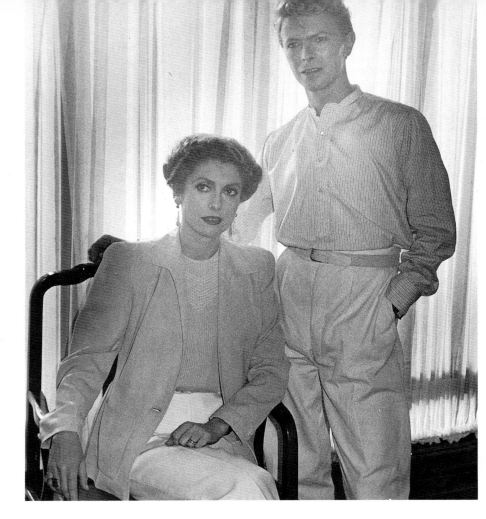

Nineteen sixty-five was **The Year of Living Dangerously** in Indonesia, leading up to the events of September 30, when the dictatorial President Sukarno was deposed in a military coup. Living dangerously were Mel Gibson, rookie Australian foreign correspondent, Sigourney Weaver, attaché at the British embassy, with whom he falls in love, and a dwarfish Chinese-Australian cameraman,

Billy, unusually and trumphantly played by Linda Hunt, who won the Best Supporting Actress for her male role; also Bill Kerr, Bembol Guzman, Michael Murphy, Noel Ferrier, Paul Sonkkila, Ali Nur and Dominador Robridillo. This first Australian picture to be wholly financed by a major Hollywood studio was directed with great virtuosity by Peter Weir, who vividly captured the tense atmos-

phere of the public happenings as a background to a love story in the best traditions of Hollywood romance in exotic climes. The screenplay by Weir, David Williamson and C. J. Koch had the ring of truth for most of the way, until the climax when Gibson's heroics began to strain credibility. The James McElroy production was shot on location in the Philippines.

ALL QUIET ON THE MGM FRONT

1984

MGM/UA began to descend in 1984 from the peak of the previous year. Output fell pretty sharply, too. MGM released a mere three pictures, of which *2010* cost the gigantic sum of $28 million, only managing to recover $20 million in US rentals. It was also a lean year for its twin company, not having a *Rocky* or a James Bond to bring any smiles to the accountant's faces. Needless to say, MGM/UA did not feature among either the box-office or Oscar winners. *Ghostbusters* (Columbia), *Gremlins* (Warner Bros.), *Beverly Hills Cop* (Paramount) and *Police Academy* (Warner Bros.) were the purely commercial hits, while *Amadeus* (Zaentz/Orion), *The Killing Fields* (Goldcrest/Warner Bros.) and *A Passage to India* (Warner Bros.) got the plaudits and awards.

Handsome, brooding, curly-haired Aidan Quinn in **Reckless** *was the latest of juvenile screen rebels in the long line descending from James Dean. (He was considered for Martin Scorsese's Jesus in* The Last Temptation Of Christ.) *As a motor-cycling youth from the wrong side of the tracks—in the screenplay by Chris Colombus—he falls for pretty, pouting, blonde rich girl Daryll Hannah, who drives around Steeltown, West Virginia in a white Cadillac. Her mother (Lois Smith) disapproves of the affair, as does her dull boyfriend (Adam Baldwin), and Quinn is in conflict with his father (Kenneth McMillan). Debutant director James Foley treated it all with surface energy and sheen, helped by German photographer Michael Ballhaus. Best moment in Edgar J. Scherick and Scott Rudin's production was at the prom when Quinn and Hannah dance energetically to Kim Wilde's 'Kids In America'. Others cast were Cliff De Young, Dan Hedaya, Billy Jacoby and Tony Kalem.*

Space travellers Robert Ulrich, Michael D. Roberts, Anjelica Huston and John Matuszak were **The Ice Pirates**, *who swashbucklingly descend on other planets in order to steal water, by now a rare and precious liquid. Piratical, too, were screenwriters Stewart Raffill and Stanford Sherman and director Raffill in their filching of ideas from* Star Wars *and* Alien, *among other sci-fi epics, and in*

throwing in an attempted parody of Errol Flynn sword-play pictures. The humans, apart from Mary Crosby's pert and pretty Princess Karina, were far less animated than the humanoids. Natalie Core, as the Princess's nanny, Ron Perlman, a smooth villain and John Carradine, the dying Supreme Commander, were the other non-robots in John Foreman's production.

Although **2010** *was set almost a decade after* 2001: A Space Odyssey, *it was 16 years since Stanley Kubrick's landmark science fiction movie. The costly ($28 million) follow-up, based on Arthur C. Clarke's sequel to* The Sentinel, *the short story that inspired the original movie, concerned a team of Soviet and American scientists, led respectively by Helen Mirren and Roy Scheider, on a mission to Jupiter where they hope to learn the fate of the spaceship Discovery. Other participants were John Lithgow, Bob Balaban, Madolyn Smith, Dana Elcar and Taliesin Jaffe. Back from the*

first picture were Keir Dullea as the lost astronaut; the embryonic baby; the mysterious black monolith; the celebrated strains from Richard Strauss's Thus Spake Zarathustra; and the egocentric computer HAL (Douglas Rain's voice again), but familiarity bred contempt among most critics and audiences this time around. Not that the visual effects by Richard Edlund on the Super Panavision 65 screen could fail to impress. The most astonishing thing about the movie was that its producer, director, screenwriter, and photographer were all Peter Hyams.

THAT'S ENTERTAINMENT?

1985

Despite *Rocky IV* and *A View To A Kill*, Roger Moore's last outing as James Bond, MGM/UA sank further into debt. In fact, it had never really recovered from a series of expensive flops. As Steven Bach, ex-senior Vice President of UA wrote, 'It is likely that the aggregate losses to MGM equalled or surpassed those sustained by UA with *Heaven's Gate*.'

For audiences, there was not much to cheer about either. Jack Haley's *That's Dancing!* didn't have the same impact as had the two *That's Entertainment!* movies, and *Mrs Soffel*, which cost $14 million, was a flop. Other companies were more profitable. 20th Century-Fox got a winner with *Cocoon*; Tristar gave *Rambo: First Blood Part II* to an eager public, Columbia did good business with *The Color Purple*, Paramount with *Witness* and Universal had *Out Of Africa*, starring Robert Redford and Meryl Streep, which won Oscars for Best Picture and Best Director (Sydney Pollack), and *Back To The Future*. MGM was wishing it could go back to its glorious past.

'What made me resolve one day to do **That's Dancing!** was the audience reaction to That's Entertainment! . . . It was the dancing that really turned people on,' said Jack Haley Jr, the co-producer (with David Niven Jr) director and writer of this compendium picture featuring dance extracts from over 150 Hollywood movies. Although MGM musicals naturally dominated, Haley also drew from the treasure troves of the other studios, notably Warner Bros. and RKO for the more spectacular Busby Berkeley production numbers and the Fred Astaire–Ginger Rogers dance routines. After a whirlwind opening montage of dozens of snippets to Henry Mancini's title song, the movie fell into six parts: 1) The Berkeley Years (introduced and narrated by executive producer Gene Kelly) 2) The Great Stylists (Sammy Davis Jr) 3) Ballet (Mikhail Baryshnikov) 4) The Golden Years (Ray Bolger) 5) The Best Of Broadway (Liza Minnelli) 6) The Future (Kelly again).

The title **Dream Lover** may conjure up cosy pictures of a romantic comedy, but the title is rather misleading. The film was, in fact, an intense and rather pretentious psychological thriller directed by Alan J. Pakula (who also co-produced with the scenarist John Boorstin), the maker of Klute (1971). Fourteen years earlier, Jane Fonda, the star of the latter film, found herself threatened from outside by a sadistic killer; here the danger to Kristy McNichol seems to come not from some external horror, but from her subconscious. She has rented a basement apartment in Greenwich Village, away from her protective father (Paul Shenar) and her boyfriend (Justin Deas) for the first time. When she has terrible nightmares of a violent and sexual nature, she turns to a dream researcher (Ben Masters) for help. Also involved in the dark doings were John McMartin, Gayle Hunicutt, Joseph Culp and Matthew Penn.

Mrs Soffel was the respectable do-gooder wife of the warden of Allegheny County Prison in Pittsburgh at the turn of the century, who fell in love with one of two brothers, both about to be hanged for murder, helped them escape and joined them in their flight to Canada. In Edgar J. Scherik, Scott Rudin and David A. Nicksay's production, Diane Keaton sensitively portrayed the woman who rebels, Edward Herrmann was her domineering husband, Mel Gibson her passionate lover and Matthew Modine his brother. Also cast were Trini Alvarado, Jennie Dundas, Danny Corkill, Harley Cross and Terry O'Quinn. On the strength of My Brilliant Career (1979), another tale of a woman who breaks with convention, MGM hired Australian Gillian Armstrong to direct this $14 million movie. But she handled it in too constrained a manner, and the screenplay by Ron Nyswaner failed to explore the potential of the true story, so that the public stayed away.

LEO BOUGHT AND SOLD AGAIN

1986

To recoup MGM/UA losses, Kirk Kerkorian sold the company to Atlanta cable and television mogul Ted Turner for $1.5 million. As part of the complicated deal, Kerkorian then repurchased UA for $480 million, which he financed in part by selling UA stock to the public. Then Kerkorian-UA bought back MGM, minus the Culver City lot and film lab which Turner sold separately to Lorimer-Telepictures in October 1986. The partnership was given a new name: MGM/UA Communications Company.

Of the few MGM movies released, Peter Hyams' cop comedy-thriller *Running Scared* earned $16.4 million, while *Poltergeist II* lost a million.

Best films of the year were *Platoon*, *Hannah And Her Sisters* (both Orion), *A Room With A View* (Cinecom), *'Round Midnight* (Warner Bros.) and *Stand By Me* (Columbia). Business was brisk for *Crocodile Dundee*, *Top Gun* (both Paramount) and *The Fly* (Fox).

With a screenplay (by Marc Shmuger and Marc Malone) that derived from the 1945 cult B-movie thriller, My Name Is Julia Ross, *and the several allusions to Alfred Hitchcock,* **Dead Of Winter** *was not the most original (nor commercially successful) of the year's releases. Yet despite these backward looking references to the past, this old-fashioned piece of Gothic hokem kept one fairly entertained and guessing. The tortuous plot had poor Mary Steenburgen as an aspiring young actress given the chance to take over the lead in a low-budget film being made in a remote snowbound mansion in New England. Even though the circumstances are less than ideal, she takes on the job, but discovers that the actress she has replaced has been murdered, and that the supposed producer, Jan Rubes, is trying to obliterate her identity. Arthur Penn claimed that his own identity as director had been usurped by the producers Shmuger and John Bloomgarden. Others involved were Roddy McDowall, William Russ, Ken Pogue and Wayne Robson.*

Poltergeist II: The Other Side *continued the story (written by the producers Mark Victor and Michael Grais) of Carol Anne (Helen O'Rourke), the little girl with innate psychic powers who, for some reason, sets evil occult forces against her. Pitted against them are the girl's grandmother (Geraldine Fitzgerald), a medium (Zelda Rubinstein), and an Indian mystic (Will Sampson). As usual the winner in this $21 million movie (it almost clawed it back) was the special effects department led by Richard Edlund and H. R. Giger, especially during two hair-raising nightmare sequences.*

As previously, Jobeth Williams and Craig T. Nelson were the worried parents, and Oliver Robbins, the brother. John P. Whitecloud and Noble Craig were also in the cast. The Brian Gibson-directed picture was dedicated to Dominique Dunne, the elder daughter in Poltergeist, *who was murdered by her lover soon after its release in 1982. Julian Beck, who portrayed the malevolent evangelist, died of cancer soon after shooting was complete, followed by Will Sampson who suffered a fatal heart attack.* Poltergeist III *would bring more bad news.*

Tap dancer Gregory Hines and stand-up comic Billy Crystal made an entertaining team in **Running Scared** as two cool, wise-cracking Chicago plainclothes detectives. Before the buddy-buddies can realise their dream of retiring to Florida, they are obliged to bust a gang of drug dealers. This delays them longer than they had wished, because underworld boss, Jimmy Smits, is out to get them before they get him. Gary Devore and Jimmy Huston's script kept the laughs and surprises coming, and Peter Hyams' direction provided some good action sequences, including obligatory car chases–one along the tracks of the Chicago El–and shoot-outs. Steven Bauer, Darlanne Fluegel, Joe Pantoliano, Dan Hedaya were also cast in this David Foster-Lawrence Turman production.

Ten-year-old Alessandro Rabelo charmingly played an Amazonian nature boy in **Where The River Runs Black**, a well-meaning adventure movie aimed at juvenile audiences. The boy is the orphaned offspring of a wayward priest (Peter Horton) and a mysterious native woman (Divana Brandaya), left with his animal playmates until priest Charles Durning finds him. Although Christopher Cain's direction moved at too slow a rate to make the Joe Roth and Harry Ufland production a winner, Peter Silverman and Neal Jimenez's screenplay, based on the novel Lazaro by David Kendall, provided enough crocodiles, snakes and even dolphins to keep the kids happy between the longeurs. Ajay Naidu and Conchata Ferrell were also in the cast.

Solar Warriors (aka Solarbabies) was a science fiction film that looked to the future with ecological pessimism. The film was set in a world that has become a vast desert, the sort of place MGM might have wished to see this motion picture lost. With many echoes of past film themes, this movie drew on movies that drew from others such as Rollerball. The script was written by Walon Green and Douglas Anthony Metrov and told of a children's camp run by warden Charles Durning, where the confined teenagers' only pleasure comes from a kind of roller-skating hockey. Jamie Gertz, Lucas Haas, Jason Patric, Claud Brooks and James Legros try to escape on their skates at the instigation of a mysterious talking shining sphere. Their escape is hampered, however, by the pursuit of nasty cop Richard Jordan. Filmed on location in Spain, the Irene Walzer-Jack Frost Sanders production was directed by Alan Jordan, who did a much better job on To Be Or Not To Be (1983), also for Brooksfilms. The film was not one of MGM great successes.

402 Caesar, Arthur 70, 94, 103, 179

403

409

Public Enemy, The 74